Charles and Indy Whitten:
SENT TO LOVE

Anne Washburn McWilliams

New Hope
Birmingham, Alabama

©1988 by New Hope
All rights reserved. Published 1988.
Printed in the United States of America

Library of Congress Cataloging-in-Publication Data

McWilliams, Anne Washburn.
  Charles and Indy Whitten.

  1. Whitten, Charles, 1922-   . 2. Whitten, Indy. 3. Missionaries—
Biography. I. Title.
BV2410.M39 1988   266'.6132'0922 [B]   88-9995
ISBN 0-936625-21-X

N884112 • 10M • 0488

Dedicated
to
my mother, Johnnie Lou Washburn,
who first introduced me to a love for missions,
and to
my husband, W. D. McWilliams,
who shares with me in all that I do.

Preface

When Joe and Lila Mefford asked John Whitten to choose a place where his family went often during his childhood, he chose the Plaza Mayor in Old Madrid. John and Ana and their two-year-old Carlos met us there in a restaurant called Las Cuevas de Luis Candelas, or by another name, the Cave of the Robbers.

During a two-hour, five-course lunch, which I began with a taste of gazpacho, John talked to me about his parents, Charles and Indy Whitten. I especially remember that he said, "They taught me to be able to feel at home with all people, at any level, rich or poor—to accept people for their own worth"; and that "they are known and accepted in many countries—not for their money or for their profession— but for what they stand for, for what they *are*."

Through Indy's press releases, sent to the *Baptist Record* since the 1950s, I have watched with interest the Whittens' missionary career. Too, I have been a grateful recipient of their friendship, of her letters, and of her encouragement in my writing endeavors.

"The Whittens love everybody." Those were among the first words of Esther Borras, when I met her at the Spanish Baptist Seminary in Alcobendas. Her husband, Jose, nodded in agreement.

From Louisiana, a letter from Virginia Wingo pointed out that the Whittens are "people who love and are loved"; and added, "We all need to know people like Indy and Charles, who make us want to follow Christ more completely, effectively, and joyfully."

Anne Washburn McWilliams

Acknowledgements

My gratitude goes
to Louise Hill Miller, for her letter to WMU, SBC, suggesting that this book be written;

to Edie Jeter, archivist, for her assistance with my research at the Foreign Mission Board;

to Joe and Lila Mefford, who showed me some parts of Spain that Charles and Indy knew best;

to Gerald and June McNeely, who welcomed me to their home in Madrid;

to many missionaries and others who answered my requests for information;

to the *Baptist Record* staff and to all the members of my family, for their encouragement;

to Joan Peterson, for being my prayermate in this project;

to Deena Williams Newman, for her expert (and kind) guidance as my editor;

to Charles and Indy Whitten, their mothers, and their children, for their cooperation in answering my questions (I have leaned heavily on Indy's writings for facts and descriptions, and on Charles's memory for dozens of details).

Foreword

After six years in Argentina, Indy Whitten and her husband, Charles, arrived in Spain in 1953. There, in the wake of civil war, feelings ran strong against evangelicals. Slowly, after 1960, the Whittens and their missionary colleagues saw the Lord reopen their churches. In 1967, the nation enacted its current Law of Religious Freedom.

During 31 years in Spain, Indy and Charles Whitten served a maturing Spanish Baptist Union. In the three years just before retirement, the Whittens helped Spanish Baptists extend their witness to Equatorial Guinea—a mission that grew out of the concern for another people impoverished by their struggle for independence.

Indy Whitten calls her four decades of missionary service "glorious years"; she celebrates the joys and tears of 40 happy years of "Charles, with Indy at his side." Mother and homemaker. Strengthener of churches, encourager of their women. Stewardship exemplar. Educator, author, editor. Contagious reporter to churches at home.

Now you can read the story of this rich and faithful pilgrimage. Indy and Charles Whitten give vivid description of the spiritual hunger they have encountered in missionary service. Overseas and on furloughs, they communicate happiness and satisfaction in being missionaries; deep conviction that doing the will of God is life's highest priority.

Reading *Sent to Love* will challenge your own discipleship. I commend it to you.

R. Keith Parks, president
Foreign Mission Board, Southern Baptist Convention
Richmond, Virginia
January 1988

CONTENTS

I. North America (1922-1947)	xi
1. Sent to Love	1
2. The Girl Who Learned the Alphabet Backward	6
3. The Boy Who Propped His Eyes Open	15
4. "And . . . the Twain Shall Meet"	24
II. South America (1947-1952)	29
5. Sent to Colombia	31
6. Sent to Argentina	39
7. A Baby with 41 Mothers	50
8. Buenos Aires	55
III. Europe (1953-1983)	63
9. Sent to Spain	65
10. Move to Madrid	81
11. Persecution Persists	88
12. Back to Barcelona	95
13. "Love in the Oven of Refinement"	101
14. "Love Never Fails"	113
15. Sharing the Bread That Satisfies	120
16. Camping at Denia	128
17. Don Carlos and Dona Nela: Encouragers	134
18. "The MKs We Left Behind"	140
19. New Work in Madrid	144
20. Sunrise of New Day	150
21. Editor of *El Eco*	156
22. "Never So Far from Home"	166
23. "One Step Enough for Me"	170
24. Sent to the Canary Islands	176
25. Exclamation Point on the Atlantic	183
26. Prayer: Love's Magic Carpet	189
IV. Africa (1984-1987)	197
27. Sent to Equatorial Guinea	199
28. A Church Grows in Malabo	206
29. A Church Comes to the Continent	214
30. "God Gives the Increase"	221
The Spanish Connection (Study Section)	231

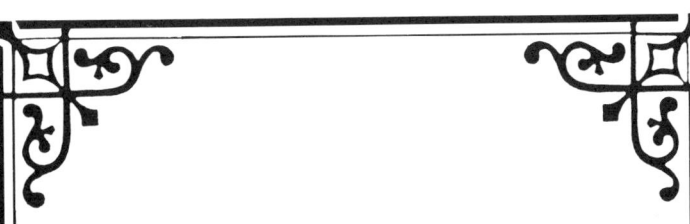

I
North America

1922-1947

1
Sent to love

"If I had to think of a single phrase as to why I am on the mission field, and what I expect to accomplish, . . . I would say 'Sent to Love.' "—Indy Whitten

THERON Rankin's voice sounded across the sanctuary of First Baptist Church, Richmond, as the president of the Southern Baptist Foreign Mission Board read the words of the prophet Isaiah, "I heard the voice of the Lord, saying, Whom shall I send, and who will go for us? Then said I, Here am I: send me."

It was April 8, 1947. The Foreign Mission Board of the Southern Baptist Convention appointed 56 missionaries, that night, breaking the record of 48 appointments set in 1923.

In 1947 terrible winter temperatures had lingered. Now it was finally spring, and two days past Easter. New missionaries-to-be had checked into the elegant Jefferson Hotel in Virginia's capital city. Their names on the register joined the signatures of Presidents Harrison, McKinley, Wilson, Coolidge, and both Roosevelts. In line with the new look, some wore midiskirts, spike-heeled sandals with ankle straps, and hats with veils and feathers.

On the evening before the appointment service, Charles Whitten met Indy (short for Nella Dean) Mitchell in the Rotunda Lobby near the grand staircase so like Tara's in *Gone with the Wind*. Victorian furnishings upholstered in mulberry, rose, and mint green created an aura of splendor. With the courtliness of Rhett Butler, Charles presented Indy with a corsage of carnations.

"That's why Mary Lee was so interested in what I planned to wear!" guessed Indy. The couple had traveled to Richmond by train from Louisville, Kentucky. Two seminary classmates had ridden with them as self-elected chaperons—Mary Lee Ernest, assigned to Hawaii; and Sophia Nichols, bound for Brazil.

"You won't forget our engagement with Dr. Sadler?" Charles asked. He had written to George Sadler, who directed the Foreign Mission Board's work in Europe:

A few weeks ago it was impressed upon me that there was an urgent need for missionaries in Spain. . . . Nella Dean Mitchell and I, who plan to be married June 1, 1947, have been thinking and praying about an appointment to some field in South America. We have presented ourselves for appointment this April. She is finishing WMU Training School, and I will have BD [bachelor of divinity] and ThM [master of theology] degrees from Southern Seminary. This great need in Spain is a constant challenge to us. . . . However, since we do not know very much about the situation, it is hard to do much intelligent praying about this. . . . Please send us information . . . about this field.

Meeting for the official photographs ranked high on the week's agenda. The 56 appointees posed on the steps of the Foreign Mission Board headquarters building, facing Monument Street. "Line up from *A* to *Z*" instructed Marjorie Moore of the Foreign Mission Board staff, as she arranged them in order.

"Could I stand in the *W*s by Charles?" pleaded Indy. You know we are to be married in six weeks."

"No," decided Moore. "You stand with the *M*s. There's many a slip between the cup and the lip."

Through the lens the photographer perused Charles Whitten, top row, second from right—a slender man wearing glasses, about five feet nine, with blue eyes and dark brown hair, high forehead, aristocratic cheekbones. Fifth row, at top left, stood Indy Mitchell, a trifle shorter than her fiance, red hair, brown eyes, and creamy skin, the velvety texture of Mississippi magnolia petals.

On their applications for mission service, both Indy and Charles had expressed a desire to work in a Spanish-speaking country. Though they talked with Sadler as planned, no definite field was designated by April 8. George and Frances Jennings were to be appointed for

Spain. Charles and Indy's appointment would be "to South America." At 24, they were idealistic, in love with the world and with each other, eager to go to the ends of the earth as the Great Commission commanded.

Their aspiration was to begin new work, perhaps in a village or rural situation. He hoped to preach and teach, and she wanted to work with young people and women's organizations, as well as help to build a Christian home, and to do some type of journalistic work.

"I want to be willing to go anywhere and to pay any price to carry out . . . Christ's will for me," he wrote. And Indy observed, "I'm sure God will open up methods of serving that I never dreamed of before."

Despite Marjorie Moore's pessimism, the wedding took place in Mississippi as scheduled. Next, since no orientation followed appointment, they would study Spanish at the Presbyterians' Evangelical Language School and Orientation Center in Medellin, Colombia. At first, Everett Gill, Foreign Mission Board director of work in Latin America, had asked if they would consider going to Brazil. They said no, because they still felt God wanted them in a Spanish-speaking country.

Indy and Charles had not given much thought to difficulties ahead. They were only sure that the Holy Spirit had communicated God's call. Now they began to grasp how hard it might be to say good-bye to their families, not to see them for five years.

On the night before they left Mississippi, they attended church with Indy's family. Afterward, as they prepared to return to the Mitchell farm, Indy noticed her 11-year-old redheaded brother H. C. sitting in the back of the family pickup. Ordinarily he would have been in the middle of whatever was going on. Suddenly she realized that he was crying. When she touched him on the shoulder, he straightened up and said, "I had a little piece of trash in my eye." He would be 16 her next visit home.

Charles's parents and brother Paul drove them to Miami. They detoured by Columbia, South Carolina, to see W. A., Charles's younger brother, who was in the army. In Miami, a city famous for luxury hotels, waves of heat mingled with loud strains of Latin music and snatches of Spanish in their nondescript, unair-conditioned hotel.

The next morning, August 15, they boarded the 6:00 A.M. Pan American plane. Indy had never been inside a plane before. Charles had only flown twice, each time for ten minutes in a small plane. Satisfying their curiosity about the plane and savoring the joy of adventure, they forgot to nurse any lurking nervousness.

They first set foot on South American soil at the port city of Barranquilla shortly after noon. From the air they could see hundreds of dirt streets running at right angles, and the Magdalena River meandering into the Caribbean. During their short walk between flights, the tropical heat washed over them in waves of perspiration. "150 degrees!" Indy imagined.

At Cartagena, two black-haired boys lugged a monkey onto the plane in a cage. The boys fed so many bananas to the monkey, they wondered if the animal would die before they reached Medellin.

Their thoughts turned to new experiences ahead. Would anyone meet them? They did not know. If not, then how could they communicate in a Spanish world? Over the Andes, the pilot began to maneuver, searching for the right place to squeeze between the mountain ranges. Because of the constricted shape of the valley, this year, for the first time, four-engine planes had been allowed to land at Medellin.

At 5:00 P.M. the plane slowed and seemed to glide downward. It looked as if they were flying straight into a mountainside. Charles leaned forward in his seat to peer out the window. "We're here," he said. But the pilot overshot the runway; Indy's eyes widened. Charles's hand reached out to cover hers. The plane climbed, circled, and came down for another try, this time successful.

"Hello, there!" someone called. The language school director, Otho Paul Daniel LaPorte, and his wife had arrived to meet them.

They found a taxi to take them to their new home on

Darien Street, but the car failed to start. The driver raised his hands and shrugged his shoulders. "Hay gasolina?" asked LaPorte. ("Does the car have gasoline?") Apparently it did not. Finally they changed to another taxi.

They arrived and met the three language students who would share their small house. The only other Southern Baptist couple in the school, Evan and Jo Holmes, would live in another house.

Their bedroom contained two chairs, a small table, and a bed. They hung clothes on hooks behind a curtain. To reach the bathroom, they had to cross the unroofed hall-patio outside their bedroom door. Though she did not understand why, Indy lay on the strange bed that night and cried.

In the streets, strange sounds struck their ears. They wanted to talk with people they met, but they could not. Gradually they realized that they had promised to spend a lifetime trying to tell the gospel story to people who didn't understand English. Could they ever learn to express their deepest feelings in Spanish?

The words of her Sunday School teacher during college days came back to Indy. The woman had quoted Deuteronomy 33:25—"Thy shoes shall be iron and brass; and as thy days, so shall thy strength be."

Among these people of another religious and cultural background, she would learn to understand their speech and customs. But first, she wanted them to know that she was there because she loved them. She knew Charles felt the same way. This was why they had been sent—to be an arm of Christ's love. In Colombia, in Argentina, wherever she might go, she wanted to help others bear their burdens, like her dad who used to drive his farm wagon down the dusty Mississippi roads, filled with four children. Sometimes he would spot someone with a heavy load on his back walking on the road ahead. He would yell, "Whoa!" to the mules, and then say, "Hop in! We are going your way."

2
The girl who learned the alphabet backward

"Time and loving people helped me to come out of the shell I was in. . . . Somewhere along the way the Lord helped me to stop comparing myself to other people and to turn my life over to Him for what He wanted to do with it."—Indy Whitten

MISSISSIPPI sunshine sizzled the logs of a sprawling country home in Winston County. A hen cackled, and deep in the woods a dog barked. Four-year-old Nella Dean stood waiting in the house's dogtrot, a bow of ribbon pinned to her red hair. She squeezed her brown eyes shut as she reached into her father's hat on the table beside her and felt the pieces of paper. Which should she pick?

Kinfolk watched her from the porch and from the shade of the tall cedars in the front yard. Her Grandpa H. M. McCully had died a long time ago, but now Grandma Mary Crosby McCully was ready to divide the land among her heirs. Numbers Nella Dean drew would decide who would get each parcel of land. Her fingers closed on one and she gave it to her daddy.

"You did good, girl!" he said. She'd picked the piece of farmland he wanted, the piece nearest this house. Mitchells and McCullys had farmed in Winston County for 100 years or more. In this house Nella Dean had been born on December 8, 1922, while her mother and father, Marie and Earl Mitchell, were visiting her grandmother. Dr. M. L. Montgomery had driven his buggy the three miles north from Louisville [LEWIS-ville] to deliver her.   Still only four in September, Nella Dean begged to start to school."You're not old enough," her mother would say.

"Please," she would keep on. So she entered Sand Hill's one-room school a few days late. However, it was not as wonderful as she had dreamed. Everyone knew how to read, except Nella Dean. Chineselike, she began at the back of the book and learned the alphabet backward.

Often she visited MaMaw Mitchell, one of her favorite people. (MaMaw was Deter Romey Mitchell, married to PaPaw, Adam Cooper Mitchell.) "Come in, Good Girl," MaMaw would say. Nella Dean thought those were special words of praise for her until she noticed that MaMaw called all her grandchildren Good Girl or Good Boy.

One morning during her fifth summer she found MaMaw outside ironing under the mulberry tree. While Nella Dean swung on the muscadine vine under the oak tree, MaMaw kept talking to her. Off and on, MaMaw would trudge into the house to exchange her iron for a hotter one from the top of her wood-burning stove.

Suddenly Nella Dean heard singing across the road at Sand Hill School, and rushed over to find out what was happening. Thus she met the Presbyterian volunteer summer workers who were teaching Vacation Bible Schools in north Mississippi that year. Enchanted, she returned every day that week to the first Bible school she had ever attended.

At her house, her parents owned a Bible, but it was mostly kept in the trunk. On Sundays, the family rarely appeared at church. (PaPaw Mitchell, whom Nella Dean adored, called himself an atheist.)

For the Bible school, the teachers had brought two shining balls, a red one and a yellow one, for use in outdoor games. They taught a chorus that Nella Dean liked to sing, though she could not understand what it meant. It sounded like a riddle.

One door and only one
And yet its sides are two.
I'm on the inside.
On which side are you?

For her "real" first grade, Nella Dean rode the horse-drawn school wagon four miles to Gum Branch. Her mother would say, "If it rains too much today, and the wagon can't cross the creek, you can spend the night with Dean." Daily she and Dean Wylie, her school buddy, would pray for rain.

When Nella Dean was nine, she and her family moved to another farm a few miles away, between Poplar Flat Baptist Church and Sulphur Springs, where once a resort hotel had flourished. Earl Mitchell grew such crops as cotton, corn, sweet potatoes, peas, and sugarcane; and he raised cattle. In his Model-T Ford he drove his daughter to school until a new yellow school bus with benches around the sides and down the middle made its appearance. Then she would walk down one long hill and up another, past Sulphur Springs, to board the bus. Much to her father's disapproval, one afternoon she generously invited everyone to hop off and help themselves to her father's sugarcane.

Nella Dean read all the books she could find, even her aunt's encyclopedias. Her bedroom was the fireplace room where the family sat at night. But her parents and her two brothers (Bruce, four; and Bob, one) would go to bed early and leave her to read in privacy. Then she would sit reading by the light of a kerosene lamp.

On her teacher's advice, she had skipped third grade. By the time she was eight, she wrote her first poem. After that, she hardly ever went anywhere without her tablet and a cedar pencil, lest she think of a new poem or a story.

For fun, she liked to swim and fish in the pond. She and her brother Bruce, and later Bob, pitched washers (similar to pitching horseshoes) and rode horses. The children of the black family who lived on the hill above their house, often played with them—baseball, football, tin cans, ante-over. Always they stayed on the lookout for Indian arrowheads lying about in the plowed fields. Nella Dean, as the oldest, felt it her duty to win at marbles, and played until her fingers were worn at the ends.

In the middle of Nella Dean's sixth-grade year, all the Gum Branch students were transferred to the school at Louisville. In the town school, the teacher listed all the sixth-graders' names on the blackboard, with numbers beside them to show deportment grades. If Jimmy threw a spitball, for instance, the teacher might say, "Go to the board and subtract three from your grade." Nella Dean, feeling new and friendless, sat quiet and miserable. That 100 beside her name made her feel different from the others. What could she do to be sent to the board? Her mind could contrive nothing.

The Great Depression had deepened, and the Mitchells' financial situation had grown worse. They no longer owned a car. That meant she could not accept a role in a play or be a member of a ball team, for she could not stay after school to practice; she would have to go home on the bus.

At lunchtimes, she would stand about alone rather than try to make friends, because she thought her clothes looked terrible and her shoes had holes in the soles. Her mother had said, "Just keep your feet on the floor. Nobody will see the holes." But she knew they were there.

Having skipped a grade made her enter ninth grade behind her classmates in age and social development. While the other girls wore hose, she still wore socks. In high school, she did have friends, though she still felt awkward and unsure of herself. She thought she was too tall. All the tiny girls seemed more popular. Actually, though, she was pretty, her auburn hair shining. One of her teachers, Juanita Hight, remarked to another, "Nella Dean's cheeks always look so rosy—so fresh and well scrubbed!"

When Nella Dean was 13, she had to swallow a severe disappointment. The baby sister she had hoped for turned out to be a third brother, H.C. Nevertheless, she helped her mother with the new baby, lugging him about on her hip. Her parents were loving toward each other and toward their children. They taught her the value of family unity, honesty, and good moral ideals; and instilled in her the value of hard work.

Because she read so much and because she was considerably older than her brothers, Nella Dean spent much time alone. She continued to express her thoughts in poetry and became a romanticist, an idealist who felt that good would in the end win over evil.

At school, any talk she heard about Jesus was vague. Never reading the Bible and seldom going to church, she thought little about God. One day she heard her teacher say, "God is as real to me as you students are." Another teacher, Louise McGee, stopped her in the school corridor and asked, "Why don't you come to church with me at Poplar Flat? Speck and I will stop by to pick you up Sunday morning." (Speck was Lawrence, Louise McGee's husband.) Since Nella Dean was fond of McGee, she accepted the invitation.

By then she was a high school senior. After graduation from Louisville High in May 1939, at age 16, she kept going to Poplar Flat Church. It was in McGee's Sunday School class that she heard the teacher read the Bible passage, "The harvest truly is plenteous, but the laborers are few; pray ye therefore the Lord of the harvest, that he will send forth laborers into his harvest." Nella Dean was sad that she could not be a laborer for this wonderful God.

At dusk on an August evening, she and Bruce left the house to walk the dusty mile and a half from their house to Poplar Flat Church. The new pastor, Joe Triplett, was preaching a revival meeting. Joe was a college student and Nella Dean liked to listen to him. It amazed her that a person so young would have enough religion to preach about it.

In the pond, frogs were croaking. Now and then Nella Dean and Bruce could hear a cowbell tinkle. Slowly the sunset glow faded as twilight came on, and fireflies twinkled here and there. A light breeze spread the scent of roses and wild honeysuckle. Nella Dean wore her tennis shoes and carried white high heels in her hand. Just before they reached the church, she said, "Wait a minute, Bruce," and jumped across the ditch, scrambled up the high red bank, and sat down under an oak tree to change shoes. "I'll leave my old ones here until we come back," she said.

In the semidarkness of the churchyard, she and her brother separated to find their own age groups. She saw her class with McGee standing in a circle, their heads bowed in prayer. Anger stirred as Nella Dean listened. They were praying for young people of the community who were not Christians. The person praying called her name. "They think I'm a heathen!" she said to herself. During the sermon that night, Joe Triplett asked, "Are you listening with the ears of your soul?" Nella Dean Mitchell was listening. Her cousin came down from the choir to stand beside her and say, "Why don't you take Jesus as your Saviour?" She did, and in that moment her life, her outlook, and her future changed.

The next day, a Saturday, she visited a school friend to share her experience. The friend's father asked, "Don't you know the Bible contradicts itself?"

But she answered, "I don't know much about the Bible, sir, but something special happened to me last night."

Shortly after her conversion experience, Nella Dean prepared to leave for Mississippi State College for Women in Columbus. Before the mirror, she turned this way and that, admiring her reflection, modeling her new green suit. She knew this gift from her parents would make a nice Sunday outfit for college.

When she picked up her suitcase, ready to leave for the bus station, her brother H. C. screamed, threw himself on the floor, and cried until his face was red. Maybe he knew bus tickets cost so much she would not be home again for almost three months.

Her father missed her too. At Thanksgiving, by pinching pennies, he hired a taxi to drive him the 40 miles to Columbus, to bring her home for the holidays.

Nella Dean gained her first newspaper experience as a cub reporter for the *Columbus Dispatch*. Through Baptist Student Union, she found a way to express her faith. The Baptist students picked her to be their representative at Ridgecrest Baptist Assembly at Asheville, North Carolina, for Student Week; they also agreed to pay her expenses.

One day at Ridgecrest, Nella Dean felt the chill of an early North Carolina mountain morning. She stood beside Lake Dew, listening to a message she would never forget. She had arrived at the assembly grounds with a busload of students from Mississippi College. "Each day, gaze into the Master's face," the speaker said, "and receive a new vision in your heart. Then turn strong to meet the day ahead."

On the final evening, when Charles Maddry, then president of the Southern Baptist Foreign Mission Board, spoke, she was overwhelmed with a deep desire to yield her life for mission service. Since she feared her parents might not approve of her becoming a missionary, she went forward to dedicate her life for full-time Christian service, but didn't admit that it might be on a foreign field.

After Ridgecrest, she spent the remainder of the summer doing volunteer work for the Training Union Department of the Mississippi Baptist Convention Board. She taught study courses and Bible schools. It proved to be a school for her too, for she grew in knowledge of prayer and personal witnessing.

Since money was scarce, she dropped out of college at the end of two years and accepted an offer to teach third grade at a school near her hometown. Her salary was $52 a month. Coaching the girls basketball team was an extra duty which provided more fun, but not more pay.

Nella Dean decided the children at Ellison Ridge Consolidated School could profit from learning more about the Bible. During noon hours she taught a Training Union study course to all who wished to listen. At the end of the course, she awarded 50 diplomas.

Soon Auber J. Wilds, director of the Mississippi Training Union Department, appeared at her schoolroom door. "Young lady, I've heard about that study course you've been teaching here. When you go back and finish college—I'm sure you will—I want you to work in the Training Union Department full time."

The Japanese bombed Pearl Harbor one Sunday while Nella Dean was still teaching at Ellison Ridge. Many young Mississippi men were entering the armed services, along with thousands of others across the nation. With wartime contracts, Mississippi's economy was edging upward. In spite of that, Nella Dean's financial situation still looked bleak.

"Mrs. Watson," she said to her former high school teacher one day, "I want to go back to college, but I don't see how I can."

"Perhaps if you would consider transferring to Blue Mountain, I know someone who might offer you a loan," Watson said. Blue Mountain was a woman's college owned by Mississippi Baptists. She did obtain some personal loans, and the college president, Lawrence T. Lowrey, secured a scholarship for her. She enrolled at Blue Mountain in her junior year and majored in English and history. Her roommate was a missions volunteer.

At Blue Mountain College in 1942 it was a fad to make up a nickname from a girl's initials. If her name were Betty Jean, she became Beejay. If her name were Nella Dean, she became Indy. "That fits!" friends gathered in her room said. "That's what we'll call you." Monte McMahan, student body president, persisted in using the name, and others followed her example. The name stuck.

Again in 1942 she worked as a summer volunteer, teaching Training Union study courses. As she boarded a bus one day at Noxapater, she met Louise Hill, a teacher at Calhoun who was on her way home to Murphy Creek near Louisville.

"I wish I could do what you are doing," Louise said.

"You can," Indy assured her, "if you want to work without pay. Some churches welcome us. Others don't. Some people are great to us. Others act as if they don't want us. But I love it! Why don't you come and begin this summer?"

Immediately Louise accepted the challenge. Their first week in Attala County at Providence Baptist Church, she and Indy taught Vacation Bible School in the mornings and study courses at night and stayed in the country home of one of the members. Late Tuesday night they blew out the lamplight and closed their eyes. Their hosts

13

had already gone to bed. All was quiet. The two young women had talked late and were tired.

Plink! Plunk! Plink!

"What's that?" whispered Indy. "Did you hear that? Is somebody in the living room?"

Plink! Plink! Plink!

"It's music!" said Louise, her heart hammering. She reached for a match to light the lamp.

"Maybe we've died and gone to heaven," said Indy. Louise tiptoed to the door and slowly opened it a crack, and then she laughed. "It's a kitten on the keys!" The animal had jumped through the open window and landed on the piano.

As a result of Indy's influence, Louise joined the Training Union Department as a paid associate on the full-time staff.

During a Religious Focus Week at Blue Mountain, Indy realized with renewed emphasis that missions would be her place of service, and made public her decision. Her attention focused on South America, partly because of her friendship with Ruth Garcia, daughter of a pastor in Argentina and the Baptist Student Union president at the college. Indy was glad she had continued a second year of Spanish.

As Wilds had promised, he gave her a job in the Training Union Department after her college graduation in 1944. During the 18 months she worked in the Baptist Building in Jackson she came to know Edwina Robinson, executive director of the Mississippi Woman's Missionary Union. "Miss Ed," as she was called, encouraged Indy to study at the WMU Training School in Louisville, Kentucky, and said that if she did, the Mississippi WMU would give her a scholarship to help with seminary study.

In August 1945, at the close of World War II, she resigned to go to Kentucky. Indy still had South America in mind. Beginning to think she might go as a single missionary, she felt she would be willing to do that if it were God's plan for her life. But God, it seems, had other plans.

3
The boy who propped his eyes open

"Always when we take a step, God gives us adequate light for the succeeding one."—Charles Whitten

THE CLOCK ticked, its broken alarm failing as usual. Charles and Paul Whitten stirred under the load of quilts their mother had piled over them the night before. They could hardly move. Their bedroom, created by enclosing one end of the back porch, had no heating system. The boys called it the icebox.

"We could stand a stick of stovewood here under the cover like a tent pole," Charles suggested.

"Time to get up," Paul groaned. They pulled on their pants and shoes, grabbed their shirts, and dashed into their parents' room to build a fire. The fireplace there was the family gathering place in winter.

Within minutes, they had a fire roaring in the kitchen stove too, and their mother had begun frying sausage. A small mountain of hot biscuits later, they pushed their chairs back from the breakfast table. "It's Charles's day to do the dishes," said Velma Whitten. And that meant it would be Paul's morning to help Willie, their father, at the barn. Since there were no sisters, the boys took turns with outdoor and indoor chores. Charles started to stack the plates, a job he hated. He glared at Paul: "I wish you were a girl!"

Charles, three years younger than Paul, didn't mind the farm work, but it upset him if others didn't do their fair share. That spring Paul broke his arm at the season when cotton needed chopping. Now Paul had a ready-made excuse for not doing his daily duties. Yet Charles knew that Paul could do more with one hand than he pretended, if he'd try. "Come on," he said to his older

15

brother. "I'll show you how you can chop cotton with one hand."

"No—no. I—I can't," Paul said hesitantly.

"You can draw water with one hand then,"Charles declared. The younger brother walked over to the well at the corner of the porch. "You can drop the bucket in the well like this. Then hold the end of the chain with your foot. See?" He stood on the chain while he jerked the bucket with one hand.

Paul (purposefully) was a slow learner, but the aggravated Charles refused to give up. "I know you could wash dishes with one hand. See?" he said.

Charles William Whitten had been born on Sunnyside Farm September 4, 1922, a couple of miles from Weir, Mississippi, in Choctaw County.

The white farm house stood on a green knoll surrounded by 150 acres of meadowland, a garden, and cotton fields. Running Branch crossed the pasture, not far from the house. It rippled over stones and flowed under a bridge to join Tilby Creek, a quarter mile away. Sweet gum trees, and here and there some oaks, edged the branch. Muscadine vines swung from the oaks. One day as Velma pulled the plump purple fruit for jelly, a fox squirrel fell out of the vines. The boys kept it for a pet. Already they had several rabbits. When Charles brought another rabbit home, his mother told him, "If you keep that one, we will have to eat it."

"No," he said. "We are not going to eat it." He carried it back to the woods and set it free.

Charles attended first grade at Weir School. One day the teacher wrote a word on the board. Then she stood back and asked, "Charles, what does this say?"

From his seat in the back of the room, the five-year-old saw some squiggly white blobs on a hazy black background. He shook his head and said, "I don't know."

An open book lay on his desk. The teacher pointed to one of the words and directed, "Read this."

To him, all the black and white shapes on the page looked as if they ran into each other in fuzzy confusion.

"I can't," he answered.

Several months passed; he still could not read or spell. When his parents asked him to read from his primers at night, he could not. They bought a set of flash cards and tried to teach him words. In spite of their efforts, he failed first grade.

"Does he have a learning disability?" Velma and Willie Whitten began to ask each other. To test this, Velma read him a story and asked him questions about it. Readily he answered every one.

"No, it's not his mind," she decided. Then finally she realized he could not see well. With his right eye, in fact, which did not focus properly, he could not see well enough to read at all. In the fall he returned to school with new glasses. His teacher assigned him a front seat. "Four eyes," his classmates called him, and he didn't like that. But his grades improved dramatically.

One source of Whitten family income was a bed of sweet potato plants. "Your mother and Paul and I are going to town today," Willie told Charles. "You stay here in case anyone wants to buy plants."

Midmorning, a car drove up and a man stepped out. "I want to buy some potato plants," he said. "I don't have any money, but I'll trade you my goat for some plants."

The young merchant thought that a good business deal, for his father had said, "Take anything you can get." He accepted the offer.

Later Paul and Charles had to go and get the goat, and then keep it tied, sometimes to a porch post. Once they found the goat standing on the porch nibbling leaves off Velma's geraniums.

"Oh!" exclaimed Velma Whitten. "I think I'll go and jump in Running Branch!" (That would hardly settle anything, for it was only ankle deep.) If she intended to punish Charles, she would usually say, "Where's my switch? You need a dose of peach limb tea!" But she could hardly punish him concerning the antics of this goat, when he had been so jubilant over his transaction. After all, he'd done what he'd been told to do.

If she and Willie ever caught him in a deliberate act of mischief and questioned him, he would not deny his deed. He'd say, "I don't want to talk about it."

Every Sunday Willie and Velma and the boys were present at Beulah Baptist Church for Sunday School. Always they were there for once-a-month preaching and the once-a-year revival meeting. Charles was taught early about Christ and His mission to the world.

At the time Charles was seven, he was singing with the children's choir during summer revival. After the song service, he listened carefully to the sermon. He sat on the third seat from the front on the left, his blue eyes solemn. On each side of the sanctuary were the alcoves where his parents taught their Sunday School classes. On three sides of the buildings was a double row of windows near the high ceiling. These windows let the sunshine through during the day. At night, Aladdin lamps shed their beams across the pews.

Sleep soon weighted the boy's eyelids; he wanted to hear the rest of the sermon, so he propped his eyes open with his fingers. The next day Velma told the preacher, C. Z. Holland, a college student who was pastor at Beulah, about how hard Charles worked to stay awake. Holland told the congregation, "I wish all of you were that interested."

Another night, the message brought a lump to the boy's throat. Charles suddenly knew he wanted to accept Jesus as his Saviour. That night at home he told his parents of his feelings, but they said, "You are too young. Do you really understand what that means?"

"Yes, I know," he said, and he began to cry. The next day the three talked with Holland.

The pastor told them, "I believe Charles knows what he is doing. He's been telling some of his friends they need to accept Jesus. That, it seems to me, is as good proof as we would want of a person's being a Christian—trying to win someone else." Thus, Charles at an early age responded to the missionary urge.

Revival time had ended except for baptismal service on Sunday afternoon at Tilby Creek. Charles took extra clothes with him, in readiness to be baptized. Holland preached a brief sermon in the pasture while cows grazed nearby. On the creekbank, he gave an invitation; the boy walked forward to make a public profession of his faith. Then Charles was baptized with the others. Afterward, he and Paul began tithing, though they didn't have much money. They used an empty box for a bank. Every day they read at least one chapter from the Bible. If, after they had gone to bed, they realized they had not read the Bible that day, one would get up, light the lamp, and read aloud at least one verse.

In high school, Charles wanted to take part in competitive sports, but his poor eyesight kept him from being good at them. Instead, he turned to more intellectual pursuits, such as the speech contests sponsored by Future Farmers of America (FFA). The time he won first place, the county agent dropped him off at Weir School. Then he walked home. His father pulled a 50-cent piece from his pocket and gave it to him. More than the money, Charles treasured his father's look of affectionate pride.

As well as speaking, another of his talents was music. A hired man on the farm taught him to play the harmonica when he was five or six. Charles did so well that his father bought him a harmonica. At school, the principal would ask him to play for the students in the auditorium. The principal would call out tune names, like "The Death of Floyd Collins" or "The Prisoner's Song." If Charles knew the tune, he played it.

While teenagers, the Whitten boys created a radio show for a station in Kosciusko, Mississippi. Local merchants sponsored the show and listeners called in requests. Charles played the harmonica (using a special harness for "no hands") and the guitar at the same time. Paul accompanied him on the guitar.

Charles and Paul entered a music competition during an FFA convention at Starkville. Their performance of "When They Cut Down the Old Pine Tree" won them first place in the state.

Charles loved music and loved to sing. He even sang while feeding the cows. One day he grew tired of the cow's tail smacking him across the face. He drew a wooden clothespin from his pocket and fastened the tail to his trousers leg. His hymn singing continued, "Lead, Kindly Light . . . lead Thou me on. . . ." Pop! The clothespin had worked loose, and the cow whacked him on the head with it. The singing temporarily ceased.

From the time he was 13, Charles began to think seriously about his task for the future. What if he were to fail in life? The question bothered him. Every afternoon, as he drove the cows home from pasture, he prayed aloud. Though he wanted to do with his life what God wanted him to do, he didn't understand how a call to ministry would come. He simply could not see the Lord calling him—Charles Whitten—to preach.

During his senior year at Weir High School, Charles won first place in the state in 4-H crop judging. As a result he earned an agricultural scholarship to Mississippi State University. However, before the fall session at State, he accepted a friend's invitation to visit Mississippi College at Clinton. The visit changed his mind about his choice of a college, and thus changed the course of his life.

With money so hard to obtain, he hated to turn down the scholarship, but he felt confident he was doing the right thing. He was graduated from Weir High School in 1940 as salutatorian. His parents bought him a new suit, and he moved to Clinton to begin college.

His first year of college Charles still struggled with what God wanted him to do with his life. On March 24, 1941, he dropped by the office of his Bible professor, M. O. Patterson, and asked for a conference. The professor listened sympathetically.

Because of limited funds, Charles told him, he had been permitted to live in the less expensive "preachers' dorm." Yet he didn't know yet what his life's work would be. He felt the Lord might be calling him to preach, and it would be an honor to serve God—but would God really call him? "Every day I go over and over this. I just don't know," he said.

"Young man, if you are sincere in what you have told me, God is calling you to preach, and I'll ask the Clinton Church to license you," Patterson responded.

Charles preached his first sermon at Beulah Church in April 1941 on "Standing Up for Jesus." The following December, events at Pearl Harbor turned the world upside down. Many of his friends and fellow students began to enlist in the army. He considered following their example, but was advised to stay in school, for he might be needed later as a chaplain.

Many in college saw Charles as consistent, reserved, studious, and quiet. When he spoke, they knew he would have something worthwhile to say. Others saw him as a person with a sense of humor, one who liked to pull a prank. While a freshman, he roomed second semester with Wilbur Carpenter, a sophomore. Charles at that time owned a tricky lamp. When he plugged it in and picked up the cord, it would give him a slight shock. Often an unsuspecting visitor would enter their room. Charles would grasp the lamp cord and surreptitiously clasp one of Wilbur's hands while Wilbur graciously shook hands with the visitor—and passed along the unexpected shock.

Too, Charles was an actor. One of his best known talents was that of imitating certain preachers and professors. His imitation of a donkey's bray was also well known.

One summer he and Wilbur were counselors at a campsite called Castalian Springs. Another summer he taught study courses for the Mississippi Baptist Training Union Department and narrowly avoided meeting Indy Mitchell when he worked in the north end of the state and she in the south.

Clinton Baptist Church ordained him to the ministry September 23, 1942. Three messages were delivered: one by his uncle, R. A. Eddleman; one by James L. Sullivan, pastor of the Clinton Baptist Church (later president of the Baptist Sunday School Board, Southern Baptist Convention); and one by P. I. Lipsey, editor of the *Baptist*

Record, the Mississippi Baptist paper. A. A. Kitchings, professor at Mississippi College, led the prayer of ordination.

For his sermon, Sullivan spoke about "The Preacher's Place in the World Today." He stressed the word *now* in Ephesians 3:10, when Paul was referring to his own call to the ministry as being something he was chosen for and not just a profession he chose. The sermon dealt with *the man* in the ministry as Sullivan talked about the character, consecration, and courage a preacher needed to do a good job. Then it turned to *the multitudes* to whom the preacher was to minister—the unlikable, the lost, the needy. Sullivan stressed that the young minister would need to love the multitudes, to lead them, and to live among them. The third emphasis was *the message* he was to preach. It was to be simple, sincere, and scriptural.

Some summer weeks Charles spent at home helping his father with the crops. This gave him a little time with his younger brother W. A. He told him, "You know God loves all the people in the world—all the races." He encouraged W. A. to include black playmates in his circle of love and concern.

While Charles was still in college, three Mississippi churches called him as pastor—Hopewell in Choctaw County; Red Lick in Union County; and Carson Ridge in Attala County. His grandfather, H. M. Whitten, had once been pastor at Hopewell and Carson Ridge. Hopewell didn't pay Charles a salary, but the congregation paid his bus fare once a month and took a love offering. Red Lick paid him $15 a month for one sermon.

While serving part-time as a pastor, Charles continued to pray about what God wanted him to do with his life. Immediately after his surrender to preach, he had begun to face the Lord's leading to foreign missions. He met Cecil McConnell, missionary to Chile, and talked with him. His thoughts then kept turning to needs of the Spanish-speaking in South America. When he considered foreign missions work, he faced two distinct challenges—the fact of a great need and the fact that so few would consider it. After a three-year study program, Charles was graduated from Mississippi College in 1943 with special distinction, with a major in sociology and minors in Bible and psychology. He knew God had called him to missions, but he did not tell others of that call until he reached Southern Baptist Theological Seminary in Louisville, Kentucky. During a Missions Day program there he made his commitment public.

4
And . . . the twain shall meet

"There be three things which are too wonderful for me, yea, four, which I know not: The way of an eagle in the air, the way of a serpent upon a rock, the way of a ship in the midst of the sea, and the way of a man with a maid" (Prov. 30:18, 19).

IN STEPHENSPORT, Kentucky, on the Ohio River, Charles Whitten slowed his pace as he neared the home of Ed Payne. He dreaded stopping to see that man again.

It was hard to talk to Ed because he was paralyzed, almost blind, and partially deaf. People in Charles's congregation had advised him, "That man won't listen to you. Don't waste your time on him. He makes fun of preachers." Ed was not a Christian. He had lived life to please himself, apparently caring little for what others or God thought of him.

Yet the fact that the community had given Ed up as hopeless was a challenge to the young pastor. Every week Charles talked to Ed about Jesus. Always he had to yell so loud to make himself heard he figured that people all over town heard him too. He'd gotten no response. Now here he was again. Hesitantly, he knocked and entered.

"Is that you, Preacher? Come on in!" Ed called from his darkened room. Inside, Charles could hardly tell if it were day or night. "Preacher," the voice from the bed continued, "I got to thinking last night, and I got to praying. And I took Jesus as my Saviour." No words ever sounded more like music! Not giving up had its rewards.

Charles had entered Southern Baptist Theological Seminary in September 1943, and soon afterward accepted the pastorate of Stephensport Baptist Church. It was a church with no prayer meeting, no Training

Union, and no budget. They had about ten in Sunday School.

Immediately Charles taught a Vacation Bible School. Average attendance for it exceeded attendance on Sunday mornings. The children's choir he had organized in Bible school sang special music in Sunday night services. Parents came to hear the children sing.

While at Stephensport, Charles preached a revival in which 11 young people came for baptism. After this, the Stephensport Church voted to have preaching every Sunday. They organized a Training Union, began Saturday night prayer meetings, and adopted a budget.

Charles was told that the community was filled with lost people. He averaged preaching one evangelistic sermon a week and made strong appeals for decisions, but the lost were slow to come. Nevertheless, through personal house-to-house witnessing, he was able to see several trust Christ every few weeks.

One of those was a 22-year-old girl who had been reared in one of the many Catholic homes in the community. Since there was no Catholic church nearby, she began to attend the Baptist Training Union meetings at his church and borrowed one of the young people's Bibles so she could read her daily Bible readings. In his visitation time on Sunday afternoons, Charles stopped to talk with her and asked, "Do you know Jesus as your own personal Saviour?"

"No," she replied. "I know that I'm lost."

"I have not come here to try to get you to become one of our church members, but I want very much for you to know the same Christ Who has done so much for me," said Charles. He explained to her the plan of salvation. A few weeks later, she made a profession of faith during one of the church services.

Charles wrote Everett Gill about his experiences at Stephensport, "In many cases I know that I fell far short, but some of the richest blessings of my life came when I saw how that God can use a weak, imperfect instrument to advance His kingdom work."

On the evening of September 7, 1945, Indy Mitchell began packing to leave for Woman's Missionary Union Training School in Louisville, Kentucky. She stopped to write her friend and former co-worker, Louise Hill:

Louise McGee told me you were in town yesterday afternoon. So was I—but down at Aunt Mabel's house trying to get my hair dry. Here's my tale: I rode Weaver (the horse) to my grandma's house and got caught in the rain with my newly washed and combed hair. I didn't want to make the people at Shower No. 2 sorry that Shower No. 1 made my hair come down. The Louisville WMU gave me a lovely shower at 8:00 P.M., and the Poplar Flat Church had a party at 9:00. I got $81 and so many nice useful things. I have almost seen you several times. One weekend I took off to Red Bay, Alabama, but had to wait in Fulton several hours. Your bags were in the bus station but I couldn't find a soul who knew your whereabouts. . . .

Bruce, my brother, is in the Naval Air School at Memphis. He got pretty homesick at first, but I think he likes it better now. He writes us every single day yet.

I leave Sunday morning at 8:51 and go to Birmingham. At 9:17 I catch a train out of Birmingham for Louisville. We are supposed to arrive at about 7:30 Monday morning, and register that afternoon. I go with high hopes and great expectations that I'll learn a headful. A head so empty as mine should be easy to work on. There's nothing much to block the entrance of knowledge.

I haven't seen you since VJ Day. I suppose your reaction to the news was much the same as my own. Isn't it a wonderful thing to have the world at peace again? . . . Write me.

Before Indy left Mississippi, friends urged her, "Be sure to meet Charles Whitten. You'll like him." Soon after she moved from Louisville [LEWIS-ville] to Louisville [LOU-ie-ville], Kentucky, the Crescent Hill Baptist Church gave a reception for new seminary students.

Another student, Olive Powell, told her she had a date for the reception with Charles Whitten, a Mississippi College friend. "If you'd like, Devee Hillman would come along as your date," Olive said. Indy agreed to the blind date idea.

"Hummm," she thought when Olive introduced Charles. "I wonder which he will do first, imitate a chapel speaker or bray like a donkey?" She had heard of his playful imitations.

As the four walked back to the Training School later in the evening, Indy sort of fell out of step with her date. Behind Olive and Devee, she walked with Charles. They found much to talk about. Though they had grown up 17 miles from each other, they had never met. They knew many of the same people and had frequented many of the same places. Both had dedicated their lives to foreign missions.

During Christmas holidays in Mississippi, Charles stopped at Lawrence McGee's brickyard to ask directions to the Mitchell house. Indy saw him drive past. He had missed the house, but in a few minutes he returned.

Later in the evening they walked under tall pines. Around them, moonlight dusted the fields and pond and white frame house with silver. Above them, winter spread a black coverlet embroidered with stars. To Indy, nothing could be more romantic.

After Charles left, Indy's mischievous mother teased her daughter by mocking the way that "spry young preacher" walked. While doing so, she sprained her back, and fell over onto the bed. "Oh," she moaned, "that's what I get for imitating a preacher. I'll never do that again!"

The following spring, back at school. Charles and Indy took walks in the park and along the river. One day, as they sat by the river and talked, they broke up some sticks. Indy saved the sticks.

"You must be in love," her roommate said, "to keep a bunch of sticks."

"No, I'm not," she declared, and she threw them in the trash can. She fished them out and thought, "This is foolish," and threw them back in. In the end, she kept them.

At school's close, the two said good-bye at the bus station. He planned to stay in Kentucky during the summer. He asked, "Will you write me?" She agreed.

Later in the summer Auber Wilds asked her to teach a Training Union study course at Beulah Baptist Church. Although she knew that was Charles's home church, she was surprised to find him there visiting his parents for a week.

A revival was also taking place that week. All week they accepted invitations to eat in homes where the pastor and evangelist ate. At the Whitten house, she tasted Velma's luscious caramel cake for the first time. At night, after revival services, they took long drives in Willie Whitten's car. By week's end they knew definitely they were in love.

Back at school that fall, Indy found a message, "Some young man surely wants to see you. He has called many times." Eventually he arrived, to ask her an important question.

She asked for a week to pray about her answer. Yet, sitting in Highland Baptist Church on Sunday morning, she thought, "You already know the answer."

To pay for the diamond, he led the music for a two-week revival in Campbellsville, Kentucky.

It was their custom, as they walked, to eat Lifesavers. On Grinstead Drive, they paused beside the steps of Barrett Junior High. "Would you like a Lifesaver?" Charles asked. She reached for one, and he slipped the diamond on her finger.

Their time was spent with classes and other activities, as well as with seeing each other. Indy had enrolled in Missionary Education—methods and history of Woman's Missionary Union work—with Virginia Wingo as teacher.

In May 1947 Charles and Indy were graduated from the seminary. A day or two before their June 1 wedding at Poplar Flat Baptist Church, word arrived that their field would be Argentina.

The couple left immediately after their wedding for a brief wedding trip to Gautier, on the Mississippi Gulf Coast. They were at home at Weir, Mississippi, until mid-August, when they left for language study in Colombia.

II
South America

1947-1952

5
Sent to Colombia

"God's grace is the oil that fills the lamp of love."—Henry Ward Beecher

FIVE days after arrival in Medellin, Charles wrote to Everett Gill of the Foreign Mission Board:

> We are running into a little difficulty in getting our personal and household effects from Buenaventura. I have talked with Dr. LaPorte of the Presbyterians, Mr. Robert Crosby of the Methodists, and Dr. Pearson of the Inter-American Mission about the situation. They said that many times it took six to nine months to receive things and quite often with a sizable duty to pay. . . .
> Language school starts Monday. . . . We are anxious to begin our study. We are learning the threefold requirements of a missionary to Latin America—patience, patience, patience.

The next day he added a postscript:

> Please disregard the part of the letter concerning the baggage. I have just heard where a couple received all of their effects from Buenaventura duty free. Grace Lines thinks that they can secure our baggage in about ten days or two weeks by rail. . . . I have learned three other requirements for a missionary to Latin America: fourth, patience; fifth, patience; sixth, patience.

Their Spanish studies included five classes a day, five days a week. Between class and study times, Charles and Indy explored their vicinity on foot, even though rainy season had not yet ended. Avenues of palms and jacarandas blended with other exotic foliage. Crude shacks, colonial mansions, and Catholic churches mingled with office buildings and factories. From any point, they had only to lift their eyes to see the mountain peaks.

Beyond the city lay groves of coffee trees. In the foothills grew vanilla and mahogany trees and orchids, which were also raised in the city.

Three ridges of the Andes stretch across Colombia, the middle range, or cordillera, rising between the Magdalena and Cauca River valleys. Medellin [Med-i- YIEN] had been built on the western slopes of this cordillera, in a steep-sided valley above the Cauca and in the center of a region that came to be called Antioquia.

In the nineteenth century, settlers from the Basque provinces of Spain had moved onto the mountain slopes above the Cauca. Later, many Negroes were imported to Antioquia. The result had been described as "a pious, proud, prosperous mestizo-mulatto people." Because of their unusual business ability, someone had called them "the self-styled Yankees of South America." It was they who had expanded coffee production in the late nineteenth and twentieth centuries and used coffee profits to make Medellin a manufacturing center.

Along the streets of the city, Charles and Indy saw descendants of those early businessmen sipping cups of *tinto* (coffee demitasse). They met priests in long skirts and Indians wearing *ruanas* (blanket-like wraps) and felt derby hats. Women in straw sandals led loaded donkeys. Street vendors, some on crutches, sold fruit or lottery tickets.

Compassion filled the two as they took note of hungry-looking children who played in alleyways. Their tongues did not yet know the right words to communicate with them.

Many old houses lined the cobblestoned streets, their carved wood doorways, tiled roofs, and inner patios souvenirs of Spanish days. In such a house on Darien Street, Indy sat in the dining alcove writing a description of the sunset:

> The clouds seemed to be having a convention just above the heads of the mountains and they were as undecided and unpredictable as a Colombian burro. Within 30 minutes they changed from brilliant red to midnight black. Finally there remained only the bulky outline of the mountains and a glit-

tering evening star piercing the darkness that seemed to hang like tar over Medellin. . . . There is a song in my heart because of God's goodness to us all.

Indy and Charles enjoyed the sunsets in Medellin. They also enjoyed getting to know the people.

One of the Whittens' first Colombian friends was their housekeeper, Rosa Holquin. Rosa, an excellent cook, was known for her baked yucca with gravy dinner. She and her daughter Margarita did the washing and ironing, cleaning, and cooking. A Latin beauty with shoulder-length black curly hair and olive skin, Rosa looked too young to have a 14-year-old daughter, a replica of herself.

Rosa and Margarita also did the marketing. Food like rice or bananas they could buy in the *tienda* (store) on the corner. Milk, meat, and vegetables they bought at scattered markets. The bread man stopped in front of the house, his crusty loaves in baskets slung over his burro's back.

The Whittens and their three language student housemates shared the costs of maid service.

At first, they felt strange permitting Rosa and Margarita to do all their work; then they perceived that maids were probably better off than many women of the city who earned less. At least the maids had a place to live and food to eat. Sometimes they also could help relatives who needed assistance. Such was the case with Rosa, whose sister and niece from time to time looked to her for aid.

"God called us to be missionary helpers," said Rosa and Margarita. They prepared special Colombian dishes; they shared their knowledge of Colombian religion and traditions; they corrected the students' Spanish pronunciation; they brought extra blankets on cold nights. Medellin, in contrast to the steamy heat of Barranquilla, seemed to enjoy eternal spring, as the temperature hovered around 72. The city's altitude was 4,880 feet. On August nights, Charles and Indy found they needed two or three blankets.

By mid-November, the *invierno* (winter), or rainy season, was nearing an end. They looked forward to *verano* (summer), the dry season. Hummingbirds thrust their beaks into crimson bougainvillea. Orchids, hibiscus, and flame trees set the world ablaze. When a new friend, Senora Zapata, invited Charles and Indy to go with her and her two daughters for a picnic in the mountains, they quickly said yes. Their English tongues still on occasion refused to roll their *R*s, but professors constantly consoled them. "The language will come to you 'little by little,' " they said. Because the Zapatas spoke only Spanish, now the Whittens would have a good chance to practice.

The train which they were to ride into the mountains looked similar to those in the United States, except it was smaller, perhaps dirtier, than some they had ridden. The cars rocked jerkily from side to side on the narrow gauge track. In spite of this, the scenery held them captivated. They crossed high bridges and looked out on waterfalls. They stopped in mountain villages and then craned their necks to look down on the thatched rooftops below them. Through the window they saw mules carrying loads of firewood on their backs, and a boy driving goats.

Senora Zapata had packed their picnic lunch in a large hamper. She kept chattering, never guessing they knew little of what she said. They explored the train and then sat down in the rear door of one of the cars, their feet dangling. At the planned destination, the Zapatas got off the train, thinking their guests would follow. But Charles and Indy sat happily unaware their hostess had left.

Soon the conductor found them. His excitement triggered wild gestures and fast flowing Spanish. The foreigners shook their heads in incomprehension. He grasped each of them by the hand, led them to the place where the hamper had been, and pointed to the empty spot. Truth hit them in the face. They did not even know where they were supposed to be going.

At the next village they stepped off the train and

started walking back down the winding mountain road. They had no idea how many miles they'd have to go to find their friends. Then below they saw a yellow bus, its wooden seats heavily loaded, weaving upward. As it neared them, it stopped, and out jumped the Zapatas! They all embraced warmly, and spread their lunch on a big rock nearby.

Every day Charles and Indy learned more about the Colombian culture and people. Rosa, their housekeeper, gladly shared her religious beliefs with them. Like most Colombians, she had been brought up in the Catholic church. She had not truly known Christ as her Saviour until five years before, when Presbyterian missionaries witnessed to her. For four years, Rosa had prayed for her sister Virgelena with no response. But God had heard. Now Virgelena had become a Christian.

It was difficult for those reared in the Catholic faith to break away from it, she told them, especially if they had to face their families' disapproval.

Celebration of *El Cristo Rey* (King Christ) Day took place on the broad front steps of the Catholic cathedral. Thousands stood in the surrounding area holding candles. A priest arose from an ornate throne and held up the golden host, or communion bread, which he said represented the presence of Christ.

All the people fell to their knees, crossing themselves. A brass band played, the church bell rang, and over the public address system someone shouted, "Praise God! Praise King Jesus! Blessed be the Virgin Mary, Mother of God."

Prior to Vatican Council II, Catholics in Latin American countries, as well as in some other lands, were often forbidden by the priests to read their Bibles. Someone said, "The Reformation never reached South America." The flavor of ancient pagan cultures sometimes intermingled with present-day practices. Indy wrote in a newsletter:

> Colombia is the most loyal Catholic country of South America, and Medellin is perhaps the most conservative city

35

of Colombia. The priests do not actively oppose Protestant movements, but often they hire the boys to throw stones when tracts are being given out. Several months ago, a language student was giving out tracts when a group of boys came up to throw stones. He started talking to them and pretty soon organized a baseball team among them. . . .

Often we hear the statement, "Politically I'm a Catholic. Personally I'm an agnostic. . . ." Christ is always an infant or a bleeding figure on the cross, much to be pitied.

Christmas celebrations began on December 8 with the Feast of the Immaculate Conception and lasted through December 31. Rosa explained that Colombians eat Christmas dinner at midnight on Christmas Eve, after they exchange presents around a tree. Every home had some kind of nativity scene, either bought from a store, made by the children, or antique carved ones handed down from one generation to another. At midnight in each home, the figure of the baby Jesus was laid in the manger of the *pesebre,* or nativity scene.

On Christmas morning in 1947, Charles and Indy exchanged gifts and unwrapped their packages from Mississippi. They spent some quiet time together, giving thanks for their most important Christmas Gift.

Though they thought their first duty was to study during this time in Colombia, they watched for chances to tell others of God's perfect Gift, the Saviour. One way to reach people, they felt, was to help them learn English. In a store where they bought records, they met several who wished to be taught English, and agreed to teach them.

Reversing the language situation, Indy also taught an elementary class in Spanish for an American family from Nashville. Mr. Padgett was in Medellin to sell buses. Once, after he'd taken a few lessons from her, he entered a drugstore to buy a soft drink. He wanted a glass, or *vaso,* but he asked for a *beso,* or a kiss.

In their own language studies, they began to realize it would take quite a long time to learn all the idioms of Spanish expression. It was not enough to scribble correct Spanish on the written page. They needed to talk and talk in order to be able to talk. Charles wrote to Gill: "One who has a difficulty in language would need more individual attention than they offer here."

Practically all their orientation work at the language school had concerned Colombia. Though this was interesting to the Whittens, they were anxious to learn more about Argentina. Originally they had planned to stay a year in Colombia. However, they were beginning to feel that six more months of hard study in Argentina would better prepare them for their missions field than to stay and continue the study in Medellin. Charles shared this opinion with Gill, but added, "I am not trying to sound discontented, but wanted to be of service to other missionaries coming this way in the future. We like our nice place to live and are willing to remain as long as you think best." They and the Holmeses had been the first Southern Baptist missionaries to study at this language school.

Another small problem emerged when the government passed a new rule that those with tourist visas could stay only six months. The Whittens' visas were to expire in February. This was solved by a trip to the Panama Canal Zone to renew them. On the way back to Medellin, they visited missionaries in Barranquilla and Cartagena to learn a little about Baptist work there.

Dorothy and Harry Schweinsberg had arrived in Barranquilla seven years earlier and had organized a church there in 1942. Carolyn and Thomas Neely had opened Baptist work in Cartagena in 1943. Others since had gone to Cali and Bogota. Now there were four churches and several missions in Barranquilla, plus a primary school. Roy and Orlene McGlamery had just arrived. Roy was a doctor and planned to open a clinic in Barranquilla.

In Cartagena, Charles and Indy were present for a Sunday night worship service. Five people who made professions of faith didn't even wait for the invitation hymn to begin, but rushed down to the front and began to give their testimonies.

A few weeks later, Charles paid an unexpected visit

to a hospital in Medellin. He "had an emergency appendectomy," Indy wrote her friend Louise. "It all happened so suddenly that he was sewed up again before I knew what was happening." Because the appendix was in an unusual location, the doctor had to search for it. Hence, the scar was large and T-shaped. The surgeon, Dr. Ochoa-Torres, told Indy, "I signed my work with my initial."

On April 9, 1948, Jorge Elicier Gaitan was murdered outside his office in the center of Bogota. That set off a chain of events that changed many people's plans, including those of Charles and Indy.

The wealthy and powerful class in Colombia was said to own 97 percent of the country's wealth; the main political parties, Liberal and Conservative, represented power blocks within the wealthy class. Naturally, since the wealthy class owned so much, that meant that the poor class was drastically poor.

Gaitan had risen as a leader of the Liberal party. Though some called him a rabble-rouser, others saw in him a hope for badly needed changes in the country's social and economic setup. Courts proved his murder to be the work of a madman and not of politicians. Nevertheless, his murder started a revolution, and Bogota exploded like a powder keg, with killings, lootings, and burnings. The violence spread all over the country.

Conservatives set up a dictatorship and declared military law in all the cities, including Medellin. Curious, Charles and Indy would walk downtown to see what was taking place. When they found a street blockaded with cannons, they would search for another way to walk past. Later they realized how easily they could have been killed.

The revolution cut short their stay at language school. In mid-April they left Medellin. On April 30 they boarded the *Santa Isabel* at Buenaventura. The ship was bound for Santiago, a stop on their way to Mendoza.

6
Sent to Argentina

"We learned to love first and not wait around to see if the people were going to love us."—Indy Whitten

THE *Santa Isabel* missed her scheduled sailing date by two days. Not until May 2 did she leave the harbor at Buenaventura. In the meantime, the Whittens struggled with yet another decision. Since a special need had arisen in Chile, the Foreign Mission Board had given them the option of serving there. Missionaries Jo and Evan Holmes, also considering Chile, had flown on to Santiago.

Fine autumn weather greeted them as they stepped from the ship in Antofagasta, Valparaiso, and again in Santiago to tour cities and visit missionaries. Jo and Evan had not as yet received an entrance permit for Argentina, while Charles and Indy had. Thus, it seemed to both couples that the hand of the Lord was working things out for the Holmeses to stay in Chile and the Whittens to go on to Argentina.

Charles and Indy left Santiago early May 21, scheduled to arrive in Mendoza that evening at 9:30. The locomotive toiled upward toward the Uspallata Pass, 12,000 feet above sea level, along the route that Indians and their Spanish conquerors had used for hundreds of years. The Andes, second highest mountains in the world after the Himalayas, loomed above and around the passengers as the train zigzagged past pillars of rock, icy lakes, snow-filled valleys, and the highest peaks they had ever seen. Through the window of the train Indy took pictures of a ski lodge and of a small church on a mountainside. She shivered, and gratefully pulled tighter around her the thick Indian-made blankets they had bought in Santiago.

They kept watching for the famous Christ of the Andes statue, but the train rumbled into a tunnel, and they missed it. Later, she hoped, perhaps they could drive back on the Pan-American Highway to see the statue and its inscription, "May these mountains crumble into dust before the people of Argentina and Chile break the peace which they have sworn to maintain at the feet of Christ the Redeemer."

At the station in Mendoza, Vada Waldron, missionary director of the Baptist Good Will Center, and several members of the Godoy Cruz Baptist Church stood waiting to welcome Charles and Indy to Argentina. For the next 12 days they walked the streets of the city searching for a house to rent, but found nothing. On one of those days, at Vada's house, they celebrated their first wedding anniversary.

Though they were anxious to begin work in Mendoza, they could not without a roof over their heads. Consequently, the Argentine Baptist Mission asked them to move 650 miles away to Rosario to occupy a house rented by a missionary family on emergency leave.

One frequent visitor to their home in Rosario was Sydney Sowell, a 77-year-old widower. "Dr. Sowell, you remind me of a ripe, red, sweet juicy apple!" Indy said to her guest.

"Why do you say that, dear?" he asked.

"Because you are kind to us new missionaries, and you act as if you understand our frustrations. You are an apple. You are delicious!" Indy was always comparing her co-workers with objects.

Sydney Sowell, the first Southern Baptist missionary to Argentina, had been there since 1903. Indy and Charles could sit and listen to him for as long as he would talk, soaking up his wisdom. Knowing him was a big plus on the side of being in Rosario. In his more than 50 years as a missionary, he had been pastor of churches in Rosario and Buenos Aires; first president of the River Plate Baptist Seminary in Buenos Aires (1918-42); and first editor of Argentina's Baptist paper, *El Expositor Bautista*.

Two other missionary guests usually arrived with

Sowell—his daughter, Anne Margrett, director of the Woman's Training School in Rosario; and Sara Taylor, an employee of the Good Will Center. "I keep a room ready for Dad all the time," Anne said. "I wish he would move to Rosario. I'm afraid he's lonely in Buenos Aires."

"Daughter, with my books and my memories, I could never be lonely!" he assured her.

For the Whittens, Sowell recounted some of the difficulties of his own early days as a missionary. "Like you," he said, "I had to learn the language. And people often did not respond because they thought they had not done anything to be saved from. 'No he hecho mal a nadie', they would say, or 'I have not harmed anyone.' Others had lost confidence in traditional religion. Some were indifferent to all religion."

During those days, he said, the rent allowance from the Foreign Mission Board had not been enough to pay for attractive chapels. Simple store buildings had been rented for worship services. As a result, ones who responded first to the gospel were the humbler people. The majority of the Argentines were Roman Catholics. "Since much wealth was attached to the Roman church," Anne Margrett said, "It was natural that the wealthy were not attracted to the simple halls used by Baptists."

In later generations, the picture changed, though, and doctors and lawyers and other professionals were included among the Baptists. "Today," Anne pointed out, "the River Plate Baptist Convention has many splendid denominational leaders, and we have many lovely church buildings."

During their time in Rosario, Charles and Indy learned a great deal about Southern Baptist missions work in Argentina. They also continued their language study with a private teacher. Their appreciation grew for their previous time in Medellin. Charles wrote to Gill at the Foreign Mission Board, "With all the household duties and other things required of one when he is actually on the field, we can see that it would be much harder to get down to a real program of study, especially for a beginner. I am sold on the language school idea!"

In Buenos Aires, missionary L. C. Quarles arose to address his co-laborers at Mission Meeting. "Charles Whitten preached his first Spanish sermon last Sunday," he said, "at the Arroyito Baptist Church in Rosario. Today I supervised his and Indy's first-year language exam. I am happy to report that they have made satisfactory grades, and I recommend that they be given the right to vote in this, their first, Mission Meeting."

The other missionaries cordially welcomed them to the fellowship, and all presented their needs in such an appealing way that Charles and Indy wanted to work in every place they heard about.

The Mission named Charles to its education committee to help make a study of the theological institutions of southern South America. The committee was to consider combining institutions to serve Chile, Argentina, Bolivia, Uruguay, and Paraguay. Uruguay and Paraguay, and Argentina were members of the River Plate Baptist Convention. However, Uruguay Baptists were in the process of forming their own convention.

On a cold, windy Sunday afternoon soon after Mission Meeting, Charles and Indy traveled to Lujan, a town on the pampa a few miles west of Buenos Aires.

Every few minutes a loaded bus stopped and let out a new group of pilgrims and sightseers. As Charles and Indy arrived, street vendors rushed up with medals of saints and of the Virgin of Lujan. Along the avenue in front of the cathedral, they passed booths selling candles, crucifixes, and statues of saints.

The enormous cathedral covered almost a whole block. Alcoves on either side of the chapel were filled with offerings people had given to the Virgin of Lujan as an expression of gratitude for prayers they said had been answered. Indy described these in her notebook:

A soldier placed his sword in the military department because the virgin had saved his life. A young woman put her bridal veil and dress in a cellophane bag and had placed them on the wall because the virgin had saved the life of her husband-to-be. Thousands of people who were cured of some disease placed little silver miniatures of the affected part of the body in a glass case designated for that purpose. There were many cases full of miniature silver arms, legs, ears, lungs, and hearts.

At every turn were basins of holy water, crucifixes, confession booths, statues of the saints, and rows of candles burning as prayers for both the living and the dead. . . . A young mother crossed the back of the chapel and entered into the open alcove where a priest was blessing the babies.

The most important activity, however, seemed to be taking place on the second floor. In an upstairs room behind the main altar, the pilgrims came face to face with the central figure of Lujan around which all activities revolved. There on a pedestal about twenty feet above the heads of the people was the famous Virgin of Lujan—a little blue doll not more than twelve inches tall.

In 1630, when the town of Lujan did not exist, a man tried to drive an oxcart carrying this statue of the Virgin Mary over the place where the church now stood, but found that it would not budge. More oxen were brought, and then more, but still the cart could not be moved. So the people decided that the Virgin Mary did not want her statue to go any further. They built a chapel for it in that spot. So many pilgrims came to see it that people built the town of Lujan and its cathedral.

Now at least fifteen people were kneeling at the confession rail. Many more stood holding lighted candles and gazing up at the statue. A teenage girl, kneeling in the middle of the crowd, kept clasping and unclasping her hands, while tears rolled down her cheeks. A priest and several of his helpers walked back and forth with silver trays, collecting offerings.

A few months after their trip to Lujan, Charles and Indy made the decision to return to the Cuyo district (Mendoza, San Juan, and San Luis Provinces). Because they still felt, as on first arrival in the country, that it was the will of God for them to work there, Charles had accepted the interim pastorate of the Godoy Cruz Baptist Church at the edge of the city of Mendoza.

Always the Whittens seemed to be moving somewhere. If they counted both houses they'd occupied in Medellin, this would be the fifth time since they left Miami. They made preparations to travel to their new area of service by train. The Cuyano, a special train, was already full by the time it left Buenos Aires. Everyone seemed to be going either to Cordoba or Mendoza for vacation. Because of that, they bought tickets for a different route, from Rosario to Rufino to San Rafael to Mendoza. That would mean a dusty trip through San Luis Province.

As he settled uneasily into the train seat, Charles said, "I feel more like a pincushion than a human being." Nine injections a day for ten days had left him feeling "holy," but much more healthy than in a long time. Ten days in a Rosario hospital had rid him of the amoeba that had kept him company since he left Colombia.

Indy had recently shared exciting news with him: she was pregnant. Packing to move had not bothered her because they had little to pack. As yet, they owned no furniture.

It still seemed strange to them that January was midsummer. The haze of dust and the hot wind blowing across the plains diminished as the train penetrated Mendoza Province. They felt as if they were leaving a desert and entering a garden. In spite of meager rainfall, irrigation had produced greenery. Vineyards began to flash by the windows; a network of canals and roads appeared, flanked by double rows of trees. In the near distance, the bare brown foothills changed colors with the changing of the shadows. Farther away, snowy peaks looked like melting ice-cream cones.

When they reached Mendoza, Charles and Indy moved into the pastorium next to the Godoy Cruz Church. They began to get adjusted to their new church and community.

One day Indy finished writing some letters and stopped to cook supper before Charles arrived home. Though at last they had bought a few pieces of furniture, they still needed a better stove. She shoved some bits of charcoal under the grate, struck a match, and fanned the little blaze. "Cooking on this," she thought, "is the hardest adjustment I've had to make yet!" In the morning, she would need to go to the open-air market to buy fresh fruit and vegetables. Could she possibly think fast enough in Spanish to bargain for what she needed?

Charles walked in from a trip to south Santa Fe Province just as she had supper ready. As usual, they were eating late in the evening as did the Argentines. In addition to his pastoral work at Godoy Cruz, Charles was acting as interim missionary in the south Santa Fe Province while the regular missionary was on furlough.

"We started plans today for an evangelistic campaign," he told Indy. He opened his suitcase. "I brought you a mending job." He showed her a pair of his pants. "The splinters in the train seat yesterday rubbed a hole in these, and I had to buy a new pair before I could preach," he said.

Earlier, on the first Sunday after their arrival at Godoy Cruz, Charles preached his first funeral message in Spanish. It was for a man who had died in a mild earthquake. The family of the man had no idea that this was the first funeral the preacher had attended in South America, and that he had no idea what he was supposed to do or say.

Another Sunday at Godoy Cruz Church, Indy stood before a class of young women teaching a Sunday School lesson from Deuteronomy. When she was ready to assign a verse to be read, she paused at the word *Deuteronomio*. "If I can't say it right on the first try," she thought, "I'm just going to say, 'Girls, turn over to page __ in the Old Testament.' " Suddenly, as she taught, she felt a sense of the Lord's presence with her and knew the assurance that He could speak through her, even through imperfect words.

The Godoy Cruz congregation was worshiping in a beautiful building paid for by Florida Baptists in honor of a Floridian, Franklin J. Fowler, missionary sent to Argentina in 1918. The sanctuary was certainly a contrast to that little rented room used for the first services in 1910. Gabriel Ostermann and a family from Rosario had begun a mission there then, and the first worshipers sat on boxes in which kerosene cans had come.

As interim pastor, Charles regularly preached three sermons a week, led a weekly prayer meeting, taught a Sunday School class, and led a chapter of Royal Ambassadors. In the first few weeks, he had also preached in four other churches, in two open-air services, and at a camp.

Besides teaching the Sunday School class, Indy was a counselor for the missions organization for girls. She had taught Sydney Sowell's book, *Parables of Jesus*, to a group of women, and had spoken to young people at a camp in San Juan. She helped to plan the programs for the Saturday night Young People's Society.

Concerning all their sudden activity, Charles wrote in a newsletter: "For such a long time we could do nothing because of the language handicap, and now we have more than we can do. Only God can make us able."

On an April afternoon, just before nightfall, Indy sat on the patio writing. "We have a new stove!" she wrote her friend Louise. "It's run by kerosene and can be transferred to natural gas when we live in a place where it's available. I like my new stove so much I'm tempted to use it for a typing table—just so I can be near it."

On either side of the patio, grapevines garlanded separate arbors. Before her, an archway of morning glory vines framed the faraway white peaks. That morning their blue blossoms had matched the sky. Now the fading light inked the bare foothills with deep purple. The sun dropped over the mountains into Chile as she closed another letter: "In my heart I have a quiet peace that goes beyond anything I have ever known before. The work here is not easy and there are problems, but nothing can compare with the satisfaction of being in God's place."

The odor of barbecue cooking at someone's fiesta and the sound of a guitar floated in on the evening air. People from all over the province were getting ready for celebration of Vendimia, the festival which honored the vineyards and the wine-making industry.

In early April, church members had told her, the farmers always placed their choicest fruit in a huge bowl onstage at an outdoor theater in the city park. The Catholic bishop of the district would bless the fruit, which was a symbol of the year's harvest. Then thousands of pigeons, painted in many colors, would be released. After a big parade, with gauchos on horseback and many floats, the queen of the Vendimia would be crowned.

One morning not long after the festival, Charles was in his study writing a sermon. He saw a woman outside, pointing to the church door as if she wanted to go inside.

"I want to ask a blessing inside the church," she said to Charles when he went to the door.

"Yes," Charles said, "you are welcome to go inside if you wish." He gave her a New Testament. "You know that this is an evangelical church?"

"That doesn't matter," she replied. As she entered, she covered her head with a black veil as most Catholic women did in church. She reconsidered, and took it off. While Charles waited at the door, she walked down front, bowed, crossed herself, and knelt between the pews. She then looked around the walls as if searching for something. Then she returned to the entrance and asked, "Doesn't your church have any images of God or of the saints?"

"No, Senora," Charles answered. "We don't have images in our church. God is spirit and those who worship Him must worship him in spirit. We believe that salvation comes through personal faith in Christ, the Son of God, and that if we have Christ in our hearts, that's all that's necessary."

Later Indy wrote a story about this woman for the *Commission* magazine. In the article she pointed out that most Argentine Baptist churches were unadorned except for a Bible text above the pulpit. "God is Love" was one of the most used texts. Though they did not display "images of God," she explained, "God's image is to be seen in the life of every regenerated Christian. Their radiant testimonies are sufficient proof of God's power to save and transform lives."

God's image was reflected in the life of Dona Enriqueta Pagliari, Woman's Missionary Society president at Godoy Cruz Church.

At the end of the worship service one Sunday morning, several members stood near the doorway of the church, Bibles and hymnbooks in hand. Indy turned to the charming, dark-haired woman who had paused beside her, and was quietly waiting for a word with her. "Will you and Don Carlos come over for tea this afternoon?" Dona Enriqueta asked. "I'd like to show you my new house. And I have an idea I'd like to talk over with you."

Senora Pagliari was of French parentage. Her husband, Don Ramon, was an Italian-born Argentine. A former taxi driver, he had swapped his taxi for a house in a new section of the city and now was in business with his cousin.

That afternoon, at the new house, Indy immediately noticed the Scripture texts hung on the wall. "We are happy here," Dona Enriqueta said, "and I want to use this house in a way that will glorify God. I have something I want to show you." She opened the door to the empty garage. "Don't you think this would be a perfect place for the Godoy Cruz Church to open a preaching point? The pulpit can go right over there."

Then the hostess prepared *mate* for them to drink. She placed the dried tea leaves in a gourd container and poured hot water on them to draw out their flavor. The three of them sipped the tea from the gourd, each taking turns sipping through the one silver tube Dona Enriqueta had placed in the tea. They kept adding sugar and water and more tea as it was needed.

Dona Enriqueta told them that she had been a Christian for 31 years. She had been living in the province of San Juan, Mendoza, when she came to know Christ as her Saviour.

"The Baptists put up a tent near my house and had evangelistic meetings. I was afraid to go to them. The first time, I waited until dark and slipped in so no one would see me. Pastor Enrique preached, and his message made such an impression on me that I kept going. I felt the burden of my sin, and not long afterward, in a regular service, I made a profession of my faith in Christ."

Her family had objected violently and had done all they could to discourage her in her new-found faith. Her young daughter had been in school, but school officials would not let her attend anymore because of orders from the priests.

"But you were baptized in spite of all this?" Indy asked.

"Yes, and the day I was baptized my niece was having a party to announce her engagement. I could not go to the party because of the baptismal service. As soon as I could, though, I called at her house. My sister would not let me come in because I had become a 'Protestant,' " she replied.

Dona Enriqueta and her husband and daughter had moved to Mendoza. Her husband had been indifferent to the gospel, but her 11-year-old daughter had trusted Christ as Saviour and was baptized. Two years later, her daughter became ill and died.

"My family blamed her death on the fact that we were evangelicals. I wrote to them and they didn't answer. But the Lord sustained me in those difficult experiences," she said. A few months after her daughter's death, her husband and her mother became Christians.

"My husband and I are happy as we serve the Lord together. I want to serve Him all the days of my life, and I pray that He will give me strength to carry to others the glorious message of salvation," she said.

"The preaching point here in your house would be a way to carry that message," Charles responded.

7
A baby with 41 mothers

"In any country, the home is an effective object lesson of Christ's transforming love."—Indy Whitten

WOMEN of the Godoy Cruz Baptist Church met regularly to knit and plan for the birth of Pastor Don Carlos's (Charles's) first baby. They kept minutes of their meetings. After their reading of the minutes each time, someone would comment, "So much expense for a lady!"

On the last Wednesday in July, as they sat sipping their *mate*, the pastor's wife, Dona Nela, as Indy was called, told them, "I won't be here next week because I'll be in the hospital having the baby."

Indy's prophecy proved to be correct. On August 3, 1949, a cloudy midwinter day, her labor pains began. She called a midwife, and her missionary friend, Mrs. James C. Quarles, who had promised the use of her car. Charles was so excited that when he climbed into the car he hung the pocket of his suit on the handle of the door and almost completely ripped it out. Later, Indy repaired the pocket while they waited in the hospital. Helen Frances was born in early afternoon, weighing in at 8½ pounds.

In the meantime, the knitting group learned that Indy had gone to the hospital. They stopped knitting and followed her en masse. When Dr. Freneau spotted them marching down the corridor, he grabbed a No Visitors sign and ran to hang it on Indy's door. He entered, closed the door behind him, and said, "Senora Whitten, I thought you said you had no relatives in Mendoza—and lo and behold, here come 40 mothers!"

Friends and relatives in many places received Indy's letters about the arrival of Helen. She wrote:

Our baby daughter is a wonderful little creature with dark hair, blue eyes that seem to turn brown, her daddy's mouth, and a puggish nose that turns up at the idea of sleep at times. She has succeeded in taking all our waking hours and a few that should be devoted to sleep. She went to hear her daddy preach when she was two weeks old and croaked out in approval in the middle of his sermon.

When Charles was not in the hospital visiting his wife and new daughter, he was taking part in a revival meeting at Godoy Cruz Church. A young seminary student was preaching. Jose Sami, a native of Argentina, had spent his childhood in Syria. The church was considering calling him as pastor.

After Jose Sami had preached at the church, the deacons said to Charles during their meeting with him, "This man is too young."

"But the church asked him to come and preach. The church must vote on this," replied Charles.

"No," the deacons insisted. They, as a board, voted that Sami was not to come as pastor.

Since Charles still felt that the church must vote, he asked the veteran missionary, James Quarles, for advice. Then Charles followed the procedure that Quarles suggested. Without telling the deacons what he meant to do, he presented Sami's name to the church and asked the congregation to vote on whether or not they wanted him as pastor. They voted to call him. However, all the deacons immediately resigned.

Afterward, Charles stayed awake all night praying and thinking, "What can I do to straighten this out?"

The next day he went to every deacon's house to apologize and to ask that the deacons return. He said, "I still believe what I did was right, but maybe I did it in the wrong way." All the deacons returned, but for some time the church did not reelect them as deacons.

Experiences with members of the Godoy Cruz Church helped Charles and Indy learn the customs of the people. To learn the language and customs of the people and to become a part of the local culture kept the Whittens ever mentally on their tiptoes.

One cold winter day Charles heard that Deacon Carmona's baby, born prematurely, was gravely ill with whooping cough. "I'm going to their house to see if I can help in any way," he told Indy. While he was at the Carmona house, the deacon's wife arrived home, carrying her dead baby bundled in a blanket. Her large dark eyes filled with tears as she looked at Charles. "I took my baby to the hospital," she said, "but while we were there, he died."

A few months later, seven women in Indy's Sunday School class made decisions to accept Christ. So did an 89-year-old woman who suddenly exclaimed, "I have seen the light!" Indy wrote to her friend Louise in October to express her joy over these decisions and added some words about two-month-old Helen:

> Her hair is becoming strawberry blonde. . . . She looks a lot like Charles. The mother has learned a baby book word for word; the father is still looking for a hat that will fit. Besides being a great blessing to the missionary's own home, a child is a means of entrance into the hearts of the people. In any country, a Christian home is an effective object lesson of Christ's transforming love.

Some months before Helen's birth, Charles had made a trip to the southern part of the province of Mendoza and seen in that desert area many possibilities for beginning new work.

"As soon as the church can get a permanent pastor," Charles had written Gill at the Foreign Mission Board, "we will be moving again. We are happy with the work here, but are anxious to reach out to the outlying districts where no new work has been opened for more than ten years."

Toward the end of October, they rented a small house in General Alvear at Calle Dr. R, Pierola 526. A row of quebracho trees led to the door. Within a few days, the three Whittens became a familiar sight to citizens of the town. Indy wanted to help Charles, so they took Helen along. Charles decided that to work as a *colporteur* would be a rapid way to meet the people. Every day, for a while, they walked up and down the streets, pushing a baby carriage and selling Bibles.

One day Indy and Helen stayed home while Charles and the Argentine pastor rode on the bus to Monte Coman, a nearby village. The Whittens had been promised a car by the Mission, but it had not arrived yet. The two men planned to make a survey to learn if anyone would like to see the chapel in Monte Coman reopened. It had been closed for seven months for lack of a preacher.

Dona Dora met them with a cordial welcome. Her house was one of the first they visited.

"I'm a Baptist," she told them. She was most unhappy that her church was closed. Because she could not read or write, she had missed the services even more sorely. Her grandchildren had helped by reading the Bible to her every day.

When she heard who they were and why they had come, a smile warmed her face and tears of joy trickled down her wrinkled cheeks. For her they were an answer to prayer. "Now that you have come," she said, "we can have preaching services again!"

The town of General Alvear was surrounded by other centers which looked promising for the beginning of evangelical churches. One of those population centers was home for a colony from Russia. Though this group had a Baptist church, services were held in Russian. The young people who had grown up in Argentina needed services in Spanish. In anticipation of their move to the area, Indy had bought a Russian grammar book.

With Antonio's help, Charles and Indy began a series of services in Spanish among the Russian Baptists of the Bowen area. Since the Russian Baptist church was out in the country where most of the believers had truck farms, the Omelanchuk family offered their home in the village of Villa Atuel as a meeting place for Spanish services. At least 30 children showed up for the Sunday School that Antonio directed at this home, and Charles preached in Saturday night evangelistic services.

One night Charles asked Senor Omelanchuk to pray.

The quiet man rose and began to pray in Russian, for Spanish still gave him problems. He and his family had moved from Russia to Paraguay, where they had been converted to Christianity. After he and his oldest son studied to become tailors, they had moved to Bowen to set up a shop.

A bond of love already bound Indy and Charles to this man who obviously longed to share his faith with the people of his village. It gave them deep satisfaction that they could be a part of the little congregation in his home. Shortly after the Russian congregation began, the Whittens received a message from Buenos Aires. A grave situation had arisen at the seminary. L. C. Quarles had retired; another missionary had resigned; another couple had moved to Chile; two couples in the States did not plan to return to Argentina. This left W. L. Cooper as the only missionary on the seminary faculty.

The faculty had recommended that during the emergency Mr. E. Swenson teach theology, that Charles teach Bible, and Indy teach church history.

This came as a surprise to Charles and Indy, for they had no thought of teaching. They had lived in General Alvear only eight weeks. Now they had to come to terms with the question, Does God then want us in another place?

On December 21, 1949, Charles wrote to Gill at the Foreign Mission Board:

> We have only begun here and have been very happy in our work. Nevertheless, we cannot turn our backs on these great needs. One of our greatest needs at the present time is for trained workers. We have some churches that have been without a pastor for over a year because they are not available. The Executive Committee met and, after exhausting practically all sources, voted to ask us to consider moving from the field to the seminary. After having faced the issue for a number of days, it seems the only thing to do. We will probably move the first of February in order to prepare fully our course of study before the school year begins.

8
Buenos Aires

"What would we do if we actually had a blueprint of tomorrow and all the tomorrows? . . . If we knew, would there be any place for faith?"—Charles Whitten

"YOUR command of the Spanish language amazes me," Kitty Cooper said to Indy. The two had eaten at a restaurant near the Plaza Flores. They had ordered steak, a food so plentiful and inexpensive in Argentina that practically anyone could have it on her menu every day if she wished. Now they were strolling in the plaza, admiring the roses while they talked about their missions experiences. Kitty and her husband, Bill, president of the Baptist seminary, had been in Argentina since 1939.

"I still feel like I'm a beginner," said Indy.

"Perhaps you do, but we came directly here without knowing a word of Spanish, and struggled through shrugging of the shoulders, gestures of the hand, and groping in general until we finally made ourselves understood. You two are fine propaganda for language study before going to the field," responded Kitty.

Indy described for Kitty some of her own early language trials in Mendoza.

"The nationals are always asking me to give a talk!" bewailed Kitty. "I would prefer to sing!"

Indy began to laugh. "Well, they're always asking Charles and me to sing and we would rather give a talk!" She added, "Helen jabbers all the time, but we don't speak her language."

A few weeks later, on a wintry July evening, Indy cleared away the dishes so she could spread her books on the kitchen table. Since she had started teaching church history at the seminary two days a week, she studied eight or ten hours for every hour of teaching she did. Though she had majored in history, she didn't feel prepared to teach church history. Beside that, she had to keep adding words to her Spanish vocabulary.

They had moved from Mendoza to Ituzaingo, a suburb 26 minutes from the seminary and 50 minutes from the central city. Their house at Laguna 970 had a big yard.

"Mercy, it's chilly in here," she told Charles. She moved with her books nearer to the stove. The woodburning kitchen stove was the only source of heat in the house. Sometimes in the evening, when the fire in the stove died, Indy would don a coat and sit in bed studying until past midnight.

"I suspect that the students don't care for a woman as a teacher," she worried. Only young men were enrolled in their classes.

"Oh, I think they respond well to you," Charles reassured her. His classes in Old and New Testament and biblical interpretation were scheduled so he could stay home to keep Helen while Indy taught her classes.

Usually they rode the subway or an electric train to school. Sometimes, though, they chose to ride a bus. Despite the traffic madness, they never tired of seeing more of this elegant city and its people. In it were combined some of the best of the old world and the new.

They rode past streets lined with large stone or brick apartment buildings, stores, exhibition halls, museums, government buildings, and churches. They passed many parks filled with trees and flower gardens, fountains, statues, and pools where children could sail their boats. Even late at night boys still played soccer in the parks.

Buenos Aires, which means "fair winds," had been named for the Virgin of Buenos Aires in Seville, Spain, because men about to make a voyage always visited her image to ask her to favor the enterprise with fair winds.

Residents of Buenos Aires, one of the largest cities in the world, boasted that their city had "the widest street on earth, and the longest; the highest building of reinforced concrete without the use of steel; and the best dressed people in the Western Hemisphere."

Its citizens called themselves *portenos,* and all other Argentines the *campesinos* (country people). It didn't matter that some lived in other cities. If they did not live in Buenos Aires, then they were *campesinos.*

The "widest street," Avenida 9 de Julio (Ninth of July Avenue), was ten lanes wide. Two famous landmarks the Whittens recognized on it were the Colon Opera House and the obelisk that looked like the Washington Monument.

The "longest street," Rivadavia, passed within a block or two of the Baptist seminary in the Floresta area of the city. Along it for miles stretched shops and restaurants, department stores, and apartment buildings.

This was truly a cosmopolitan city. Many of its parks were named with English or Italian names. Its downtown architecture was French. Its industries had felt the influence of the Germans. And Italians had helped to build its harbor on the Rio de la Plata.

Since Ituzaingo had no evangelical church, the Whittens began attending a small new church in a nearby suburb. Before they had even stashed their suitcases in the closet, though, they considered organizing a mission in Ituzaingo. Then just as Sunday School and WMU meetings began in their house, Charles was named interim president of the seminary. Bill and Kitty Cooper were leaving soon for furlough. To better fulfill their duties, Charles and Indy moved to Bolanos 164 to an apartment a half block from the seminary.

Rainstorms in mid-October lashed the city of Buenos Aires. Day after day the deluge recurred. Thunder and lightning mixed with downpours that even Noah might have felt kinship with.

October 14-17 was the date set for the 1950 Spiritual Congress, planned by and for Baptist young people of Argentina. Banners and posters advertised the theme, *Rios de Agua Viva: en Cristo Vida Abundante* (Rivers of Living Water: In Christ the Abundant Life). Charles had been invited to be one of the guest speakers. Because the congress would be held at the seminary, students and faculty helped youth committees to prepare for it.

For a meeting place, youths pieced together a big tent from several smaller ones and pitched it in the seminary garden.

The night the congress was to begin, a group of leaders met inside the seminary building. They heard the crash of thunder and saw the sheets of rain wash against the windows.

"We must not be discouraged," said Jacobo Vartanian, chairman of the Spiritual Congress committee. "Let us pray that the rain be stopped in time if it's God's will that we have this meeting." In less than ten minutes the downpour stopped long enough for the arriving crowd of young people to find their seats in the tent and for the meeting to begin.

The next night it rained again, and water piled on top of the tent. A big gust of wind sprayed it through a crack in the tent onto someone's surprised head. Once the water hit the young man who was preaching. He calmly picked up the pulpit and moved it a little way and kept speaking. Still he was standing under a leak, but he didn't stop. When he got too uncomfortable, he just moved again.

On Saturday afternoon the young people went out in twos to give out tracts and Gospels and invite people of the neighborhood to the evangelistic meeting the next day.

Sunday afternoon the tent was full; young people were standing in the aisles and outside the tent. Ramon Vasquez used as his text, "If any man thirst, let him come unto Christ and drink." More than 20 made professions of faith.

The day after the congress ended, a barbecue was held in a park outside the city. The "propaganda table" held copies of the young people's publication, the *Evangelical Tribune* which was celebrating its fifth birthday.

In December, Charles traveled to Asuncion to a meeting of the trustees of the Paraguayan Baptist Hospital. Back home, he untied Christmas packages as Indy handed them to him. Their best present, they felt, would be a little belated—a new baby due around February 1. But the gift was not as belated as expected. Indy arrived at the British Hospital on January 14 at 4:15 P.M. David Charles arrived at 6:56 P.M. He weighed 7½ pounds. "Helen's Happenings," a news sheet edited by Indy, gave the "stork market" reports and announced the second visit from "the famous old bird."

Helen at age 1½ spoke most words in English, but she had also learned a few Spanish ones from the maid. "*Pobrecito* (poor little one)," she said when she saw David. She tried to give him cookies and toys, but could not understand why he would not accept her offers.

During the same month that David was born, workers began cutting trees and cleaning up the seminary grounds for construction of two dorms and a new administration building.

As well as caring for the two young children and working with Charles at the seminary, Indy discovered another avenue of service, "Do what you can." The admonitions of her professors at the Training School kept ringing in Indy's ears. Maybe that was why she accepted a job in Woman's Missionary Union that everyone else was scared to take.

Minnie McElroy, who had given long service as a missionary, wanted to see an associational Woman's Missionary Union organized in Buenos Aires, so she called for a meeting of representatives of the various Baptist women's societies. Attendance was good and the women enthusiastically voted to start an association in Buenos Aires. But they needed a president. One person after another was nominated, but declined.

Then a woman nominated the youngest missionary present—Indy Whitten.

For a moment, the introvert within, a remnant from her early school days, tried to reassert herself. Apprehension crept over her. This would be a big, and perhaps, difficult job. Quickly, though, her desire to serve the Lord showed her what a large opportunity she would have here, and she answered, "All right."

Her friend, Teresa Pluis, was there to congratulate and encourage her after the meeting. She and Teresa had met on the train on the way back from the Argentine Baptist Convention in Rosario the previous year. Teresa, another pastor's daughter, was an active worker in Woman's Missionary Union. Though they had only been on the train together for four hours, they had immediately liked each other. They learned that they were the same age, and a friendship had blossomed. Teresa admired Indy's rosy cheeks and eyes which expressed a good, sensitive, and sweet nature.

In the first months of its existence, the associational Woman's Missionary Union in Buenos Aires organized a music festival, sponsored evangelistic meetings among the women, and emphasized the celebration of Christian Home Week in the churches. Various committees of the association met in Indy's living room.

Also, during August and September the WMU of Buenos Aires sponsored four sectional prayer meetings to pray for simultaneous evangelistic crusades being planned in the churches. C. Y. Dossey from the Home Mission Board of the Southern Baptist Convention was in Argentina for four months to help prepare for and to participate in the campaign.

The Woman's Missionary Union Association of Buenos Aires and its young people's organizations staged a rally prior to the crusade. More than 400 attended, in spite of the bad weather. Boys from two churches served as ushers, and a quartet from Velez-Sarsfield Baptist Church sang.

During the two weeks of revivals in 15 cooperating churches in Rosario, at least 600 persons made professions of faith.

While Charles preached during the crusades for two weeks in Tucuman, an area where many Indians lived, Indy taught his classes in New and Old Testament, as well as her church history class.

While Indy was thus involved in WMU affairs in Buenos Aires in 1951, she heard that Alma Hunt was coming to Argentina for a visit. In 1948, the same year Indy and

Charles had first set foot in Argentina, Hunt had been installed as executive secretary of Woman's Missionary Union, SBC. Eula Mae Henderson, the executive director of Texas WMU, would be traveling with Hunt to South America.

The Baptist missionary wives in Buenos Aires met and decided that each of them would invite Hunt and Henderson to eat in their homes.

Neither Indy nor Charles had met Hunt. They wished that Helen were old enough to make some clever remark, and just hoped that she would behave. "I guess we won't seem very Lottie Moonish or William Careyish to her," Indy sighed.

Alma in Spanish means "soul." Right away, they found this meaning applied to Alma Hunt. As soon as she sat down on their couch, they forgot about trying to impress her and felt at home with her.

She related interesting experiences that she and Henderson had been having in Colombia, Paraguay, and Chile. Hunt found her automobile ride in the Buenos Aires traffic more frightening than interesting. The traffic always moved at a wild pace through streets with no stop lights, the right of way granted to the driver who blew his horn first. "How," she asked them, "after a collision, is one able to prove who blew first?"

Two months after the visit from Hunt and Henderson, Charles and Indy attended Mission Meeting. The other missionaries surprised Charles when they elected him president of the Mission, for at 28 he was the youngest of the male missionaries. Indy was elected historian and reporter.

By October the concrete skeletons of the dorms were taking shape. The buildings were expected to be ready for use by April 1952. Plans by the architect called for a clock in the steeple of the administration building and a cross at the top.

Because of the study instigated by Gill of the Foreign Mission Board, with the help of various nationals, a decision had been made to establish four seminaries in South America, on a sound basis—two in Portuguese-speaking and two in Spanish-speaking sections. The seminary in Buenos Aires had been chosen as the site of the one for the southern half of the Spanish-speaking section, and its name had been changed to International Baptist Theological Seminary. That was an apt term, for students in 1951 included those of Russian, Spanish, Italian, French, and German descent.

As soon as the new buildings were ready, the Training School for women in Rosario would be moved to Buenos Aires to be combined with the seminary. W. L. Cooper would be president and Anne Margrett the dean of women.

The seminary faculty met and set commencement exercises for November 30, 1951, so that Bill Cooper would be present. He and Kitty were to return from furlough in early November.

The number on the faculty had increased since the Whittens had agreed to help out in time of emergency. Others now included Hugo Culpepper, Judson Blair, S. H. Cockburn, and Thomas B. Hawkins, besides Cooper and Anne Margrett. Charles and Indy had begun a friendship with the Hawkinses, longtime missionaries to Argentina, while they were in Rosario.

Early in 1952 Charles booked passage on the S. S. *Del Norte* for their May 8 return to the States for their first furlough. It had been almost five years since they had seen their families and Mississippi. Expecting in a year to return to Buenos Aires and the seminary faculty, they stored their furniture, little suspecting they would never see it again.

III
Europe

1953-1983

9
Sent to Spain

"Be like the little duck on the boundless Atlantic Ocean. Ease yourselves into world missions where it touches you."—Evelyn Hughey

DURING June 1953, the Whittens were on board the S. S. *Excalibur*. Somewhere between New York and Barcelona, Charles sat writing an article for the *Commission*. He wrote: "God has always led me one step at the time. . . . Little did we know when we went to Colombia and later to Argentina that one day God would point us to Spain."

A year earlier, the Whittens had sailed from Buenos Aires. As their ship had edged farther and farther out to sea, the last thing they saw on land was missionary Judson Blair holding up his child's blanket and waving it in a gesture of farewell.

After a visit with their families, they moved to Louisville, Kentucky, for a year. Charles continued graduate studies in Old Testament at Southern Seminary.

Long interested in Spain, they heard a speech by missionary George Jennings that tipped the scales of their concern. "Who will take over the work in Spain?" Jennings asked. He and his wife, Frances, who had received appointment there in 1947, had returned to the United States. Missionaries J. D. and Evelyn Hughey, who also had served in Spain, had transferred to Switzerland. The two couples had helped to reorganize Baptist work in a country recuperating from civil war.

Charles wrote to George Sadler at the Foreign Mission Board, asking for more information about the situation. Sadler asked the Whittens if they would like to transfer. Charles replied that they were happy in Argentina and had no desire to leave. However, if the Foreign Mission

Board requested they transfer, then they would be glad to do so. Sadler suggested they go for three years, with the understanding that if they wished, they could then return to Argentina. Sadler knew that no Southern Baptist missionaries had ever gone back to Spain for a second term. The field was a difficult one because of lack of religious freedom.

Certainly the need for missionaries to Argentina was still great, they reasoned. But Argentina had several dozen Baptist missionaries, while Spain had none.

On July 1, as the S. S. *Excalibur* neared the harbor at Barcelona, Charles and Indy looked toward land with a touch of uneasiness about the future that awaited them. Spain's largest port lay before them. The Mediterranean metropolis was on a plain between two rivers, with mountains rising in the background like a balcony. From one of those mountains above the city a roll of cannon fire sounded. Indy thought, "Have they discovered that Baptist missionaries are aboard this ship and they are after us already?"

Shipboard acquaintances had inquired, "Do you know anyone in Spain?"

"No," they replied.

As the ship pulled up to the dock, a group of people stood waving and calling out to them and holding up bouquets of flowers.

"Who are those people down there?" the others on ship inquired.

"They are our friends," the Whittens declared.

"Please make up your minds!" pleaded the others.

As Charles, Indy, Helen, and David, stepped off the gangplank, they were engulfed with handshakes, smiles, and kisses on both cheeks. *"Bienvenidos!"* rang in their ears from all directions. "Welcome!"

The little group of Spanish Baptists, much buffeted by the tragedies of war, had waited in excitement; many hopes and dreams revolved on the coming of the Whittens.

Representatives of the Spanish Baptist Union had been holding a board meeting in Barcelona that week.

Among those at the dock was Pedro Bonet, pastor of the Badalona Baptist Church in Barcelona and president of the Young People's Union of the Spanish Baptist Union. Also there were Joaquin Pastor, another of the Baptist pastors of Barcelona, and his wife.

Senora Pastor called to Charles, "I guessed which was you when I saw your hat!" She thought it looked like a Texas hat.

Missionary J. D. Hughey had come from Ruschlikon to meet them; he brought the news that Theron Rankin, president of the Foreign Mission Board, had died during their ten-day voyage.

From the time their feet touched the ancient soil of Barcelona, Spain held a place in their hearts. Indy wrote a friend, "We were plunged into a world of religious persecution, isolated Christian people, and larger responsibilities."

For them, Argentina had been a good learning experience. They had faced nationalism and realized that if not excessive and negative, it is the natural feeling of patriotism. They had learned the importance of loving first and not waiting to see if the people were going to love them.

They could not have coped as well in Spain had it not been for their experiences in Colombia and Argentina. Those countries had introduced them to the Spanish language and to Catholicism as the predominant religion. Teaching in Buenos Aires, they had unknowingly prepared themselves for teaching in the Baptist seminary in Spain.

Leaving the harborfront, they looked up to a statue of Christopher Columbus on a towering column, based in a fountain. They rode into the city on the Avenida de Jose Primo de Rivera, a wide street lined with palms and other trees. (Spaniards renamed streets with nearly every change of government.) Carts pulled by donkeys mingled with taxis and buses and cars. For the time being, the Whittens would work in Barcelona, where Charles would be interim president and teacher at the seminary. Indy, pregnant with her third child, would teach English at the seminary.

After a few days in the empty seminary building, they moved to an attic apartment at Tavern 34. It was comfortable, with bookcases on either side of a stone fireplace. Above the mantel Indy hung a picture of a magnolia blossom painted by Charles's Aunt Podie. A balcony across the back gave a view of houses built close to the street, decorated with iron grillwork, geraniums in window boxes, and fountains in rear gardens.

On the Whitten family's first Sunday morning in Spain, the Bonanova (Good News) Baptist Church welcomed them with bouquets of flowers. Sunday evening, the Badalona Church also presented flowers, and the children gave bags of candy to Helen and David.

One of the pastors suggested the Whittens hire Vicenta Ramos as their maid. Vicenta had come from Alicante, a city on the southern seacoast, looking for a job. They needed help with the house and children, so Indy followed his suggestion.

Right away Vicenta said to Indy, "I know you are a Baptist and I don't want you to be talking to me all the time about the church and religion."

"All right, I promise," said Indy. "But first, may I explain to you just one time what it means to be a Christian?" she asked.

Their conversation lasted for a couple of hours. Then Indy kept her promise to say no more on the subject. Since Vicenta had Sundays free, Indy did not know what she did on those days. One Monday morning Vicenta asked, "Do you know what I did yesterday?"

"No," Indy responded.

"I went to the Barceloneta Baptist Church." Not waiting for a response, she rushed on, "I took Jesus as my Saviour!"

"Why, I think that is wonderful," said Indy.

As the Whittens had relied on Rosa to teach them customs and traditions in Colombia, so they learned much of Spanish folklore from Vicenta.

At the time of their arrival in Barcelona, David and Helen still spoke mostly English. When Charles and Indy went out at night, Indy would ask Vicenta to listen to the children's prayers before they crawled into bed. Often Vicenta complained that the children prayed endless prayers; she didn't know how to stop them. Indy instructed her to say, after a prudent length of time, "In Jesus' name." It pleased Vicenta to find this worked.

When two more missionary couples arrived in Spain on September 13, 1953, the event was an answer to prayer. Francisco Fernandez, pastor of First Baptist Church, Madrid, from 1931 until his death of cancer in 1951, had let it be known he was praying for three Southern Baptist missionary couples to come to Spain, at least one to work in Madrid. No more than two such couples had ever worked in Spain at the same time.

"Why don't you pray for just one couple at a time?" Fernandez was asked. "Then you can ask for the other two when that prayer is answered."

"For one thing, I don't have that much time left on this earth," replied Fernandez. "Anyway, it's as easy for the Lord to send three as one." He did not live to see the answer when it came.

"*Bienvenidos!*" The Whittens and a group of Spanish Baptists welcomed the Meffords and the Wyatts as they walked down the gangplank in Barcelona harbor early on a Sunday morning.

Later, the three families got together in a hotel—Lila and Joe Mefford with their children, Tony, Sylvia, and Janie; and Roy and Joyce Wyatt with their son, Mike. Indy had brought a bag of sugar cookies and some bananas for the children because they were going to church and it would be a long time before lunch. Worship services began at 11:00 and Sunday School at 12:00.

The pastor welcomed them all to the Bonanova Church. It looked like an apartment house. "Remember that I told you all the churches that look like churches in Spain are Catholic churches?" Joe asked the children. "In Spain people are not free to worship as they please. The buildings must not look like churches or have any kind of a sign to say that there is a Baptist church there," he explained.

Most of the women at the church were wearing black

as a sign of mourning, for many in their families had died in the civil war of the 1930s. On their heads they wore black lace veils. While someone in the balcony played the organ, the congregation sang hymns from little black books that looked like poetry books. Deacons took up the offering in red velvet bags with short handles. The pastor introduced the new missionaries. They were given flowers and, after the service, many kisses on both cheeks.

One evening the next week, Charles returned home from an exploratory trip around the country to check on needs and opportunities in the churches.

"I met the ex-Catholic priest, Jose Borras," he announced at suppertime, "in Albacete at the home of Senor Juan Antonio Lopez."

"What is he like?" Indy was curious. "Does he look—well, priestly?"

"Not really. But I was impressed. You'll see for yourself soon. He will be studying with 11 others in the seminary," replied Charles.

As promised, she did meet Borras a few days later, on October 5, opening day at the school. Borras, handsome with dark hair and eyes, at first appeared somewhat reserved, but he greeted her with a friendly smile. He told Indy that as a Catholic priest, he had studied for the purpose of helping to stamp out evangelicals in Spain, but through a study of the Bible he had come instead to a personal acquaintance with a Saviour he had not previously known. Now he was studying to be a Baptist pastor.

Borras was one of only 12 students accepted for the three-year program. Limited space and faculty made it necessary to limit enrollment. It was exciting to start the school year. For two years the seminary had been closed due to lack of personnel.

First on the day's agenda was a meeting of the faculty and students to make plans for the school year. Later they stood on the patio talking and eating. Here was a student from a village and there one from the city. One had come from near the French border and had worshiped only in services in his home; another had been converted while in jail as a political prisoner. They represented the largest number yet to study for the Baptist ministry in Spain.

That evening at 8:30 the formal opening exercises took place next door to the seminary at Bonanova Baptist Church. Charles Whitten, Roy Wyatt, and Joe Mefford were seated on the platform, along with Spanish Baptist leaders. Charles brought the message on "The Kind of Preacher God Wants."

During that same month, word came that Baker James Cauthen had been elected as president of the Foreign Mission Board of the Southern Baptist Convention. Missionary J. D. Hughey returned to Barcelona to teach Charles how to keep the books as Mission treasurer. This was a job Charles did not want, but someone had to do it. Since no one else was available, he said he was willing. His administrative ability coupled with his personal integrity enabled him to learn quickly and to perform exceptionally well what often was a grueling, thankless task requiring more than a little patience. His less than perfect vision made the paperwork even more tedious.

As treasurer, Charles was destined to spend untold hours unwinding the red tape of church property deals. Only a few days after he arrived in Spain, a letter arrived from Lerida, a city west of Barcelona on the Segre River. "Come as soon as possible," the pastor had written to Charles. "We want you to help us solve our problems." The Whittens had come to a land with no freedom of the press, no economic freedom, no religious freedom. Many church doors—Lerida among them—had been closed and sealed by the government. But evangelicals courageously continued to meet in homes or other unusual places.

On October 18, Charles met with 41 Lerida Baptists gathered in the home of their pastor. From their explanations and what he already had heard, he pieced together the story. When winter drew near, the pastor had asked permission to break the seal that the government had placed on their old meeting place and to enter the building to retrieve two stoves. The governor told the pastor to go ahead. A policeman was instructed to reseal the doors. However, when the door to the basement apartment was opened, the pastor found the place a foot and a half deep in water from recent heavy rains. All the furniture had to be removed and stored elsewhere. Five policemen had inspected the place, and then removed the seal altogether. But the congregation did not think it wise to meet in that location anymore because of the flooding hazard.

Now one member asked Charles, "Will you, with Southern Baptist aid, help us obtain property where we can build?" It was extremely difficult for any evangelical group to buy property, and next to impossible to gain government permission to open a new church.

"It would be impossible to get a permit to build if it were done in the name of the Baptist Mission," the architect reminded Charles.

It seemed that the land for Lerida would have to be bought in the names of two Baptist laymen in Barcelona, for no one at the moment could think of another solution. Charles remembered that two or three properties J. D. Hughey had bought when he was in Spain had been in the name of Spaniards. Yet in this practice he could foresee trouble, for even the best and most trustworthy men would someday die. Then someone would inherit the property who might not be sympathetic with Baptist ownership of it.

How had it come about that a Spain which in her golden age colonized a new world now had so little freedom?

In 1931 a republic had been established. The next five years had been a time of great religious liberty for Spain. But then a part of the army rose against the republic. In the civil war that followed, hundreds of thousands died. General Franco won and came to power as dictator in 1939. Franco supported the political-religious state, meaning loyalty to the Spanish government and loyalty to the Catholic church were the same. Not only did religious liberty get squashed, but the salary scale fell unbelievably low. Most men had to work two jobs to support their families. Often every member of the family worked. Yet the Spaniards, as always, remained courteous, full of fun, friendly—and proud. "We are as noble as the king—only not so rich," one saying went.

A person strolling in Barcelona most any day could turn a corner and see a band playing on the steps of a cathedral and rings of dancers in the square circling in the infectious rhythm of the *sardana*. Of all folk dances, the *sardana* was most revered by the Catalan. When Franco captured Spanish Catalonia, he had burned the Catalan classics and excluded their language from schools, theaters, and public offices. Because of this, the dance had come to be used as a sort of political demonstration.

In spite of restrictions, Baptist progress under Franco had been steady. Baptists in the early 1950s numbered around 2,000. Southern Baptists had assumed responsibility for Baptist missions in Spain in 1920. Before then Swedish Baptists and the American Baptist Missionary Union had at various times established Baptist work in Barcelona, Valencia, Alicante, and Madrid.

Indy wrote in an article for *Royal Service*, a missions magazine:

> Spain is religious by nature and temperament. Traditionally she is 99 percent Catholic, but in practice her heart is far from the faith she professes. . . . Spain is receptive to the message of Christ. Outward appearance would indicate that many doors are closed, but the doors of human hearts are open. . . . The message cannot be broadcast by radio, but it is spread abroad by those who love Him. The good news cannot be announced in public squares, but there are ambassadors of the living Christ who faithfully represent Him before the public. The churches are beset with difficulties, but the word of God is not bound.

Once in a Sunday School class, Indy talked with a visitor about the Saviour. The visitor objected, "Don't talk to me about changing religion. I was brought up on religion. I have tried all my life to be religious. What do I get as a result? Nothing but an empty heart!"

"Oh, I beg your pardon," Indy replied. "You have misunderstood what I wanted to share with you. It is not a question of changing religions. Jesus Christ, the Son of God, will come into your heart and change you."

The Whittens were alike in their dedication to the Lord in their missionary efforts. Yet the two of them were as different as daylight and dark. She was always bubbly with excitement and enthusiasm. It was evident she was made to be a missionary in Spain. Living in the middle of history, so to speak, she was in her element. An effervescent, outgoing night person, she was happy with the Spanish time schedule—late breakfast, leisurely lunch, long siesta, work until 7:30 or 8:00, dinner at 10:00 or 11:00 lasting until midnight or later. He was forever busy in a quiet, unassuming manner getting his work done—using his gift of wisdom well, and yet witty as well as wise. He was unselfish, kind, and thoughtful of others' feelings. For example, one day a student opened the door for Charles. He was not ready to leave the room, but left anyway rather than hurt the student's feelings, and then shortly returned to complete his business there. The Whittens made a good team partly because they were so different and yet so alike.

Besides his work as treasurer and in various roles at the seminary, Charles assisted in the Spanish churches when needed as pastor or interim pastor. His reputation grew as a powerful, persuasive preacher. Particularly he was effective in leading in stewardship campaigns in the churches, which resulted in leading many of these churches either to or in the direction of self-support. Self-support was always the goal of foreign missions, and a concept primary in Charles's thinking.

Both Charles and Indy contributed to the music in the churches. Sometimes they would sing a duet. One of their favorites was "Some Day the Silver Chord Will Break." Other times he played the harmonica, or sang, accompanied by Joe Mefford on the accordion.

Indy was good at entertaining and at directing recreation. She often gave parties at home or led the games for church fiestas. Her love for people was evident; her sense of humor kept people laughing. Her letter writing continued unabated. As press representative for the Mission, she wrote newspaper articles as well as articles for missions magazines. She threw herself wholeheartedly into Woman's Missionary Union and youth work. Also she had accepted the editorship of the WMU magazine, *Nuestra Labor* (Our Task).

On November 25, 1953, Margaret Dean Whitten was born at the Hospital of the Foreign Colonies in Barcelona. She weighed 8¼ pounds. While Charles was at the hospital with Indy, missionary Roy Wyatt stayed with Helen and David. Seminary students pooled their resources to buy a pink blanket, and delivered it to the hospital. While Jose Borras stood beaming, Adolfo de Silva issued congratulations for the group. When Charles next entered the classroom, all the students stood and bowed to the proud father.

Early in the following year, Indy accepted an invitation from Malaga to help organize missions organizations for preschoolers, children, and women. On the Costa del Sol, not far from the chapel where stood de Mena's statues of Ferdinand and Isabella, she climbed two flights of stairs to the small apartment where the Baptist congregation held its meetings.

Short benches and chairs had been taken out of a closet for the women and children who filled every inch of space. French doors, opened wide, blended the two rooms into one. "I hope the floor doesn't break," the hostess whispered to Indy, who had squeezed behind the pulpit assembled piece by piece in the doorway.

Indy, remembering that the Lottie Moon Christmas Offering for the year would include $20,000 for a new Baptist chapel for Malaga, said to the group, "I bring you greetings and Christian love from more than a million Baptist women and young people in the United States. They pray and give because they love God and because they love you. Do not forget to pray for them that they may know how to appreciate and use religious liberty and that they may see their missions responsibility toward the world, even as we see ours."

One bent little woman of 75, who had climbed the stairs with difficulty, looked up with a smile on her face and tears in her eyes. "Praised be the Lord!" she exclaimed.

Spanish Baptist women often asked, "How can we be a part of the world missions enterprise? We are so poor. Our opportunities are so limited."

The rich Spanish senora had few hardships, but most Spanish Baptists were near the other end of the social ladder. The typical Spanish home in 1954 did not have refrigeration. Thus, every day included a trip by foot to market. If the housewife got to market with 25 pesetas, a good daily wage for a blue collar worker, she usually found that a basket of food cost 75 pesetas. Cooking was mostly done on charcoal stoves. In the villages, women washed clothes by hand in a stream and carried water from the public fountain. During rush seasons, they worked in the fields. Tile floors always shone—for this was a mark of decency. Women scrubbed them every day on hands and knees.

Though centuries of Moorish domination had left their mark on the attitude toward womanhood, Spanish Baptist women had been remarkably successful in breaking away from the old molds. Back in 1895, Antonio Zapater had been the first woman among Baptists to begin a union of Spanish women, which took the name Priscilla. In 1929, during the Baptist convention in Barcelona, the women present met together to organize. In 1935, women agreed to work under the name of Baptist Woman's Union and an executive committee was elected. Sadly the activities of this union were soon suspended due to the beginning of the civil war in 1936. This was a period of trial in which the women showed stout faith and trust in the Lord. Little by little they carried out their testimony silently but effectively. In some of the churches the women began to meet together again to pray and seek God's direction.

They saw their prayers answered in the arrival of

missionary Evelyn Wells Hughey in 1947. Hughey called a meeting of Spanish Baptist women in Barcelona March 17-19, 1948. Twenty women came as delegates from different churches. The purpose of their union was fixed: "Establish Christian homes and promote missionary work."

Another forward step in the work of Spanish Baptist women was the arrival of Frances Jennings, who encouraged the organization of missionary groups for youth. Then in 1953 the Baptist women took an offering to establish an old folks home in Vilafranca del Penedes, Barcelona.

When the Spanish women asked Evelyn Hughey how they could be a part of world missions, she said to them, "Be like the little duck on the boundless Atlantic Ocean. Ease yourself into world missions where it touches you." She was referring to a poem by Donald Babcock. The poet was describing the experience of realizing God's love by resting our lives in it where it touches us.

Many a woman in Spain had thus eased herself into missions by offering her home as the evangelical center of the community. Sometimes her family had borne the brunt of persecution for this.

While Indy was engaged in promoting Woman's Missionary Union, Charles as treasurer and as legal representative for the Foreign Mission Board, found plenty to keep him occupied.

"Senor Carlos," Vicenta called one day, "The telephone is for you."

He picked up the receiver. "How long? Forty-five days? You can't be serious. Yes, I'll do what I can."

Charles's friend, Aurelio del Campo, an elderly Baptist pastor, had been arrested and sentenced to 45 days in jail in Valencia.

Charles repeated the charge to Indy, "He had moved to Navarres and had not even had a chance to hold services when he got a notice to appear before the governor of Valencia Province for—(he counted on his fingers)— 'blaspheming the Virgin'; 'interfering with Catholic unity in Spain'; and 'distributing Bibles and other unauthorized literature.' He was told to leave the province at once, or the officials would not be responsible for the safety of his family."

"But he didn't leave?" Indy asked.

"No, he was fined 3,000 pesetas, and refused to pay the fine. So they arrested him," replied Charles.

And then Charles started laughing. At Indy's strange look, he quickly went on: "He took his Bible and a suitcase full of biscuits with him in case the jail food was bad!"

As he had promised, Charles as legal representative visited the American Embassy to ask for their aid with del Campo's case. After 15 days of negotiations, the governor of Valencia said the pastor might be released if he would not return to Navarres.

When the prison doors swung open early, and Charles and others were there to meet him, del Campo complained, "You could have left me until I finished my ministry!"

Jail officials had been surprisingly sympathetic, he said, and he had received good treatment. They listened as he talked to them about his faith in Christ. One made a profession of faith. Four others said they would like to visit Baptist church services (they did, and at least two continued to attend). The prison priest came by one day and del Campo persuaded him to sit down and read Psalm 24 with him. All this was remarkable because it was against the law for one to witness of his faith outside the church building.

As well as being legal representative, Charles continued to work in churches. When controversies arose, Charles tried not to take sides, but to be a middle-of-the-road person. Occasionally that meant he got hit from both sides.

After Charles accepted the pastorate of the Bonanova Church in Barcelona, a former pastor wrote letters of bitter criticism against him and the Baptist Mission. Charles simply answered nothing and did nothing. "I think people know what kind of person I am," he said, "and what my motives are for being here. I will not engage in a countercampaign of slander. Everybody knows that by his own actions he is no longer pastor of this church." Later on, letters of criticism circulated in regard to his stand as mission treasurer; he replied not a word. The matter enhanced peoples' opinion of him as a person and as a leader among the Baptist missionaries.

One day Charles and Joe Mefford attended an unusual service at Barceloneta Church. With the help of Southern Baptists the church had been building a new and modern place of worship three blocks from the dimly lighted, narrow place they'd been meeting. A permit had come from the government to finish the building.

The people had saved money in little clay pottery banks for the building fund. On this day they were bringing the banks, glad to have a part in giving.

The service opened with hymns. A deacon, Senor Celma, said that the members had thought and thought about how they might show their deep appreciation to friends in America who through their gifts to foreign missions had made such a beautiful new building possible. They decided they could do only one thing.

The deacon called the pastor to the front; then he called Charles Whitten. Representing the church, the pastor gave Charles a tremendous bear hug and a couple of back slaps. Then the pastor took a blue-handled hammer and smashed all the banks; the money fell into the offering box.

Since Charles already knew the language well, he was constantly giving pointers to Joe and Lila Mefford in their early language study. On one of his journeys with Joe, Charles parked his small English Morris-Minor while Joe registered at the inn. Joe announced to the clerk that the "other *caballo*" (horse) would be in in a minute. He intended to say *caballero,* or gentleman. The astonished clerk said to Charles when he came through the door, "I was watching for a horse."

At Christmastime, the three missionary couples usually would celebrate together. On December 28, 1954, Joe heard Charles call out from the street below: "Come on over for breakfast." They did, and ate bacon, eggs, cereal, hot biscuits, *leche de almendras* (almond milk), and coffee. Then Joe and Charles had an accordion and harmonica session. The wives told them they changed from "Saved, Saved" to "Beer Barrel Polka" awfully abruptly. Next the men went to look for a used car for the Meffords. Christmas dinner and the "family tree" had been at the Wyatts' home that year.

On December 31, Indy and Lila shopped for rare things, one of which was cornmeal. Most Spaniards did not like cornbread, for they remembered it as it had been during the civil war, when cobs were ground up with the meal to stretch the food rations. Late in the day Joe and Charles went to Bonanova Church for the watch night service. Others family members stayed home and tried the grape swallowing custom at midnight. Each tried to eat 12 grapes, one with each chime of the clock as it tolled the year's end. For every grape swallowed, a wish would come true for the new year. The Whittens and their friends hoped God would bring many good things to pass in the coming year.

10
Move to Madrid

"Lord, speak through me to the persecuted and to the persecutor."—Indy Whitten

CHARLES and Eric Ruden, European secretary of the Baptist World Alliance, walked through a series of arches and into the cobblestoned Plaza Mayor in Old Madrid. King Philip III had masterminded this elegant place in the early seventeenth century. What once had been a bakery house and royal lodgings, butcher shop, and mercantile guilds now housed cafes and souvenir shops. At El Pulpito Restaurant, Charles and Ruden met with Spain's minister of foreign affairs to talk at length about the problems of evangelicals. For instance, Second Baptist Church, Madrid, had been closed since the middle of 1954, and was still meeting in the pastor's apartment. First Baptist, Madrid, had been closed briefly in the fall of 1954, for "various infractions," even though it had written permission to meet.

Not long after this conference, on February 3, 1955, a telegram turned up in Barcelona, addressed to Charles. "I am at your disposition in Madrid until Sunday," the message said. It was signed by Jose Maria de Areilza, Spanish ambassador to the United States. Already Charles had gotten a letter from George Sadler of the Foreign Mission Board, praising Areilza's tolerance. Sadler added, "The Honorable Ambassador would like a conference with you." So at 8:00 the next morning Charles returned by plane to Madrid. By midafternoon he stood face-to-face with the ambassador.

"How many churches are closed?" Areilza asked. Charles listed four: "Lerida; Second, Madrid; Elda; Second, Valencia."

As the ambassador wrote, he remarked, "You know there are two kinds of religious people in the world?

First, those who are fanatical, intolerant, radical, and religious bigots. Second, those who want to be fair, tolerant, liberal, just, and to live at peace with other religious groups. Naturally, I like to include myself in the latter." He said he wanted to help, and asked, "Surely the opposing groups can coexist happily?"

"This is what we desire," Charles assured him. "You can count on our cooperation. We will make every effort to be prudent in the exercise of our religious faith.

"I hope the chapels can be reopened," Charles said. Charles pointed out numerous cases where churches did not have written permits for services. "Our congregations have asked for permits, but almost half of them have never received a reply," he said.

"I can see that they would not want to refrain from worship services for months while they wait for a reply, and I will make every effort to see that such requests do get their deserved answer," Areilza promised.

Charles was impressed with Areilza's seriousness and sincerity, and wrote to thank him and again to offer full cooperation in seeking solutions. "We realize we live in the framework of Spanish civil law," he wrote, "and I can truthfully say that all of the Spanish Baptists I know want to be loyal citizens of their country."

In the spring, the Whittens packed to move for the 11th time since 1947. Roy Wyatt had taken over as seminary president the fall before, so Charles and Indy planned to work in Madrid as the first Southern Baptist missionaries to live there. Since the Spanish government had signed a treaty with the United States to build air and navy bases in Spain, many things had changed. Lots of Americans in Madrid were paying $300 a month for house rent. Charles was able to rent a large house for $90 a month. He also rented a mission office on San Geronimo near the Plaza Mayor.

The Whitten family arrived in Madrid June 22. Before they even unpacked, they left for London and the Baptist World Alliance Congress. They traveled by train to Paris and Calais, and by ferry to Dover.

In Royal Albert Hall, they heard Lawrence North of New Zealand give the opening address on "Jesus Christ the Same Yesterday, Today, and Forever." They could barely begin to grasp the width of God's love as they heard citizens of 60 countries answer the roll call of nations. It seemed to Indy that the entire congress was a symphony set to the music of "blest be the tie that binds our hearts in Christian love."

That year a procession of Baptists visited Spain on the way to and from the congress. Indy wrote in a newsletter, "They are a source of encouragement to the Spanish believers and something like a shot of vitamin B to the missionaries." Since Indy had by then learned to drive, she would chauffeur anyone anywhere they wanted to go. Her reputation as the "fearless driver" grew rapidly, for it was jokingly said she could maneuver through Madrid traffic with her eyes shut. She could talk while she drove, sometimes illustrating a point with her hands.

Earl Waldrup, Charles's former classmate at Mississippi College, came to visit on an assignment with the Foreign Mission Board. During his visit Earl learned about Charles's superb language skills. One of the missionaries told Earl about the day Charles entered a hardware store to make a purchase. Charles greeted the sales clerk and told him what he wanted. The clerk replied, "I'm sorry, but I just sold the last one we had to a foreigner," never realizing Charles was a foreigner.

Edna Frances Dawkins, assistant secretary of missionary personnel for the Foreign Mission Board, had visited the Whittens in Barcelona before they moved to Madrid. She had driven with them into the mountains to the famed Catholic shrine of Montserrat, where the mountain rises from a flat base of strangely serrated rock. A monastery had been founded there in the eleventh century. During the Middle Ages a legend grew that Montserrat was the hiding place for the Holy Grail.

On the day of their visit, women were carrying their babies up to the small, glass-enclosed statue, the Black Virgin, for hope of a blessing. Many legends have been woven around the powers of the image to heal the sick and wounded. Many invalids travel there, hoping to be cured. Around the case where the statue stood were precious stones; in the rooms outside were jewels and other offerings of value made to the Black Virgin. Teresa Pluis, a friend of the Whittens from Argentina days and president of the Argentine WMU, came after the congress. Her Argentine sisters had collected a special offering for her to take to the Baptist Home for the Elderly in Villafranca, and had asked that she visit Spanish women's societies in their name.

Teresa arrived at the Madrid airport on a Sunday morning. After she accompanied the Whittens to First Baptist Church, she and Indy talked about her schedule of activities. Indy thought all visitors to Spain ought to see at least 1 or 2 of the 1,420 castles. She offered to take visitors to Madrid to the Prado Art Museum, El Escorial, the palace of kings, the flea market, or whatever other historic places they chose, as well as to churches and other Baptist places of interest.

Indy and Teresa talked and talked, trying to catch up over the years. Suddenly Teresa remembered her baggage. She had washed her clothes before leaving Longdon, but needed an iron. "I'd like to press my dresses," she said.

Indy called Vicenta and asked with a conspiratorial smile, "Where is the iron in this house?" Vicenta returned the secretive smile.

"There's so much to do," Indy explained, "that I have tried to simplify housework. We never iron our clothes except on special occasions, but just fold them neatly."

Teresa, knowing Indy's commitment to the Lord's work, said she agreed with this plan entirely.

While in Spain, Teresa toured several provinces and visited churches where Spanish Baptist brethren had found it so difficult to live their faith. She wrote in her notebook:

> Once, on a bus trip, I was sitting next to a Spanish lady, and we began a conversation. She realized by my accent that I was Argentine, and she asked me why I had come to Spain. I told her I was a Baptist and that I was visiting my brothers and sisters in the faith. She was so shocked! Sitting next to

a Protestant! She moved all she could toward the window, as if by being close to me she could be stained. I tried to make her understand that evangelical Christians love God, her God, and the Virgin Mary. Yes, all I said was fine, but she was desperate to reach her destination. When we got off the bus, she shook her clothes, as if she had been sitting next to somebody unclean. I was very upset to see how some people have such a mistaken idea about evangelical Christians.

After Teresa's visit, Baker James and Eloise Cauthen of the Foreign Mission Board arrived to stay with the Whittens for several days. The Whittens took them to the Plaza Mayor. While people walked leisurely by, a little girl and her grandfather fed the pigeons. Sounds of flamenco music floated from the window of a basement cafe. Cauthen stood quietly, looking at the center of the square where so many martyrs had died for their faith, burned at the stake during the height of the Spanish Inquisition. Charles noticed the tears running down Cauthen's cheeks.

At Christmastime, Joe and Lila Mefford arrived from Valencia for the holidays. "I'm determined we're going to have a good time!" Indy announced. And they did. The four adults and six children drove to Toledo and spread a winter picnic. They ate *paella*, a favorite Spanish dish, with their gloves on. Back at the house, they played games and sang Christmas carols.

While Charles kept writing the Foreign Mission Board and meeting with various Baptist World Alliance and government officials about the lack of religious liberty, Indy kept many in the United States informed about the problems and needs through her steady flow of magazine and newspaper articles. At the same time, she continued her work as editor of *Nuestra Labor* (Our Task).

After she prepared the copy for the magazine in Madrid she shipped it to the printer in Barcelona by a moving van. The inch-thick manuscript looked strange in the van next to threshing machines or couches, but Indy had to consider the problem of censorship. If the material were sent through the regular mail, it might be stopped and not reach the printer at all, or even if it did, she might be expelled from the country for editing an unauthorized publication.

The printer, Senor S. Salvado, and his wife and son had become Christians because of their contacts with *Nuestra Labor* and another Baptist magazine, *Eco de la Verdad*.

In January 1947, a Baptist pastor had asked Salvado if he would print *El Eco*, and he refused. Before then Salvado had printed only books for collectors. He was rightly proud of his work, for on each book's flyleaf was written, "This book was printed by the master printer."

But the pastor said to Salvado, "Very well, but if you will reconsider, we will be very indebted to you, and we will ask our readers to pray for you."

In the first issue of *El Eco* that Salvado printed, readers were asked to pray for the new printer. Six months later, the Salvados visited an evangelical church. A year and a half later they came to know Jesus in a personal way.

Salvado had told Indy that his slogan had been changed. "The 'master printer' no longer exists," he said. "Now he is 'the printer for the Master.' "

Nuestra Labor carried monthly programs for the missions organizations. It contained articles, missionary features, promotional plans, methods, study outlines, news reports, and daily devotional readings for the family. At times there were articles in big print for persons learning to read and evangelistic messages for non-Christians who might see its pages.

Indy described the magazine as a "love letter circulated among Spanish Baptists. . . . She often changes her appearance with a new dress or a new mantilla (lace scarf), but the content of her message is always the same. . . . She is glad tidings written on paper."

Before the Spanish Baptist Union met for its 1955 sessions, the Baptist Women's Union met for two days in Madrid. Indy invited all the women present at the convention to her house for refreshments and fellowship. She noticed a policeman stationed across the street, watching, she supposed, to find out why so many busloads of Protestant women were arriving there. When she invited him inside for a cup of coffee, he accepted.

She had a chance to show him the women were not doing anything to harm anyone.

On her birthday in December, Indy received a letter from a friend. In the letter the woman recalled that she and Indy were the same age. Teresa wrote, "This year I celebrated my 33rd birthday and now you too are the same age as our Lord when He fulfilled His ministry on earth."

Indy replied, "How far I am from being like the Master, but I long to be like Him."

Indy recorded many of her experiences, and Baptist newspapers printed them so Baptists in America could share the missions vision.

MANY PASS JUST OUTSIDE THE DOOR

It was the first Sunday in the new year and my heart sang as I approached the new church building in Figueras, Spain. The sky was blue, and the sun transformed the ice in the little mud paddies into sparkling diamonds.

The pastor pointed to the snow-covered Pyrenees Mountains in the distance and I made a mental note to describe the scene on paper when I got home. Those majestic peaks seemed to stand as a reminder that purity and beauty have not disappeared from the earth. "Though your sins be as scarlet, they shall be as white as snow" came to my thinking.

Then suddenly I heard a child's cry and my rejoicing was interrupted. There in the garbage dump not far away were a mother and three sad-faced undernourished children. They were going through the garbage sorting out what might be good enough to eat.

"I found one good orange," said the youngest child joyfully. He stuffed it in the pocket of his ragged short trousers and fell to his knees to continue looking.

I walked on toward the church, but I stumbled over the curb for I was looking back. "There you have a parable for a sermon," I remarked to the pastor. "There are millions of people at our door going through the garbage of life physically and spiritually speaking."

"Yes, that is true," said the pastor.

By this time we were at the entrance of the church. My husband, the pastor, and I went in and shut the door behind us—leaving the garbage, the woman, and her three skinny, big-eyed, hungry children outside.

Indy Whitten
Baptist Record
February 12, 1959

11
Persecution persists

> "We are troubled on every side, yet not distressed: we are perplexed, but not in despair, persecuted, but not forsaken" (2 Cor. 4:8-9).

"OUR CELL was there on the ground floor," Manolita Duet Diaz pointed out the drab gray jail to Indy. "We stood by those windows and sang hymns." Their fellow church members outside in the square would hear, and answer by pacing up and down, whistling hymns. This was the only way they could communicate.

"How long did you have to stay?" Indy asked. "Eight days. Truthfully—eight happy days. The Lord taught me many things," Manolita responded.

Twenty-four members of the Jativa Baptist Church had been fined for gathering on the Albaida River for a baptismal service. Though Baptist churches took an offering to pay the fines, 3 young women and 2 young men refused to pay. Police arrested them; 3 were sentenced for 8 days and 2 for 15 days. As they proceeded to jail, their families walked with them, singing hymns of praise.

"It would have been easier to pay the fine," Jose Garcia Arnau explained, "but I had made up my mind to go to jail. I had the conviction that my Lord had need for me thus to testify of Him."

In the jail they held worship services, with prayers, Scripture reading, and testimonies. Other prisoners and one jailer came to listen. Outside, church members continued a chain of prayer for them the entire time.

In 1955 it was not easy for anyone to cast his lot with the evangelicals. If he were employed he would likely lose his job; if he were a businessman, his establishment might be boycotted. In many cases it meant alienation from his family. Yet, scores continued calmly to stand

and say, "Today I take my stand with Jesus." They had already counted the cost.

Another friend of the Whittens who went to jail was Juana Lumbreras, a middle-aged woman of Tabernes, a Valencian village.

Senora Lumbreras had invited her sister-in-law and a few friends to her house to read the Bible. Five friends were reading with her when neighbors told a policeman about it. Senora Lumbreras was fined 2,000 pesetas for holding a religious meeting without permission, and the others were fined 500 pesetas each.

She didn't think she should pay, for she had done nothing wrong. But when she didn't pay, she received a sentence of 15 days in prison. Her four children stayed home with their father. When the 15 days were up, authorities added 15 more days without giving her a reason.

Every day for 30 days, the Woman's Missionary Union of First Baptist Church, Valencia, sent Senora Lumbreras a basket of food. A prison guard saw the food and asked, "Are these your relatives who send food?"

"No," she answered, "they are my sisters in Christ." Surprised, the guard asked for the address of a Baptist church. Later he visited it, and accepted Christ as his Saviour.

When Senora Lumbreras returned home, several neighbors said, "If you think enough of your faith to go to jail for it, we want to hear more about your faith." Five of her neighbors also accepted Christ. Until then, the pastor at Denia had gone to Tabernes to preach about once a month. Soon afterward, a small church was formed in the village.

Early in 1956 Charles had another interview with the ambassador, and he and Theodore Adams, president of the Baptist World Alliance, talked with the minister of foreign affairs. Yet, there seemed to be little noticeable result.

Later that year Charles became interim pastor of Second Church, Madrid. The church was still closed, the brown paper seal still glued to its doors because "they had bribed children to go to Sunday School." The "bribe" was a bit of candy given at a Christmas party. Printed above the sealed doors were the words, *"Entrad por sus puertas con reconocimiento,"* from Psalm 100—"Enter his gates with thanksgiving."

The congregation continued to meet in the pastor's apartment and held some services in First Baptist Church's building. One afternoon Indy was teaching a Bible study for a women's group on the outside patio of the pastor's home. An apartment window above the patio suddenly opened. A woman stuck her head out and called, "Speak a little louder, please. I can't hear you."

Within a few months, the church called a new pastor, Jose Nunez.

When spring came to Madrid, the sidewalk cafes filled with people sitting in the sun and chatting leisurely. Pomegranate trees and yellow jasmine blossomed. After working hours, the *paseos* (sidewalks) along the wide tree-lined avenues filled with strollers. Since the winter had in no way resembled travel folders' ads of sunny Spain, the Whittens were glad to see the warm days.

Indy opened a letter one day in early spring. "It's from Roy and Joyce," she said. The Wyatts had returned to the States. Both had hepatitis and doctors advised rest. "They say they probably won't be back until fall." Yet three more months remained in the spring session at the seminary. Someone would need to fill in for Roy there.

Charles called Joe Mefford. "What do you suggest that we do? Could we take turns, do you suppose?" he asked.

"If you want to take Thursdays through Saturdays, I'll take the other part of the week," Joe said.

So Charles flew to Barcelona early on Thursdays and stayed until Saturday night, and flew back to Madrid so he could preach in the city on Sundays. Joe drove or flew from Valencia to stay from Mondays through Wednesdays until the school year ended.

Thus Charles was ready for the family vacation trip

to Switzerland in their Morris-Minor. At Ruschlikon-Zurich they met with 20 missionaries and 24 missionaries' kids at the first conference of all Southern Baptist missionaries in Europe, June 24 and 25. They crossed the Alps by car for the first time. It seemed they were skimming along on the top of the world looking around at white-tipped peaks and down at shining glaciers.

On the way home they stopped in Rome to visit Virginia Wingo, then a missionary in Italy. Through the years since seminary, she and Indy had kept in touch through letters. Wingo had told a friend about Indy, "She's as good a correspondent as C. S. Lewis was described to have been! She's faithful and prompt in writing, yet never insisting, 'Please write more often,' or apologizing for not having time to write." Every time Spanish Baptists sent a young woman to study at Armstrong Memorial Training School in Rome where Wingo was director, Indy would introduce the young woman to her by way of an advance pen-picture—brief, but enthusiastic and appreciative, capturing the best of each personality.

As Wingo drove the Whittens about in Rome, Charles showed her how to shift down instead of wearing out her Fiat's brakes as she drove down the Roman hills, especially the Janiculum and Monte Mario.

In August, the Whittens began teaching a study on love, courtship, and marriage. Youth from across the country gathered at the church for classes, recreation, eating, and sleeping. It was a lovely city for such a meeting. The Castle of Santa Barbara towered on its hill, and the Mediterranean was such a special deep shade along the shore that it was called Alicante blue.

The conference began with enthusiasm. But on the second day, policemen delivered a threat: "Everyone here who does not live in Alicante is to leave the town within 24 hours. If this order is not obeyed, this church will be closed." They adjourned, and all left.

Altogether, they spent a good year in Madrid. Yet when the seminary opened again in the fall, Charles and Joe felt they could not continue commuting so far weekly as they had during the spring. Though Roy and Joyce Wyatt had returned from sick leave on September 17, their doctors had warned them not to overwork. Thus, the six members of the Mission conferred together and the Whittens agreed to move back to Barcelona as a temporary solution.

Since the churches in Madrid were somewhat isolated from those on the coast, the Whittens were needed there. But as usual, they were willing to be adaptable. George Sadler from the Foreign Mission Board had written that two more missionary couples were on the horizon for Spain.

Charles would teach New Testament in the seminary and do general field work with the churches of Catalonia, in addition to his work as treasurer. Indy would teach Christian ethics in the seminary and a class for pastors' wives. With her characteristic sense of humor, she remarked to Lila, "A person has to be somewhat silly and quite daresome to think she can teach just any subject in the seminary."

Charles, in a few days, wrote to Sadler:

> Since the beginning of our foreign mission experience we have always felt that we ought to be willing to do the work and to live in the place which seemed to be the greatest need at that particular time. And now with a definite feeling of divine guidance we joyously make this move. . . . Of course, it gives us some sense of sadness to leave Madrid.

This time they found a house with a yard outside Barcelona's city limits, at Esplugas.

In the Barcelona area, Indy launched herself into promoting the literacy project begun by the Baptist Women's Union.

"Here comes the reading lady!" children called when they saw Indy. She had made so many visits to one housing project that children knew her car.

In the dining room of a small home in the suburbs Indy sat at the table beside Senora Mercedes Garcia, the Laubach primer open between them. While Garcia's three children sat on the floor, all ears and eyes, she fingered the edge of the table nervously and mumbled, "I'm scared I'm so dumb you can't teach me anything."

With patience, Indy guided the woman through the first page. Garcia, ready to try a sentence, took a deep breath and slowly said the Spanish words for "Papa calls the cow!" A look of relief crossed her face. "Thank God, children!" she cried. "Mother can read!"

Some months previously, Frank Laubach, "apostle of the illiterates," and his co-worker in world literacy, Richard Cortright, had been guests of the Spanish government and also guests in the Whitten home. Due to conversations with Indy and Charles, Laubach had given permission for his primer to be printed in Spanish for Baptists' use.

Churches had adopted a goal of teaching every illiterate member to read. Lila Mefford was elected chairman of the WMU committee for promotion of the literacy effort. The women taught the Laubach method to pastors and to seminary students. Indy presented the idea many times to her class of pastors' wives. Also, she worked with a committee on literacy in the Badalona Church. Indy took advantage of opportunities to reach her reading students for the church program.

Esther Frances Garcia translated Laubach's primer and also his *Story of Jesus* into Spanish so they could be published by Baptist Women's Union. Esther, a Baptist pastor's daughter, had come from Alicante to Barcelona to study in the university. She lived in the home of the Salvado family, the printers for *El Eco* and *Nuestra Labor*.

While in Barcelona Esther met Jose Borras, the seminary student who was an ex-priest, and they fell in love. When the Salvados invited Charles and Indy to lunch one day, they did not expect the surprise that awaited them. Jose arrived dressed in stiff collar and tie and holding a bouquet of flowers. During the luncheon, his engagement to the vivacious, brown-haired Esther was announced.

Jose was admitted to study in the European seminary in Ruschlikon. Esther continued in the University of Barcelona and became the first Spanish Baptist young woman in Spain to receive a university degree.

Jose and Esther wanted to be married the next summer, in 1957, but it looked as if that might be next to impossible. The Spanish government would not permit a priest—not even an ex-priest—to break his vow of celibacy, though he had officially left the church.

At length, Esther and Jose reviewed the various solutions to their dilemma. Finally they decided to establish residence in England and be married legally there (at least, legal everywhere in the world except Spain). Then Jose would go back to Switzerland and Esther would return to complete her university studies. The next summer they could have their real wedding ceremony at the Baptist church in her hometown of Alicante.

When Esther was leaving for England, Indy went with her to the train station. "Am I doing the right thing?" Esther asked. Tears quivered on her eyelashes. Taking such a bold step frightened her.

"You know you are," Indy encouraged. She hugged her, kissed her on both cheeks, and waved as she stepped onto the train.

Indy herself would be leaving Spain soon, for she and Charles and the children were preparing to leave for furlough. Not long before they left, George Sadler came to Spain for the last time before his retirement. A banquet given in his honor at the Badalona Church served the double purpose of welcoming a new missionary couple, Patsy and Russell Hilliard. Sadler told Charles he had never seen anything on the missions field to compare with that banquet.

As the Whitten family left to sail from Cannes, a Baptist woman in Barcelona gave them a little plastic sack filled with dirt. She said, "As the ship pulls by the Statue of Liberty, throw this Spanish soil at her feet and tell her that one day we will be free and we will lift our torch."

12
Back to Barcelona

> Barcelona is "the flower of the beautiful cities of the world, honor of Spain, dread and terror of near and distant enemies, joy and delight of its citizens, haven for foreigners, school of chivalry, and exemplar of all that a great, famous, rich, and well-founded city should be."—Cervantes

WHEN the S. S. *Excalibur* once again pulled into the Barcelona harbor at 6:00 A.M. September 1, 1958, it carried the first Southern Baptist missionary couple ever to return to Spain for a second term of service. This time a large group of Spanish friends met them with kisses and tears of joy. Among the missionaries on the pier were Gerald and June McNeely, who had arrived on September 2, the preceding year.

Gerald was teaching New Testament and archaeology at the seminary, and June was librarian. Charles would continue as treasurer and act as interim president in Roy's absence. (The Wyatts and Meffords had gone on furlough.)

Indy had been elected as president of the Mission in 1958, no doubt because she had done such an efficient job in that office during 1955 and 1956. The Hilliards also would be helping them in Barcelona.

The Whittens moved into a fifth floor apartment three blocks from the seminary on Avenida General Mitre. Their children enrolled at the American Navy School, thrilled to ride a school bus for the first time.

All the Spain Baptist Mission had always been like one big family. Immediately the McNeely girls, Linda and Marsha, and the Whitten children became friends. Linda owned a mouse named Benjy, "the wise one," which would sit on her shoulder. Because Benjy could crawl between the bars of the bird cages Linda tried to keep him in, Tony Mefford had made her a special cage with wire mesh.

95

It was a sad day when Benjy died. Linda spent all her weekly allowance to buy black-edged stationery to send out death notices. She wrote on each formal announcement that "Benjy has gone to his reward." Her "Aunt Indy" cared enough to send her a sympathy card.

For picnics together in the mountains above the city, they could reach Mt. Tibidabo by cable railway. From there they could see the city spread below, a great tangle of Gothic arches and stone lacework—and the blue sea beyond, edged with wharfs and liners. For weeks ahead of the week of prayer, talk of the Lottie Moon Christmas Offering dominated family worship time at the Whittens' house, and mealtime conversations too. The goal for 1958 was $6,800,000. Spanish Baptists had adopted their own Cooperative Program the year before. With Charles's stewardship revivals and Indy's Woman's Missionary Union work, the topic of giving often arose.

"What would you do if you had $1 million?" David asked one night at the dinner table.

Tenderhearted Helen started listing ideas, but then said suddenly, "Oh, I know! If I had $1 million, I would give at least half of it to the Lottie Moon Christmas Offering."

"But what are you planning to give even without having $1 million?" Charles asked. This required further thought and discussion.

Later, as Charles walked to David's bedroom to hear his prayers, David said, "If I had 1,000 daddies, I would send them all away and keep you, Daddy."

Though they were members of First Baptist Church, Barcelona, the Whittens often visited other churches. One Sunday evening they walked up the stairs to a third-floor apartment to the night service of Third Baptist Church, Barcelona. They carried their Bibles and hymnbooks wrapped in newspaper, not because they were ashamed of the gospel, but because they wished to avoid any public demonstration of their faith, as required by law.

The entrance hall was filled with people. The living room, 8-by-14 feet, was packed. A few even sat in the kitchen and bedrooms.

Several weeks before, the police had threatened the pastor and told him the church would be closed if they didn't stop meeting in it without a permit for that locality. Since then, the congregation had been divided, meeting in this home and two more.

They sang hymns softly to avoid attracting attention. Every time the doorbell rang, the people glanced nervously toward the door, as if half expecting the police to enter.

The pastor preached on Christian hope, and led in prayer that God would use these present circumstances for His glory and to make the members strong enough to carry on despite difficulties.

After many affectionate farewells, the people quietly left, a few at the time, down the dark stairway. Charles and Indy, Margaret, Helen, and David came out the front door and walked toward their little car parked on a side street away from the building in order not to attract attention. They did not turn to wave good-bye to their friends because they were not supposed to be thus congregating in groups; they climbed into their car and drove home for their Sunday night supper of pancakes.

Indy had met for women's meetings at all hours of the day and until midnight. She had attended meetings in big churches, little churches, homes, a garage, and under a tree. The national Woman's Missionary Union president, Noemi Celma Bonet, wife of the pastor of the Badalona Church and one of her dearest friends, had been active in Spain's Woman's Missionary Union since its beginning. Indy, Bonet, and other leaders had faced all kinds of problems—no members, no literature, no transportation to get the women to meetings.

In November 1958 Indy added a new experience to her list. She and Patsy Hilliard were invited to lead a study for the women of Third Baptist Church.

The 12-by-16-foot kitchen where they met also served as a dining room. In it were seated 22 women. She and Patsy edged around to chairs saved for them. From there, Indy could see in the corner facing her a charcoal fire, an aluminum pot, and two skillets hanging on the wall.

Patsy and Indy were introduced as "those who have come so far as an expression of God's love and the concern of Southern Baptists in the United States."

After the study ended the president said, "I think we could use this time to plan the program for the close of the Week of Prayer for Foreign Missions." They decided exactly what they would have—a play by the young women, a song by the children, and a filmstrip. Various women agreed to take part.

But suddenly the vice-president asked, "Where will we have this meeting? These plans include the whole church. We have only one group to put on the program, but we would have to meet in at least three different places."

With a sigh of disappointment, they began to make other plans.

Once a man visiting Spain had said to Charles, "My son, don't ever forget that there are kinds of persecution worse than throwing stones. Refusal to grant marriage permits is one."

Though on December 10, 1958, the United Nations had celebrated the tenth anniversary of the Universal Declaration of Human Rights, scores of young couples in Spain still looked in vain for notice from the government that they could be married in a civil ceremony. Civil law forbade Protestants to marry people who had ever been baptized as Catholics. Almost everyone in the country had been baptized into the state church as infants. Evangelical young people who had been thus baptized and later left the state church especially felt the law's severity.

To write an article for the *Commission* on the topic of marriage, Indy interviewed several couples. She especially wanted to talk with Santiago Rodes and Ana Rocal, whose case had been denied in the highest court that deals with such matters. She met them in front of First Baptist Church, Madrid, and talked with them at length.

They had been waiting for 18 months for permission

to marry. Their parents had spent a lot of money for legal fees. The district judge had refused to marry them so they carried their case to the Supreme Court. There their request was denied "because people who have been baptized as Catholics and have left the state church cannot be legally married."

They could not with a clear conscience go ahead and marry in a Catholic ceremony and promise to rear their children in the state church. One alternative would be to marry before a notary public and let him make out a statement that they had done all they could to marry legally. But if they did that, it would give authorities further chance to say that evangelicals were breaking the law.

Even with all the odds against them, the couple told Indy they had not thought of giving up.

During the Easter holidays in 1959, the Whitten family made an 1,100-mile round-trip journey to south Spain. In Murcia, they watched elaborate Holy Week processions parade along the streets. Fireworks and cannons flickered and roared.

In all, on the trip, they took part in eight church services, including one in a cave home of members of First Baptist Church, Valencia. Indy wrote in her notebook:

At Aguilas, the group of Baptists was small. The walls in the plain room needed repairs and painting. A rectangle of liquid sunlight fell on the rough concrete floor and a piece of blue sky was wrapped around the rocky hill visible from the narrow window at the back. Fifteen people had met in the city of 25,000, in that room, to worship the Risen Christ.

Along the way, David, aged eight, said he wanted to write an article:

I am going to tell you how Spain is like a candle. When a candle is lit, it burns until the fire goes out or the candle melts. That is just what happened in Spain. The light of the candle is the gospel in this country. During the first years it was going fine. The missionaries at that time were Dr. and Mrs. J. D. Hughey and Dr. and Mrs. George Jennings. These missionaries had to leave Spain, and that's the way the candle went out. When the Meffords, Wyatts, and our family came to Spain, we lit the candle again. Signed: David Whitten, son of Charles William Whitten, a foreign missionary.

Helen, aged nine, kept a journal on the trip. One part of it reads:

I am going to tell you about a little church mission in Alcoy. It was a small room for church services with about 30 chairs. They started out with 2 people. They had never had over 22 people to come. On Friday before Easter the chairs were full and some people were standing. On that night 42 were present.

Mother and Daddy sang, and Daddy preached. At the close of the service Daddy asked those who wanted to accept Christ to stand up. They had never had an invitation given because this is a new church. The result was three grown-up ladies who gave their hearts to Jesus. Then the service finished and we went to our hotel happy.

June 10: Indy circled the date on her 1959 calendar. That night Helen was to be baptized at First Baptist Church in Barcelona in the new building made possible by the Lottie Moon Christmas Offering. Indy had organized a Girls' Auxiliary in that church in January, and by May Helen had earned her green Maiden armband.

On June 11, the Whittens once again moved to Madrid, this time to a two-story house on San Telmo Street.

13
"Love in the oven of refinement"

"We heard the unmistakable Voice of Love say to our troubled hearts, 'My children, lean hard. My Grace is sufficient for your every need.'" —Indy Whitten

RAIN began to fall over Barcelona as the green mission car left the city and headed for Madrid. It was September 4, Charles's birthday; his mother's was two days later. "We'll celebrate with ice cream and cake for both of you when we get home," Indy said.

David and Helen were squeezed between their grandparents on the backseat. Margaret was in the front seat between Indy and Charles, who was driving. All of them had just returned from a tour of France, Switzerland, Germany, Austria, and Italy, and a stop in Barcelona for Mission Meeting. Velma and Willie Whitten had been in Spain since July.

The road climbed around the southern end of Montserrat and crossed the Segarra, a wheat-growing plateau dotted with ancient villages. Those in the car, excited about being together, talked and laughed. The children could hardly wait to get home to see their new dog, Lassie. Ahead of them, the wet pavement glistened as the car followed it through the drizzly dark day. One by one the children hushed, their eyelids growing heavy with sleep.

They drove through Quinto, a quiet place where storks flapped their wet wings. An old woman in black sat dozing in a doorway, a dog asleep at her feet.

Indy leaned her head back. "I'll drive later," she said. "Right now I plan to take a nap."

Down the road in front of them, a truck tried to pass another on the narrow road. Charles stepped on the brakes but could figure no way to miss the truck. From the backseat David saw a bulky shape loom through the grayness, and he felt an enormous impact. Then the car stopped on the right side of the road, its front smashed in and its steering-wheel shaft driven into Charles's abdomen. Charles was conscious but could not speak because of his crushed diaphragm. Indy was unconscious, blood trickling from cuts on her face. Velma could not move her left arm. Helen held her hand across her mouth where something had struck it. Margaret, David, and Willie were all right, but in a state of shock. David got out and walked around, rubber-legged, while they waited, not knowing what to do. Willie looked at his watch. It was one o'clock.

None of them knew exactly how long they waited before a Spanish diplomatic car stopped to take them to the nearest first-aid station, which happened to be in the village of Pina on the Ebro River, 26 miles from Zaragoza and about halfway between Barcelona and Madrid. As the men carefully moved Charles into their car, Helen tried to hug him. "You are going to be all right, Daddy," she said.

At the first-aid station, Willie tried to call the local doctor. Since he only knew the words for *good morning, good-bye,* and *thank you* in Spanish, he had a nerve-racking time trying to get the message through. David, eight, and Helen, ten, acted as translators.

When Indy opened her eyes, she saw that they were in a strange place. Where? Velma was lying on another bed, her face pale, her eyes closed.

Indy heard a groan. Her eyes searched for Charles and found him on the examining table. The man beside him—he must be the doctor—kept making alarmed exclamations. By that she knew Charles was hurt badly. Something oozed down her cheek; she reached to wipe it away, and her hand came away wet with blood. Willie was making signs to the doctor, trying to persuade him to give Charles a shot. The children stood beside him with tear-smeared faces, telling him the words to say.

The compassionate couple in charge of the station had called an ambulance. Eons passed, and no ambulance appeared. Charles was in agony, and his pulse grew more and more feeble. When the doctor suggested they call the American Air Force Hospital in Zaragoza to send an ambulance, Willie did. They waited and waited. Still no ambulance.

Margaret began to cry, "My head hurts." Again the couple in charge thought of something to do. They pushed two chairs together and draped them with blankets to make a bed for her. They gave all of them some bread and oiled potatoes and sent out for soft drinks, thinking Americans would like them.

Finally at 4:15, the Spanish ambulance arrived. It looked antiquated and uncomfortable, but they didn't know when the other one would arrive, if ever, so they thought they had better take this one. (The other one, with confused directions, had gotten lost.)

As they came through the door, first with Charles on the stretcher, they saw a crowd of people from the village standing near the entrance gate, waiting in silence. Indy would never forget their faces. The men pulled off their flat, round woolen caps and clasped their chests as a gesture of respect. Several women wearing black lace mantillas fingered their rosaries and began to pray aloud.

"*Pobrecitos* (poor people)," they said. "They are so far from home."

When Indy saw them, her head cleared and she thought, "They don't know us, but to them we are fellow victims of the labyrinths of life and death. They are doing for us the best that they know."

She wanted them to know that their caring made a difference. She wanted to say, "Go back to your homes and read your Bible. No, excuse me. I know that most of you don't have Bibles. I mean . . . talk to Jesus Who loves you and Who can save you. . . . He will bring light and life and hope into your lives." She wanted to say those things to them, but her head ached and she didn't feel like talking. She turned and said, "*Gracias! Muchas gracias!*"

Helen sat in front of the ambulance with her grandparents. David and Margaret and Indy sat in the back on the floor beside Charles's stretcher. Indy kept her finger on Charles's pulse. To her his wrist felt cold and lifeless.

"Mother," David asked, "will Daddy live?"

"Mother doesn't know what God wants to do with Daddy," Indy said. "We must ask God to let Daddy stay with us."

"We are asking God that," David told her. Indy felt God's presence there in the ambulance, enfolding her. She knew Charles was near death, and she prayed, "Oh, God, do what You know best." There in that old, creaky ambulance she gave Charles up to God, if God wanted to take him.

Velma, in almost unbearable pain, drifted in and out of consciousness. Finally at 5:00 in the afternoon they saw the four distant bell towers of the Basilica del Pilar and knew they were nearing Zaragoza and the hospital. When at last they did arrive, Charles received first attention. Because of a shortage of doctors, only Dr. Blumberg was available to tend them, so Indy's facial cuts and Velma's broken arm and leg could wait until after Charles's surgery.

Dr. Blumberg, a surgeon who had been in Spain only a few weeks, began an exploratory operation on Charles at 7:00 P.M. At 8:00 P.M. the Zaragoza Base Radio Station went on the air for the first time. Five minutes later an announcer appealed for A-negative blood for Charles.

Donors from many places gave him 15 pints of blood during the operation and 3 afterward. The doctor found two broken ribs, a crushed liver, perforated small intestines, and an abdominal cavity filled with blood. Every stitch taken to try to mend the liver simply meant another hole stuck in it with the needle.

The doctor finished the surgery at 10:00 P.M. Around 11:00 P.M. he told Indy, "I put him back together. Only God can make him live. I'd say he has a 30-70 chance, with the odds against him."

At last he took the necessary stitches in Indy's face. It was nearly midnight before he set Velma's arm (broken in five places and the elbow dislocated) and a small broken bone in her leg.

As Indy lay in the darkness, she remembered for the first time since early that morning that it was Charles's 37th birthday and he was listed on the prayer calendar that day. People all over the Southern Baptist Convention had prayed for him. Then she was able to take the tablet the nurse gave her for pain and go to sleep.

As they had entered the hospital that afternoon, they had met a woman who recognized Indy. Mary Dean Graham and her husband, Lt. Charles Graham III, were stationed at Zaragoza Air Base. They were Mississippians and Indy had met Mary Dean when she was teaching in a world missions conference in Charleston, Mississippi.

Immediately Mary Dean swept the children into her protective arms and said, "I'll take them home with me." When Indy was away at the hospital, she would make the children take baths. David would only take a quick dip, with no soap. Once she checked the water and made him get back in and take a real bath.

David lived with the terrible fear that his daddy was going to die. It seemed a long time before they let him see him, and then only for just a few minutes.

Word of the accident spread swiftly, because of Strategic Air Command's role in securing blood to save Charles's life. As a result, many in the United States knew within a few hours and were able to pray for him. W. A., Charles's brother, heard about the accident on television in Jackson, Mississippi. He called his brother, Paul, in Anniston, Alabama, and the Mississippi governor, J.P. Coleman. The governor called Sen. John Stennis, who contacted the American Embassy in Spain to try to learn more.

At the time, there was only one transatlantic telephone cable available, and W. A. did not even know where the accident had taken place. But with the help of government authorities, the Spanish police, and the telephone company, he was talking to Joe Mefford on the phone within a few hours.

As soon as the other missionaries in Barcelona heard about the wreck, they wanted to go to Zaragoza then, but the hospital staff urged them to wait until morning. On Saturday they arrived, all except Patsy Hilliard and June McNeely, who stayed with the children. Though Charles was unconscious most of the time, he realized they were there.

And he must have known Patsy and June wanted to be there and were praying for him, for he told them later he thought they were there, but that they were slicing tomatoes!

Sometimes, as he lay there, a half-smile would cross his face. When he was able to talk again, he told Indy, "I heard a choir singing 'Longing for Jesus.' I know they sang it at least 100 times! Is the chaplain playing records in his office upstairs?"

"That's your imagination. You're hearing the air-conditioner," a nurse insisted.

But he was hard to convince. Another time he imagined he heard choirs of at least 500 voices marching by his window. The air base must be preparing for a music festival, he thought. He had never heard "How Great Thou Art" sung so beautifully.

On the Sunday morning following their "day of miracles," Indy sat beside Charles's bed wishing she could talk to him. But even if he had not been in a semiconscious state, he had too many tubes in him to be able to talk much.

She wrote a letter to her mother, and then, with tears dripping on the paper, she wrote another to Charles.

My beloved husband,
This awful Sunday morning when you are struggling for life, I am so near to you physically, yet so far away in what I can do to help you. One thin partition separates me from your bed, and I can imagine that just one fragile open gate is between you and eternity.

I could easily cry out in my anguish, yet I must not. You are in the hands of God Who gave you to me and Whom we have tried to serve during our 12 years together. There are no accidents with Him, and His immeasurable love makes me certain that He will spare you if His purposes can be accomplished. If God has other plans, I would be altogether unworthy of your love and dedication to Him if I should cry out for you to stay.

How I love you at this moment! I long for just one more chance to tell you that you are the most wonderful husband in the world. If I tried 1,000 years, I couldn't begin to deserve your love and partnership in life.

I am forced to think what life would be without you, and I can't see beyond the moment. The way is altogether dark, yet I know that God is there and will lead me on.

I thank Him for every wonderful moment we have had together. Truly "Life is ever Lord of death and love can never lose its own."

And so I wait . . . loving you and looking up.

She placed the letter in her billfold, not really thinking of delivering it. (Forty-five days later she gave it to Charles and together they looked back on the day God spared their lives.)

In a corner of the hospital patio, Indy found a special place of refuge. Many times she sat there among the September flowers and searched the Bible for words of comfort and looked up into the autumn sky to talk with God. Each time she found renewed courage to say, "Thy will be done, O Lord."

Her natural impulse was to cry out, "Oh, God, let him live, no matter what. Let him live." Yet the words refused to come. She knew that in the light of Calvary's cross no real Christian could pray that kind of prayer. Jesus in Gethsemane had cried, "If there be any other way to accomplish your purposes, save me from this crucifixion experience; nevertheless, I want your will to be done and not mine."

Through the days she scribbled notes of the thoughts that came to her. She wrote on discarded envelopes, on address cards in her billfold, in the margins of her Bible, and on little scraps of paper that she kept in untidy heaps on her dresser.

On one of them she wrote:

To say "Thy will be done" at any time in our lives should be an intelligent, purposeful decision. It is not stumbling blindly into the unknown because we have no other choice.

It is not a stoical resignation to the inevitable. It is cooperation with the plan of God to accomplish His purposes. With His hand in ours, we stand before the great loom of our lives, weaving a pattern that can only be seen from the other side. We are in His hands and He sees everything from beginning to end of our lives. He knows why this seeming tragedy had to happen. He permitted it. Whatever, the outcome is BEST.

About five days after the accident, Velma Whitten was moved to a hospital in Madrid to have her elbow reset by a bone specialist. Soon afterward, the children and Willie Whitten also returned to Madrid so that the children could enter school.

Willie took care of the children. He would buy a chicken, growl *"gracias"* to the grocer; thrust it in front of Rita, the current maid, and say,*"Paella."* David continually ran around with him to translate.

From all over the world cards and letters brought messages of love and assurances of prayer. On Sunday after the accident, many of the Spanish Baptist churches turned their regular services into prayer meetings for Charles.

Many in the United States wrote that they had prayed for Charles on his birthday. Louise McGee, Indy's former Sunday School teacher in Louisville, wrote, "When we saw that Charles's name was on the prayer calendar Friday, we prayed for him in our devotional time that day, but for some reason I felt a special need to pray for him again Saturday morning." Letters came from dozens of others, including Rev. and Mrs. B. B. McGee, Willie and Velma's pastor at Weir.

Indy, in one of her prayertimes on the patio, came across Paul's words, "But I would ye should understand, brethren, that the things which happened unto me have fallen out rather unto the furtherance of the gospel" (Phil.1:12). Yes, she realized, God was using this tragedy for the furtherance of the gospel in more ways than one.

He was using it to bring her and Charles closer to Him, to make them more effective in His service. He was using the suffering to draw the ten missionaries in

Spain together in a closer bond of understanding and to draw the missionaries and the Spanish believers closer, to make them realize anew their dependence on each other. The other missionaries had taken over many of Charles and Indy's responsibilities. Roy Wyatt was substituting as treasurer.

The Spanish Baptists came from all over the country to visit Charles. This missionary had loved first, and in return, he was loved. Perhaps it could be said that he had an old-fashioned way of looking at people—for he always looked for the best in them. Even if someone did something mean or ugly to him, which did not happen often, he would not say anything bad about them or speculate that their motives had been wrong.

Two pastors from Madrid rode the slow night train to Zaragoza. Senor Juan Perez, pastor at Albacete and president of the Spanish Baptist Union, traveled to Zaragoza, and then sent out a newsletter to the churches telling of God's mercy and care for Charles.

Indy wrote on one of her scraps of paper, "The pastor from Huesca sat beside Charles's bed, clutching a package of cookies and some apples from his orchard. Tears rolled down his cheeks. "I know you don't need these things, Don Carlos, but I wanted to bring you something."

For 12½ years Charles and Indy had not ceased to marvel at their happiness together. Yet God used the accident to deepen their dedication to each other. Brought face to face with the possibility of her husband's death, Indy suddenly thought, "I have shared the days, the activities, the thoughts, the dreams, the life of a great man of God and have often taken him for granted. His purity of heart, his devotion to us, his family, and his consecration to the cause of God's kingdom on earth stand out as clearly as the stars on a crisp autumn night."

She absentmindedly pulled off an earring of Toledo gold and sat looking at it. Threads of pure gold had been tapped into a piece of scratched metal and the two baked in an oven until the gold looked brilliant against the blackened metal.

As Jesus had once told Mary and Martha that Lazarus's suffering was not unto death, but for the glory of God, Indy wrote:

He promised that in proportion to my faith I would see the glory of God. Then came the answer to our prayers, and God's healing hand brought Charles back from death.

I realized that God was permitting my husband to live for a purpose. He had allowed our human love to be refined in the oven of suffering and the uncertainty of life. In and through it all, we saw God's glory and knew that our marriage had mounted up to a higher level of awareness and dedication.

One morning when Indy went into five-year-old Margaret's bedroom at the Graham house, Margaret asked, "Mother, is Daddy the only person who is sick in the hospital?" She began to think she should look around and see if she could help to bear others' burdens instead of keeping her eyes always on her own. She made an effort to share with some of the sick people the comfort that she knew in Christ. She thought then of those who worked at the hospital who had never heard about the Saviour. The Spanish scrub women spoke of room 9 as "the room where they pray," because every pastor or church member who visited said a prayer before he or she left. Sometimes the nurses' helpers or the scrub women stood in the doorway to listen.

Primitivo dell Vall, the driver of the American ambulance which was sent out to look for them, came to Indy and said, "I'm sorry I could not find you."

"Don't worry about that now. God saved my husband's life in spite of the delay."

Primitivo began to ask questions about her faith, so she gave him a New Testament, which he often sat in the lobby reading. One day another ambulance driver sent word to her that he would like to see her. When she met him on the front steps, he asked, "Could you please give me a book like you gave Primitivo? He's always reading his and I never get to see it."

Indy kept tracts and New Testaments that she gave

away at every opportunity. In the hospital cafeteria she answered questions about her religion.

An American airman was engaged to a Spanish girl interested in the evangelical faith, but not convinced. One night in the base chapel, Indy translated the sermon for her. Before Charles was transferred to the British American Hospital in Madrid, this couple visited him. He was still so weak that he had to stop to catch his breath between every two or three words.

Later, the girlfriend told the young airman that the gospel must be true. Why else would a person who talked with such difficulty make the effort to tell her more about Christ?

In the two hospitals, Charles stayed for 40 days. He lost 30 pounds, due to an infectious fever. At last, on December 14, he returned home, 6 days after his parents left for the US.

The next day he wrote Cornell Goerner, who had succeeded George Sadler at the Foreign Mission Board:

I am very grateful to God for all the wonderful blessings I have received from Him during this experience. Romans 8:28 has certainly been a reality to me, and I can truly thank God for having permitted me to be so blessed and to feel so close to Him during these past weeks. . . .

I would like to ask you to convey to all the Foreign Mission Board family our deep appreciation for prayers and encouragement which I have felt so keenly during these weeks.

Soon afterward, Vicenta, who no longer worked for the Whittens, arrived by train in Madrid and announced, "I will stay as long as you need me."

Indy tried to pay her train fare to Madrid, but Vicenta protested, the tears shining in her eyes. "What are friends for if not to help in times of need?"

The first time Charles was able to go back to church and conduct prayer meeting, Senor Bonifacio, a member of First Baptist Church, Madrid, prayed, "Oh, Lord, we asked you for a miracle and you gave it to us. We are absolutely certain You spared this, our brother, because You had work for him to do in Spain."

As never before, Charles felt the stewardship of his own life. For the whole family, the simplest everyday activities took on a new joy, because once again they were all together.

Indy wrote a book about what God had done in their lives in those months. She called it *We Camped at Heaven's Gate*. She included the stories that have been told in this chapter. In the closing paragraph she said:

We will never know all the purposes God had in permitting us to go through such a terrible, wonderful experience. Of one thing we are certain: as we camped at Heaven's Gate, we heard the unmistakable Voice of Love say to our troubled hearts, "My children, lean hard. My Grace is sufficient for your every need."

And it is.

14
Love never fails

"If we could give our family anything, what would it be? (1) An understanding of the importance of love in this world . . .; (2) a deep respect for all people . . .; (3) a sense of humor . . .; (4) a deep abiding faith in God."—Indy Whitten

MADRID theaters wanted to sell their own concessions just as American theaters do. Naturally, they took a dim view of patrons bringing their own food. Indy, Charles, Helen, David, and Margaret filed into the dark playhouse. They leaned back in their seats, ready to enjoy the Friday night double feature.

Indy opened the plastic bag she'd brought and handed out sandwiches. Mixing the drinks would take a bit of maneuvering. From large bottles, she quickly poured soft drink into hard plastic glasses and added *gaseosa* (carbonated water).

Pop! Psst! Pop! Fizz-z-z! Just as the movie began, lids began to blow off the glasses, making sounds like bombs ready to go off. An usher frantically flashed his light their way, but they hid the drinks. These weekly family nights were always fun. Yearly children's days were too; then the children chose what the family would do all day.

On birthdays, everybody went to great lengths to surprise the birthday person—write a poem, sing a song, shop for an unusual gift. On Helen's birthday, Indy handed her a sealed empty envelope. "Take this down to the corner at (she named a certain place). Wait until Mrs. Calero comes to meet you and pick up this letter."

An hour later, the car loaded with the rest of the family stopped in front of Helen. "Mrs. Calero is not coming, but we'll take you to the place you choose to eat. Happy birthday!"

All during that summer of 1960, Charles constantly worked out legal details for churches buying properties. In fact, the job as treasurer had occupied the major part of his days, and many sleepless nights, for a lot longer than he had intended to keep it. But he did such a good job no one wanted him to give it up.

The negotiations for property required unlimited patience and rare skill in public relations. For instance, in one city he learned that a family was still living on the property he was seeking to buy for a church. If the church bought the property thus occupied, the law said those people could never be made to get off the land.

Compassionately, but firmly, Charles told the owner, "No, I'm sorry, but the deal is off."

But the owner said, "Don't leave. I'll have them off the property today." (They were his relatives.) As good as his word, the owner set their belongings out on the street. Charles regretted that, but knew it was impossible to deal fairly otherwise.

In another place, he had to round up 15 heirs to sign the deeds for the property a church was buying. When he finally got them all together, one refused to sign. Several got into fist fights. Then it took nine more months to complete the transaction.

The church in the harbor city of La Coruna bought a three-story building. Charles and Indy had helped to organize that church in 1954, the first in north Spain.

As the Whittens were en route to La Coruna, David and Margaret kept hitting each other. When a strange silence fell over the backseat, Charles asked, "What happened?" Hesitantly, Helen explained, "Margaret hit David's glasses, and they flew out the window." That called for retracing some kilometers, without success. They bought new glasses in La Coruna.

Once, when Charles and Indy were showing Mrs. Childs, British justice of the peace, around Madrid, David and Margaret kept up their backseat fights. Charles repeatedly warned them to quit. Finally he stopped the car, took them out, and spanked them both. They were so embarrassed that afterward any time he wanted to stop a quarrel he had only to say, "Remember Mrs. Childs?"

In their house on San Telmo, family council meetings helped to settle disputes. "We can't keep six dogs," said Indy. "We must choose two." A month or two before, when the postman had left the gate open, Lassie slipped out. Finally, with tears, they gave her up for lost and got Laddie. Then Lassie came home and soon added four puppies to the family.

"But we can't give Lassie away," Helen protested. "How would you like to be given away just because you had a child?" The majority ruled; only two puppies stayed.

As autumn's cool days set in, Rita Duran Torres and Helen began knitting a coat for Helen's doll. (Rita, a lovely Christian who sang often at home and at church, had come to them as maid from Galicia.) One chilly morning Helen tried the doll's coat on a puppy; it fit so well she gave it to him.

At home Indy and Charles kept a world map on the wall, usually beside the dining table. In family devotional time, when the prayer calendar was read, one of the children would point out the countries where the missionaries worked.

As Indy wrote a letter one night, Charles sat on the side of Margaret's bed and listened as she prayed.

"Would you like to go with me to the office tomorrow?" he asked.

"Oh, yes!" It was her favorite way to spend a Saturday morning. She would sit and draw while Charles did his work. She knew she must be quiet so he could think. Later, they might walk the block or two from the office to the Plaza Mayor and feed the pigeons, or stop on the way home to drink a milkshake. She and Helen and David took turns doing this on Saturdays, so each could have a private time with Charles.

Each January 6, Spanish children set out their empty shoes on the Day of the Three Kings, to be filled with gifts. But a different kind of gift for the Whittens arrived on Christmas Eve 1960 at 1:45 A.M. at the British-American hospital—a new baby, John William. Later in the week, the baby's mother announced through the "Whitten Weekly" that a new staff member had checked in at his desk at San Telmo 10, and that the editors predicted he would throw his nine pounds around considerably. The baby's father said, "Our family is balanced now—two boys, two girls, two born in North America, two born in South America, two born in Europe."

Five months later, on June 1, 1961, Charles and Indy's 14th wedding anniversary, Rita caught the celebration fever and bought a large white cake with red rosebuds and *Congratulations* on top, plus a heart with an arrow in it and the words *Love Never Fails*. Rita and the children had all emptied their pockets to buy gifts. Rita brought John to the table with a flower in his hand (which he almost ate).

Later in the summer, when the children began to act bored, Indy taught Vacation Bible School at home for them. The three older ones, sometimes with John present, listened to Old Testament stories, memorized Scripture verses, and worked on crafts projects.

Military and construction workers on new air bases had added a pinch of American flavor to Madrid's atmosphere. This gave Indy opportunity to teach in Vacation Bible Schools for children of American military couples. In one of her groups, 30 children made professions of faith.

At nine o'clock on Thanksgiving morning 1961, members of the new Immanuel (English-speaking) Baptist Church of Madrid gathered for a praise and baptismal service.

Charles, the church's interim pastor, waded into the pool, a garage's car greasing pit that had been deepened and cemented. He reached out his hand to a young air force man who stepped into the pool to be baptized. Next, he baptized two children—David, ten, and Margaret, eight. About a year before, Margaret had one night listened closely to her father's sermon. When he talked about sin, she remembered doing things that were wrong and decided she wanted to change and to give Jesus her life. In Spanish churches, people raised their hands to respond to the invitation rather than walk down the aisle. When Charles did not see Margaret's hand, she stood on a chair.

Like a jigsaw puzzle, the pieces had gradually fallen into shape to form Immanuel Church. Among other projects, an English-speaking Woman's Missionary Society sponsored fellowship suppers among Southern Baptist families in Madrid. A group of men connected with the military organized a Brotherhood. Representatives of these groups had invited Charles and Indy to meet with them August 25, 1961, to discuss organization of an English-speaking Baptist church.

Charles told the group that two conditions would need to be met—permission from the Spanish government and permission from the American military high command.

Seeking government permission, Charles interviewed the director general of the political section, Ministry of the Interior, who dealt with the granting of permits for all non-Catholic worship services. No proselytism of Spaniards would be involved. Thus the man said, "No problem."

Yet it took time to get the permits. Charles made so many trips to the man's office that the elevator boys began to recognize him and punch third floor before he could say "Three."

However, to his surprise, the senior chaplain at the American air base said, "Some of the other Protestant chaplains don't like the idea of a Baptist church being established. Can you tell me a bit more about who is doing this and why? Will the Spanish government approve?"

"I have no doubt they will."

"Then I can see no reason why the other chaplains should raise further serious objections."

"Of course, all our members won't come from the military. Any English-speaking foreigners will be welcomed—personnel in the American embassies and consulates, American businessmen and their wives, American students in the city's universities."

A four-story building was rented; then the church was organized October 22, 1961, two days after permission came from the Ministry of the Interior. Members named it Immanuel, or "God with us." They called Charles Whitten as interim pastor, since he felt he could not give as much time as the church would need from a regular pastor. The congregation asked the Foreign Mission Board, SBC, to send a missionary couple to work with them, if possible.

Until furlough time, beginning July 31, 1962, Charles remained as pastor. Under his leadership, the church by its third month had voted to give 33 percent of its offerings to outside causes—15 percent to the Southern Baptist Convention, 15 percent to the Spanish Baptist Union, 2 percent to local missionary work, and 1 percent to the Association of Baptists in Continental Europe. Thirteen members had publicly decided to enter church-related vocations, 5 saying the Lord was leading them into mission service.

On February 13, 1962, Charles wrote Goerner:

> Due to a health problem, it is not recommendable that I pursue the intensive doctoral program that we had anticipated. The fact is that I have never fully recovered from the physical, psychological, and emotional shock of the automobile accident which our family experienced.
>
> Lately, due to the strain of my accepting again all my former responsibilities, an ulcer of the duodenum developed and for some time gave me quite a bit of trouble. Since it has been brought to my attention that further medication and convalescence will be advisable while in the States, the wise course now seems to point to a period of time when I will be freed from as much responsibility as possible.

Gerald McNeely would take care of the treasurer's duties for a year.

During June the Whitten family spent a week at Santa Severa, the Italian Baptist camp near Rome. During that time of rest, they made plans for furlough at 602 West

College Street, Clinton, Mississippi. Already, speaking engagements were lined up "from sea to shining sea." Perhaps David could squeeze in time to see the Yankees play the Kansas City Athletics in New York City, they thought hopefully.

15
Sharing the bread that satisfies

If we with humility and love break bread with the nations of the world, the "image" will take care of itself.—Indy Whitten

WHILE deacons of Second Baptist Church, Barcelona, passed trays filled with bread for the Lord's Supper, Indy sat praying silently, head bowed. Next to her, John, two, blue eyes wide open, tugged at her sleeve and whispered, "Wake up, Mother! It's time to eat!"

Though amused, she thought, "Yes, my son, it is time to wake up and realize that the world is starving for bread that satisfies."

When the *Exeter* plowed across the Barcelona harbor on August 11, 1963, the Whittens had stood on deck, ready to begin a third term in Spain. Through the fog, they had seen their friends at the dock raise clasped hands as a sign of welcome.

Once more, while Charles was interim director of the seminary, they were living in Barcelona, in an apartment which looked out on the Pyrenees on one side and a palm-shaded garden on the other. Charles's office was across the hall from the dining room in the seminary's two-story white concrete building. Gray wooden shutters flanked the upper windows outside the students' bedrooms. Black iron grillwork covered the lower windows. At one side grew a small garden, a lemon tree in one corner. Many times policemen had come to the door in the high wall along the front of the property to talk with the director and report back to the government.

Spanish Catholics during their lonely centuries of war with the Moors had come to look on themselves as the only true defenders of the faith. As a result, in the Spaniard's eyes, Catholicism had become interwoven with nationalism and patriotism. But now a new attitude of tolerance was said to be abroad in the land.

In October 1963, for the first time, Spanish Baptists gathered in convention with written permission from the government. Small groups clustered along the mosaic esplanade and in the beachside cafes, talking excitedly of recent events. Elche Church had reopened with permission. So had Second Church, Madrid (which had joined with Third Church and taken the name Good Shepherd). *YA*, a leading newspaper in Madrid, had called on Catholics to be good hosts to Protestant tourists.

A spirit of optimism continued in the biennial meeting of Woman's Missionary Union which followed the convention. Indy was a featured speaker. The women re-elected her friend, Noemi Celma de Bonet, as their national president for a fifth two-year term.

Senora Bonet was daughter and wife of Baptist pastors. Born March 12, 1921, in the home of a Baptist pioneer, she and her family had faced many trials during the civil war. Their church had been raided and her father had faced serious dangers. Later she had married Pedro Bonet, who was now pastor of the Badalona Baptist Church in Barcelona. Her father had baptized the two of them the same day, August 15, 1934.

For the WMU convention, Alicante women had prepared a surprise. A small boy with olive skin and dark hair stepped forward with Spain's red and yellow flag. "Oh, Christian friends," he said, "we must hold high the flag of Spain." Children dressed to represent different regions marched across the platform. "But more than that," he continued, "we must hold high the flag of Jesus."

Regardless of other assignments, Charles and Indy rarely missed a chance to "start a new work." On most Sundays that year in Barcelona they crowded into a small shed room with the Cornella Mission members, and Charles preached. If poverty flourished among these proud people, no one could have guessed. Everyone wore a good dress or suit (even though it might be the only good ones some owned) and white shirt and highly polished shoes.

Cornella's Sunday School overflowed the shed; Indy taught her children's class in the front yard, and Charles taught adults in the kitchen. Fourteen-year-old Helen walked to a nearby house to teach, followed by at least 20 preschoolers.

All too swiftly the year passed. Russell Hilliard was named seminary director. Cornella Mission organized as a church. Indy received a diploma in Spanish Studies at the university as Charles had done previously.

When new missionaries, Tom and Betty Law, arrived in February 1964, Charles and another missionary, Dan White, borrowed a station wagon to pick them up at Algeciras, across the strait from the Rock of Gibraltar.

"To be a *sevillano* is to be the most fortunate person outside of Paradise." So goes a Spanish proverb. Sevilla was a city of Arab gardens, bullfights and roses, huge cathedrals, and the horse fair where aristocrats rode in black suits and wide-brimmed hats. By the time the station wagon reached there, the fountains in the Parque Maria Luisa had frozen. It was so cold that Tom backed up to a heater in the hotel room and scorched his pants.

"When you find an apartment, perhaps you can warm your feet like the local families," Charles told him. "Set a pan of coals on a shelf under a table. Then prop your feet on the shelf and drop the tablecloth onto your lap."

To Betty, Charles said, "You'll need an inventory list to get your belongings out of customs. Do you want me to help translate your list?"

Betty, as dark-haired as most Andalusians, could not find a plug-in for her electric typewriter except in the bathroom. So they sat in the bathroom while he dictated and she typed.

The Laws and Charles met again soon at Mission Meeting in March at Immanuel Church, Madrid, where James Watson was missionary pastor. Just a week before, Immanuel had marked its first anniversary by posting a sign outside to show it was a church. At last this was possible!

While the adults attended to Mission business, the older missionaries' kids, including Helen and David, taught Vacation Bible School for the younger ones. Usually the seven-, eight-, and nine-year-olds were a bit hard to manage. Yet, the first night, not a sound was heard from them beyond their room.

The next morning Charles asked at breakfast, "How did you keep such good order last night?"

David grinned, "We tied them to their chairs."

"My daddy is Mission treasurer!" bragged Marsha McNeely to the other MKs. (Gerald had been interim while Charles was on furlough.)

"No!" Margaret quickly corrected her. "My daddy is Mission treasurer!"

As the ever-careful treasurer, mindful of using Foreign Mission Board money wisely, Charles was forever asking his fellow missionaries for copies of receipts. Thus, it seems, he'd built a reputation!

"Uncle Charles," asked young Dickie Law, "do you really sit on the moneybags?"

Later during Mission Meeting the grown-ups produced a skit. An actor playing Charles sat on the moneybags. Another asked, "Can't you get up and give out the money?"

"Charles" looked at his watch and said, "No, it's not midnight yet."

Spring turned to summer again, and the Whittens moved back to Madrid to a house at Francisco de Goya, 5. It was a good thing Indy had brought 50 sheets back from furlough, for a constant stream of visitors broke bread with them during the year. They included J. D. Hughey, the new secretary for Europe and the Middle East, and Becky Rowden, 16-year-old former MK in Israel, daughter of Marjorie Rowden and the late Paul Rowden. Becky lived in Mississippi where Helen had met her at GA camp.

Before Becky left home, Indy wrote and sent her reams of background information about places of historic interest she might visit.

On arrival, Becky met all the family and Rita. Then Indy led her to her room and said, "Sleep until you feel like getting up."

For breakfast, Indy served her crusty bread fresh from the bakery, spread with butter and marmalade. Later she showed her how she made cold gazpacho soup, adding vinegar to tomato soup, plus chopped cucumbers, green peppers, bread crumbs, and onions. It's refreshing to drink this in hot weather," she said. And she explained how the Spaniards ate meals in courses—soup, then omelet or fish, then a meat (perhaps roast lamb) or a vegetable, and fruit for dessert. Every course required clean plates.

At Plaza de Espana, Becky admired the bronze figures of Don Quixote with his lance and Sancho Panza on his burro. And one day the whole family plus Becky folded themselves into their compact car to visit El Escorial, burial place of Spanish kings. Leaving Madrid and its surrounding plain, they headed toward the snow-capped peaks of the Sierra de Guadarrama.

One high hill near the monastery almost defeated them; the car got halfway up, stopped, and rolled backward. On the second attempt, the same thing happened. Everybody was ready to give up but Indy. "Come on, Charles. Let's try once more." He turned around and drove back to the top of the hill behind them. Then he stepped hard on the accelerator and gathered enough speed to make it to the top of the next! There before them sunlight glinted from the turrets and towers, pavilions and courtyards of the architectural wonder which King Philip II had created.

As Becky observed Indy's unquestioning acceptance of people whose personalities and ages and beliefs and backgrounds were different from her own, she herself felt entirely comfortable with her. To the teenaged girl, the missionary became teacher, friend, surrogate mother, and model.

She noticed that Indy seemed at home with the richest or the poorest. Indy eagerly and enthusiastically shared "her Spain" with this 16-year-old. And Becky wrote down what she remembered most about her:

She merged into the culture and became part of it, learned it and perceived acutely the life-style and values of the people of Spain as if to say, "I am the outsider. I will learn your ways, not try to mold you to mine. I value your culture because you value it. I will accept your customs and speech and life-style—because if you are ever to value me as a person—what I believe about life—you must first believe that I genuinely like you and accept you and honor and respect your traditions and will humbly try to live among you, and then maybe when you have accepted me as a caring person, you will also listen to what I believe about my God."

In August they set out for Switzerland and the meeting of European Baptist missionaries. Those in the backseat swapped places every two hours so no one would fuss about sitting in the middle.

Doing without modern conveniences didn't bother the Whittens, Becky saw. All along the way they stopped for picnics and spent the nights in inexpensive small inns. If the rooms didn't have enough beds, someone in the family quickly made a pallet on the floor.

At Ruschlikon, a Girls' Auxiliary coronation service was held in the chapel to honor the missionaries' kids. Helen was recognized as Queen Regent, and Becky as Queen Regent in Service. All the Whittens took part—Margaret as Lady in Waiting, John as Helen's cape bearer, Indy presiding at the coronation, David giving out programs, and Charles standing outside the door keeping three-year-old John in the mood to carry Helen's "little coat."

"All Hail the Power of Jesus' Name," the girls sang as they took off their crowns, a symbolic act.

From Zurich, Becky was to fly to New York City; her mother met the plane at Kennedy Airport. No Becky. Marjorie panicked and called John Watts, president of the seminary at Ruschlikon, not thinking (or caring) of the time difference.

At 2:00 A.M. Watts groggily answered his phone and told the distraught mother he didn't know where Becky was, but he'd find out. He pulled on his bathrobe, located the Whittens' dorm, and knocked on their bedroom door. Indy opened it.

"Is Becky Rowden there? Her mother is on the phone.

Come and help calm her down." Becky slept through this. Indy in her housecoat walked across campus to the Watts's house at 2:30 A.M. "Yes, Becky's fine. We'll send her to you on the next flight," she assured Marjorie. It turned out that the person who had written Becky's plane ticket accidentally dated it a day later than the date on the itinerary left with Marjorie.

Leaving Switzerland, the Whittens set out for Amsterdam, to camp during the congress of the European Baptist Federation, in their green tent. The first night, David could not get his air mattress adjusted. All night they could hear the hiss of air being added or let out. The next night heavy rain drenched the city of canals, and also the canvas floor of their tent. Such problems could be assuaged, if not solved. "Don't drown in a glass of water!" they said, reminding each other of the Spanish proverb.

Walking down the street to the congress hall, they saw a man throw a piece of linoleum into the garbage. "Do you mind if we take this?" Charles asked. The man said no, and the linoleum made a fine waterproof floor for the tent.

As usual, they'd brought along several good books. In late afternoons, they sat in front of the tent, taking turns reading aloud. Passersby might have seen them wiping away tears or heard a voice choke up when they reached the sad parts. Sometimes Indy told them stories that her mother had told her.

On that same trip they cooked on a portable butane stove or made sandwiches with the big, red, juicy tomatoes they bought along the way.

All that summer in the United States, racial strife flamed so high that it would go down in history as "the long, hot summer of 1964." Indy, like many other missionaries abroad, found herself living intensely with the matter of the "American image." She felt herself on both ends of the question, for the more she loved her adopted land, the more patriotic she felt toward her own land.

In the past she had felt tempted to explain unchristian

actions which took place in the United States. While Indy was teaching an ethics class in Barcelona, a student had asked, "Why doesn't Christian America do more to clear up the race problem?"

Her impulsive reply was, "I don't excuse my fellow countrymen, but let me ask you how you feel about other races who live in Spain—the gypsies, for example?" Then she realized she had tried to explain away a violation of Christian love in her country by pointing a finger at the same weakness in Spain. Two wrongs did not make a right.

Later, she wrote an article, "In the World's Mirror," for *Royal Service*. In part, she said:

Being reflected in the world's mirror is not so distressing or uncomfortable if we aren't trying to live up to a false image. Our failings—though lamentable—do not prove Christianity has failed. It has yet to be tried by most of the people of the world—including the people of the United States. . . .

If we with humility and love break bread with the nations of the world, the "image" will take care of itself. The blessed point of emphasis will forever be Him before Whom "every knee must bow and every tongue confess that Jesus Christ is Lord to the glory of God the Father."

Let us take out citizenship papers in the human race. There is never a barrier that can continue to stand in the presence of real Christian love—whether the barrier be race, language, educational background, social position, or any other circumstance.

> We are needy creatures,
> We stand together on level ground—
> With stained hands outstretched to God,
> Certain that it's mercy we must have
> Not justice.
> We are needy creatures.
> God's love is color blending.
> He does not see in red or white
> Or any other color that Separates.
> We are needy creatures.
>
> From "Common Ground"
> by Indy Whitten

16
Camping at Denia

"The most important question is not whether you belong to a Baptist church or a Catholic church. The most important question is whether or not you know Jesus." —Charles Whitten

DURING the night, the sound of the wind flapping a loose corner of their tent wakened Indy. Then she heard a scream. And another. And another, mixed with shrieks and laughter. She peeped through a slit in the tent.

The wind, she saw, had split one tent completely down the middle and left its occupants sitting out in the moonlight. Most of the other tents had blown down, some of them torn. Girls inside them were rolling around tangled in canvas. By the time June McNeely, camp director, had lighted the gas lantern, they had all freed themselves.

June, a five-foot, 95-pound brunette, didn't look big enough to handle this situation, but she was a live-wire youth director for the national Woman's Missionary Union. Her husband, Gerald, soon set the tents up again, but it was obvious some must be mended.

For this Girls' Auxiliary week at the Baptist camp in Denia, Charles and Indy had brought their own green tent. Some summers they had worked in camps for as long as ten weeks in a row, and this year would be no different. Since Indy had had experience in being national WMU youth director, June had invited her to help with the program and with recreation, and Charles to be camp pastor.

"Any volunteer seamstresses?" June asked. Indy and Lila Mefford and Noemi Bonet, armored with flashlight and big needles, challenged the night wind. With coarse thread, they mended the rips. Senora Bonet had found a red-checked strip of oilcloth, a former tablecloth, which she sewed to the tent that had split in half, and used it to pull the sides back together. "These girls will win the prize for the most colorful tent in Denia!" she said.

Up on the hillside with their flashlights the women looked like fireflies against the backdrop of an enormous bare rocky mountain called Montgo. Far below them, the moonlight sketched a silver path across the wind-whipped whitecaps of the Mediterranean. Ruins of Denia's castle on its private hilltop stood as sentinels over the harbor and lighthouse and the little town beside it. Leaves of the almond trees flickered to and fro.

The younger girls seemed to be sleeping through all of this. "Do you know that I kissed all 40 of them good night?" June laughed. "When I kissed Marsha [June's daughter], then all the others wanted a kiss too!"

Linda McNeely, the Queen with a Scepter in June's family, had made the program folders and name tags and helped to assign sleeping space to everyone. When her count revealed more girls than beds, she had pushed two beds together in several places. Thus, some of the younger girls had the honor of sleeping in "big beds." The older girls she had assigned to tents.

"I think by next summer the new building will be finished," Charles said. He had bought the camp property in 1963 with the aid of Southern Baptist money after the pastor, Joaquin Pastor, had located this choice site.

Sunrise over the sea the next morning tinged with yellow the palms that curved along the beach and the white adobe houses and their red tile rooftops, and sent its beams up the winding road to the camp.

Hungry girls, some still sleepy, drank chocolate milk for breakfast and ate sardine sandwiches on thick bread. For tables, boards had been spread across sawhorses a few feet from the miniature kitchen building.

Mornings were occupied with Bible classes and mission study. At morning watch each day, a girl talked about one of the Star Ideals: Abiding in Him Through Prayer; Advancing in Wisdom by Bible Study; Acknowledging My Stewardship; Adorning Myself with Good

Works; Accepting the Challenge of the Great Commission.

From 11:15 until 1:15, campers swam in the big pool near the gate. "Come and get your *horchata*," Indy called. The milky-looking cool drink was made from *chufas* which grew under the ground like peanuts. *Churros*, long sticks of fried sweet dough, tasted good with it. So did sunflower seeds. Later, after lunch and a siesta, prayermates met for 15 minutes.

That left late afternoons free for excursions. The first day, as the girls walked down to the beach, Senora Bonet told them about an old woman who had come to the camp. She said the old woman had never seen the ocean before, and the water in her part of the country was so scarce she had only seen small rivers.

She had not brought a bathing suit to camp, and probably had never owned one. "No, I'm not going down to that water," she declared.

Her roommate, almost as old as she, kept insisting, "You ought to see the beach, even if you don't touch the water!" Finally she assented.

When the woman saw the dark blue waves breaking on the warm sand, she ran across the beach and into the water in her clothes—never even stopping to pull off her shoes. She scooped up the water in handfuls and poured it over her head. "I've lived all my life without enough food, enough clothes, enough medicine, enough anything," she cried. "Here's one thing I've found enough of!"

The girls, on their way back to camp from the beach, stopped to buy flowers from a vendor who was selling them from his donkey cart. They presented bouquets to the women who had repaired their tents.

The second afternoon, as the girls who had come from all parts of the country started out on a bus tour of the town, Indy told them, "Denia is one of the oldest towns in Spain and is named for the Roman goddess, Diana. Greeks founded it.

"Some history books say, though, that Phoenician traders had a port here 1,500 years before Christ was born. Once the town was a wedding present, when James the Conqueror gave his wife a choice of lands he had conquered. She looked them over and decided the most beautiful spot of all was this point of land on the Mediterranean."

After they saw the castle and the rock museum, they stopped at the Baptist church. The cream-colored building was joined to others in the block; on its front hung a brown cross. Inside, over the baptistry archway, were the words, *Dios es amor*, meaning "God is love."

They drove through acres and acres of orchards around the town—lemons and oranges and almonds and other fruits. Villages they passed had such names as Beniali and Benisiva. "If Beni and Ali are the village names, that means they are Moorish names," Lila Mefford explained. "Arabs first terraced the land like this with stone walls, to conserve the water."

They waved at four women sitting in front of a house, one of them holding a dog on her lap. And they waved to the women scrubbing clothes in a wash house like an open pavilion, in water that ran from a nearby spring.

Indy pointed out another mountain across from Montgo. "Do you think that looks like a sleeping woman?" she asked. "I think Montgo looks like a giant gray *flan* (pudding)."

On the way back through town, they stopped briefly at the cemetery to see the grave of the first wife of Aurelio del Campo, the pastor who had gone to prison for his beliefs. The girls had studied about him.

The Protestant cemetery here, as in most of their own towns, was separated from the Catholic cemetery by a concrete wall. One tomb had a sculptured boat on it. "Perhaps that was a fisherman or sailor drowned at sea," said Lila.

That night the wind was still blowing. "How can we have a campfire service?" June worried. "We don't want to burn down half of Denia." The ground was very dry. "The girls will be so disappointed."

"Well, let's don't drown in a glass of water," Indy answered. "There must be a way. How about a campfire service without a fire?" Since there was no electricity, the girls had all brought flashlights to camp. They could point those to the outdoor "stage" to floodlight the skit which Indy had written and was directing.

Four girls walked out and sat down at a table, representing officers of the Spanish Baptist Union. Different items or groups which needed money, such as the camp and the magazine, *Nuestra Labor*, and the old folks home, came to the officers and asked for money. The officers sadly shook their heads and said, "There is no money." Then the officers exited and returned carrying a big pot labeled *Cooperative Program*. Together they said, "Let all the churches put money into this pot and then everybody can draw out."

In other fun times during the week the girls from Sevilla entertained with flamenco dances, or Indy-directed games on the soccer field. In one game, campers divided into two circles, going in opposite directions while music played.

David played the accordion which his Uncle Joe Mefford had given him. Like his father, David could play almost anything by ear, and he could play the piano, the trumpet, and the violin, as well as the accordion. Helen could play the piano and the Autoharp, and Margaret the guitar. When the music stopped, each facing couple had to act out Bible scenes for each other to guess. They also debated on which was worse, to be a 1,000-legged worm with corns or a giraffe with a sore throat.

One day a group succeeded in climbing Montgo, a mountain quite steep and dangerous.

On one walking trip into Denia, the campers joined the fun of the village fair. Bulls were turned loose to run through the streets as a contest between the bulls and the older boys of the town. Bulls chased the boys while people stood on the sidewalks and cheered. The boys stood on a platform which had been built out into the sea, and waved red capes to try to get the bulls to charge them. If the bulls rushed on so fast that they fell into the water, the boys earned a point. But if the boys got scared and jumped into the water, the bulls scored a point.

On Sunday morning, the girls gathered for a preaching service under the big algarroba tree between the kitchen and the swimming pool. Encarnacion Gil picked up one of the wrinkled brown pods under the tree, smelled it, and wrinkled her nose. How did the prodigal son eat that for food, she wondered, or even the pigs? Charles sat in a chair, facing the girls on the ground. A quartet of young people from the Denia Baptist Church sang, and then David played the accordion.

Charles had named his sermon "Take a Giant Step," from a game he'd played when he was a boy in Mississippi, where the leader stood in front of the others and told them what size step to take: a wee baby step, a kangaroo step, or a giant step. He said:

I remember how happy I was to be able to take a giant step. Today some of you are going to take the most giantlike step of all your lives. Jesus said, "Behold, I stand at the door and knock" (Rev. 3:20). It's up to you to decide whether you are going to hear that knock and open your door to Him.

I am not asking you to join the church. The most important question is not whether you belong to a Baptist church or a Catholic church. The most important question is whether or not you know Jesus. I am just giving you a chance to say before the rest of these campers that you are going to take the giant step of faith.

Encarnacion, her brown pigtails shining in the sun and her blue eyes sparkling, stood and raised her hand. She was ready to take the giant step. So was Marsha McNeely. And then one by one every girl present who was not already a Christian—18 of them—made similar professions of faith.

Many happy girls left Denia early the next morning. "*Adios! Adios!*" Charles and Indy and June and Lila and Senora Bonet and others on the faculty called. "To God I trust you!"

17
Don Carlos and Dona Nela: encouragers

"Sometimes I would have 'suffered' less if I had empathized less and had been less able to put myself in the other person's place."—
Indy Whitten

FOR MILES before they reached Salamanca, Charles and Indy and Dennis and Judith Hale could see the cathedral campanile rising over the plain. Pale golden yellow houses and the city's two cathedrals posed regally on the opposite bank of the Tormes River. In the far distance, mountain ranges rose in layers, beyond hills covered with dark green olive trees. As the four crossed the Roman bridge that spanned the river, they could see women kneeling on the banks below, washing clothes.

When the Hales had arrived in Barcelona August 9, 1965, the Whittens, always encouragers of new missionaries, tucked them under their wings. As treasurer, Charles had located an apartment for them. As a member of the missions language study committee, Indy had checked out language study possibilities at the university in Salamanca.

At the hotel, Indy and Judith had just managed to get two-year-old Janet into bed for a nap when they heard a key turn in the door. "It's us," called Dennis. He and Charles had been supervising the unloading of the Hales' household goods at their apartment.

Dennis looked at Judith. "There's been a little accident. The movers were hauling the furniture up by rope outside the building and—well—they dropped our new refrigerator from the fourth floor window!" Thus did the Hales' missionary career begin with a bang.

The trip to Salamanca was only the beginning of years

of the Whittens' loving support of the Hales and their ministry. During the Hales' second year they moved to La Coruna, 450 miles from the nearest missionary colleague. After the excitement and newness wore off, Judith had trouble adjusting, more in the second year than the first.

Indy, sensitive and perceptive, wrote, "I'll come if you need me. Distance doesn't matter."

"No," Judith replied. "Just knowing you care that much gave me the boost I needed."

In a similar way, the Whittens helped William and Dorothy Jean Ligon find a place to study Spanish at the University of Santiago de Compostela, and assisted Jesse and Beverly Bryan, who also arrived in 1965. Early one morning Charles and Indy, along with Ruth and James Watson, left for Valladolid, to visit its university and seek information the Bryans would need for their Spanish studies. Also they learned that a house in Valladolid would be practically impossible to rent. Charles would return later to find an apartment for them. Indy wrote the Bryans:

We found the same foods available as we have in Madrid. They have pasteurized milk which seems to us to be reliable. . . . The winter gets quite cold, and in most cases heating facilities are not as good as those in the States . . . so you would need some items of warm clothing. Men wear sweaters under their suit coats—women and children too! Fur-lined boots have been the order of the day for women. You might like to bring heavy underwear for Skip and for yourselves. . . . The point is: just don't let yourself be too carried away with this "sunny Spain" deal. . . .

Our most sincere wish is that you will be very happy and satisfied among us and that you will be used mightily to help bring Spain to a knowledge of the Living Christ.

While absorbed in the Spanish culture and in the workings of the Mission, the Whittens also managed to fit themselves into the American community in Madrid. Friends at Immanuel Church introduced them to Col. James Lindsey of the Strategic Air Command at Torrejon, and his wife, Marge. On at least one occasion,

Charles used his ability as interpreter to do a favor for the colonel—and for a member of the national police.

The Guardia Civil, which under Franco had complete authority, had a complement stationed near the Lindseys' residence. Several Sunday mornings, when the Lindseys set out for Immanuel, one of the young Guardias, in his olive green uniform and black patent leather hat, would thumb a ride.

They never said no, for it was a good deed—and also they were afraid not to. Inwardly, they chuckled at their efforts to speak his language, but they did get across that Jim was a pilot and that they were en route to a Baptist church. By then the English-speaking congregation had bought an old summer palace and moved into it near the Avenida de Americas.

One Sunday morning, unknown to the Lindseys, the Guardia, relaxing on the backseat, unbuckled his gun. When they let him out at the usual spot, James noticed in his mirror that the man waved and waved. "He's unusually friendly today!"

Getting out at the church, Marge exclaimed, "Look! He left his gun on the seat!"

A Guardia losing his weapon was probably an unpardonable offense: yet they didn't know how to help him. If they called his post, that would be tattling, but they knew no other place to locate him. They hid the pistol under the seat and hurried on to Sunday School.

Some minutes later, Charles walked into James's class, saying, "A Guardia is here asking to see the pilot with a red car. That has to be you!"

When the policeman had entered the English-speaking church, someone had remembered seeing Charles that morning and sent for him to translate. Thanks to him, the Guardia retrieved his pistol, gave Lindsey a big hug, and left, beaming.

During a week of prayer program at Immanuel, Indy met Grace Wetherell, whose husband, Charles, had business connections in Spain. Both had four children; and both were intensely interested in missions, so their friendship flourished. When the Wetherells went on trips, Margaret often stayed at their house to baby-sit. A natural teacher, she had taught John to read when he was quite small, and had been teaching Sunday School in a mission where her parents were working at the moment.

"I'd like for Margaret to have more fellowship with English-speaking girls," Indy told Grace, "so that when we go to the States on furlough again it would be easier for her to adjust."

"I would be thrilled to have her in my class at Immanuel," Grace said. She invited Margaret and the rest of her class to a pizza supper at her house, on the garage rooftop deck. For fun, she demonstrated her twister, an apparatus on which she stood and twisted, to trim her waistline. The girls all roared with laughter, and all wanted to try it. When they found out that Charles Wetherell had been sitting in a foyer window taking pictures of them acting silly, they were embarrassed.

Encouraging Grace in her effort to learn Spanish and to teach it to other company wives, Indy remarked on her ability to pick up the language with such ease. Indy had a knack for building people up when they didn't even know they needed it.

Also she encouraged Grace in her efforts to learn more about the country and its people. Unconsciously, she became a role model as she witnessed to people they met. One memorable trip they took together in the company's station wagon. Clumps of yellow broom dotted boulder-strewn fields on the road to Avila. As the vehicle wound upward toward the indigo mountains and topped a ridge, suddenly there on a low hill was the granite city with its twelfth-century walls.

While swallows flew in and out of Avila's towers, Grace and Indy stood in thyme-scented grass beside the wall and Luis, their driver, took their picture.

They invited Luis to join them for lunch, which he reluctantly did, as employees did not ordinarily dine with their senoras. Indy thanked him for his thoughtful suggestions during their tour that morning and easily changed the conversation topic to Jesus, the only Way.

On another day, in winter, Grace and Indy invited three other women to drive out with them to a small village where the townspeople gathered at a central well to secure water and buy bread. Since Indy knew the location, she drove Grace's car. They arrived while the women at the well were filling their jars and buckets. Just then, a little French truck arrived and the women gathered around to buy *pan* ("bread").

Beyond the village, in the open country, they saw a group of women in an olive orchard, beating at the trees with long poles to harvest the last of the old dried-up olives. Indy explained, "They are too poor to buy processed oil, so they knock down the last of the olives that have not fallen or been picked and take them home to press out the oil for cooking."

When Indy stopped to greet the women, and they saw how fluently she spoke their language, they readily agreed to have their pictures made. Again, Indy shared something of her belief in the Living Christ, and gave each of the women a leaflet about Him.

Never was she too hurried to stop and enjoy a bit of beauty or chat with anybody she met on the street or elsewhere. Sometimes when she and Charles were driving a long distance, and she saw an unusual mountain or castle, she'd suggest a brief stop for the drinking in of beauty, for refreshment physically, mentally, spiritually. "I'm taking a five-minute vacation," she'd say. One day in Grace's backyard she watched Grace, busy with her children. Beyond her, yellow roses flowed over the fence. "Grace, don't forget to take time to smell the roses," she said.

In late 1967, thousands of Cuban refugees were passing through Spain, en route to the United States. At least 30,000 of them were living temporarily in Madrid. These Cubans came to the attention of the Whittens when a group of them formed the Cuban Baptist Fellowship and began meeting on Friday nights at First Baptist Church of Madrid. Feeling empathy for the Cubans in their exile, Charles agreed to become their pastor-adviser, and Indy said she'd be the fellowship's treasurer.

Furthermore, they did something besides give verbal encouragement to the Cubans. At the back of their patio, they set up a "clothing store" and stocked it with used clothing. As winter approached and the temperature fell below freezing, Cubans came hurrying to this "store." In the hopes of replenishing her stock, Indy wrote in her November 1 newsletter to the US: "If any of you could send clothing, please send the packages to Sgt. Robert Jones, 98 Strat, Wing, Box 1925, APO, New York, New York."

Not only in Spain, but also across the United States, they reached out with words of encouragement.

The Whittens were going on furlough. When their ship, the *Leonardo da Vinci*, sailed from Barcelona on June 5, Helen, then a freshman at Mississippi College, had written, "I'll be waiting for you in the Jackson airport, my nose smashed flat from peering through the glass."

While they were living in Clinton in 1969, Indy spoke to girls gathered at Broadmoor Church, Jackson. Dressed in a Galician costume and wearing a mantilla, she talked about "Witnesses Today and Tomorrow in the Land of the Long Yesterday."

Afterward, Nancy Jordan, a third-grader, came down front to meet her, and Indy gave her three Spanish coins. Quite a few years later Nancy's mother met Indy in a beauty shop in Clinton and said, "I have always wanted to meet you. My daughter Nancy lost her Spanish coins, and she was so sad."

In 1987, Nancy Jordan Rowe and her husband, Bryan, a preacher, were studying at New Orleans Baptist Theological Seminary. She is only one of the hundreds of girls and other young people influenced by Charles and Indy's letters and furlough addresses to give their lives in full-time Christian service.

The next time they left for Spain, they would be in need of some words of encouragement for themselves.

18
"The MKs we left behind"

"Being an MK makes me feel special. When I'm in Spain, I'm the tall Americano, and when I'm in the US, I'm the fellow who knows Spanish and lives overseas."—David Whitten

HARDLY had the Statue of Liberty disappeared from view when Indy sat down and reached for a pen. Maybe it would ease the anguish if she could transfer it to paper:

Today I experienced a weightless feeling of suspension between where I came from and where I'm going. The S. S. *Raffaello* slices the murky greyness of the Atlantic, and every radar-controlled moment takes us further from those we left behind.

Two nights ago, in a New York City hotel, we talked by phone to our oldest daughter Helen in Colorado Springs, Colorado. She could not come to see us off because her student summer missionary work was keeping her in the West until the end of the month. Her words tumbled over each other as she spoke with enthusiasm of her second summer in Colorado.

"We wish you were here, Helen," I said when Charles (my husband) handed me the telephone. That remark almost ended the conversation.

"Yes, Mother," I heard and wondered if she were catching a bad cold.

"It won't be long until we'll be together again," I managed to say.

"Yes, Mother," Helen replied.

"Take care of yourself, Helen," I said, through a lump too big to handle.

"Good-bye, Mother."

"Good-bye, Helen."

Then there was yesterday, when we left our oldest son David. Five of us Whittens, with Helen noticeably absent, had been together for two days in New York City. We checked out of the hotel early in the morning, and a taxi whisked us to the port. We went aboard the ship and had fun exploring, as our family always did before a voyage.

This time we were uneasily awaiting the announcement, "All ashore that's going ashore."

David suggested that the family sit together on a long bench by the wall, just to the right of the visitors' exit. We didn't say much. We just sat, with our shoulders touching, and watched the people file out—some sobbing their last farewells to loved ones who were going away.

David reluctantly joined the slow-moving stream of people when the voice over the loudspeaker became insistent. We raced up and down steps, trying to find the spot on the deck closest to where David was standing.

Charles made several unsuccessful attempts to throw a streamer of colored paper from ship to shore. He called David's name each time, and the people standing around him groaned when the streamer fell short of our son's outstretched hand.

Finally David caught a yellow streamer. Everyone cheered.

One thin yellow strip of paper was the last physical tie between us and our son. The *Raffaello* moved slowly out, and the paper snapped in the middle. At that moment our separation began.

The sun wasn't shining, but I felt more secure wearing sunglasses. We fixed our gaze on Pier 90 until the only thing we could see about David was his boyish hand, held high, waving back and forth.

Finally we turned away from the deck and slowly went downstairs to our stateroom. I had often wondered how I would act and feel when the time came to leave the children. Now I know.

I have no better way to say, "I believe in world missions" than hearing the choked voice of Helen over the telephone or seeing David standing alone on Pier 90.

"Am I American, or am I Spanish?" all of the children had asked at one time or another. With time, they would discover they were both, with a capacity to take in the rest of the world.

As she continued to sit and reminisce, Indy considered the pros and cons of being a missionaries' kid (MK), from the standpoint of her own four. In Spain they had taken a bit of teasing because one pronunciation of their last name came close to the word for buzzard. They had sometimes had one set of friends at school and another at church because many of their church friends had to work instead of going to school. Their social life was different from that their American friends wrote them about, for dating customs in Spain differed from those in the United States.

Now those left behind must make their own decisions based on Christian convictions and not on what others did. She knew they would be tempted to identify with their peers in order to seem less foreign.

Yet, being world travelers held its advantages. It meant they could speak two languages. It meant having friends in both countries, and a better perspective for dealing with people, because they knew the different points of view of the two cultures. It meant having an enlarged and supportive family of missionary "aunts" and "uncles" and MK "cousins."

Once David had remarked, "Being an MK makes me feel special. When I'm in Spain, I'm the tall Americano, and when I'm in the US, I'm the fellow who knows Spanish and lives overseas." To him, the hardest part about moving back and forth from country to country had always been leaving his friends behind, no matter which direction they were traveling.

Margaret, because she was born in Spain, loved it and missed it when they were on furlough. Sometimes in the United States, she felt a little out of place among the small-town kids who had grown up together.

Suddenly Indy rose and left her stateroom for a walk about the deck. "Hello, there," she said to a woman reclining in a deck chair. "You have a nice smile," she told her, and, brown eyes radiating friendliness, she sat down to begin a conversation.

Just then Margaret appeared. "Hi. Are you on the way to dinner? Come meet my new friend."

As the two redheads entered the ship's dining room, Margaret said, "Mother, do you remember the time when the teacher criticized me for taking the plates off the table in the wrong order? I just knew you were going to say the teacher was right. But I was so proud of you when you took my side. I felt so vindicated!"

In a home economics course in junior high, Margaret had had a personality conflict with her teacher. When one day she served a meal and removed the plates in the wrong order, the teacher had humiliated her before the class. At first, she hesitated about telling Indy. But when she did, Indy immediately went to see the teacher to say she didn't like the way Margaret had been treated.

Margaret, a teenager during the sixties when newspapers constantly referred to the hippies and to the generation gap, sometimes felt her parents were too busy with their work to be in tune with their children. Anxious to maintain family harmony, though, she simply avoided subjects she felt were too volatile. Thus, she thought she got along better with her parents than many of her friends did with theirs.

Her friends, in fact, loved to come over to her house because her parents were easygoing. Of course, they had rules, and were strict about them, but they were always fair. When she was tempted to do something she knew she shouldn't, she would remember that Charles had told her he trusted her, and she didn't want to violate that trust.

On board the S.S. *Raffaello*, she and her mother met John and Charles at their table in the dining room. John, nine, and blue-eyed like his brother and sisters, had been exploring the ship some more.

Several days later, on August 20, 1969, the four stood by the rail and watched the sun go down and lights come on over the Rock of Gibraltar. One month before, two Americans had been the first to walk on the moon.

"He shall set me up upon a rock." The words of the psalmist came to Indy's mind. She would miss Helen and David, but she was as sure as that rock was secure that since God had called her to missions in Spain that He would give her the strength for the times of heartache also.

19
New work in Madrid

"Just as the astronauts set foot on the moon, we who represent you overseas dare to dream of entering as yet untouched fields for Christ."—Indy Whitten

WE HAVE had several weeks of trying to get settled back in Spain," Charles wrote J. D. Hughey, October 7, 1969. "Our old house was torn down in our absence, and we took an apartment near Plaza de Castilla . . . on the subway line. . . . The astronauts arrived in Madrid last night. . . . It is indeed a challenging time to be alive and in the Lord's work."

Charles took the treasurer's duties back from Jesse Bryan, who'd filled in for him while he was on furlough. With patience and stamina, he kept traveling over the country, unraveling red tape, doing the job he'd been given and doing it well. Yet his heart was that of a pastor. His missionary colleagues said he was their best evangelistic preacher, and many nationals felt the same.

Both he and Indy remained deeply interested in starting new churches and missions; however, they didn't believe in waiting for an ideal situation to begin ministering. They went ahead, using whatever situation they found themselves in.

When the pastor of First Baptist Church, Madrid, Juan Luis Rodrigo, and the deacons offered Charles space for his office in their church on General Lacy, he accepted the offer. Almost immediately, the pastor asked, "Would you consider being pastor of our Vallecas Mission?"

First Baptist Church was continuously sponsoring several missions in Madrid. Also churches in La Coruna, Sevilla, Malaga, Bilbao, and San Sebastian owed their start to this church.

Vallecas Mission had previously met in a mechanical

shop, but thanks to missionary James Buie and others, the members had secured a chapel, transformed from an old potato chip factory.

On a Sunday September evening, Charles and Indy arrived at the chapel by subway and found a large crowd gathered for opening night. The Vallecas congregation was international—Japanese, Cuban, American, and Spanish. Hence, Indy felt sure that the Japanese university student, Yashimi Miyamoto, would enjoy going there. Indirectly from missionary Charles Whaley in Japan, she had learned that Yashimi, a Christian, was studying in Madrid. She "sort of adopted" her, inviting her to their house and to the Mission.

At Vallecas, Yashimi made a hit, especially with the young people, who formed a circle around her to make her feel welcome. They divided her name into syllables: *Mi* (my); *ya* (now); *moto* (motor) scooter. She thought that funny.

Not knowing either Spanish or English too well, she said to them, "Christian—alone—No, No, No! Christian with other Christian—Yes, Yes, Yes!" Indy thought that incident itself was a good reason the church should exist.

Cristo Unica Esperanza (Christ the Only Hope) was the theme of the evangelistic campaigns held all across Spain in May 1970 while the Whittens were still at Vallecas. The campaigns, as Indy described them, were a united effort "of the 56 churches of the Spanish Baptist Union to go outside the walls and love people into the kingdom of God." Indy wrote:

> It wasn't easy. Many obstacles still remain rooted in the religious persecution of the Spanish Inquisition. It is not easy to shake off the centuries of being told that Protestants teach a false religion and that it is dangerous as well as sinful to attend their services. Ignorance and fear stand at the doors of the Baptist churches, and many people are turned back by these frightful figures.

She could not forget the woman from Albacete who rode across town on a motorcycle, wiping clammy hands on her husband's jacket and dreading their moment of arrival at the Baptist church. Maruja Bernalte said she had prayed, "God, or whoever it is who looks after such things—stop me if this be as sinful as I've always been taught. You could let us have an accident or I could have an attack of appendicitis." But she arrived and heard the message of Him Who said, "Fear not."

Every Sunday morning at Vallecas, the blind organist emerged from the subway exit, tapping her white cane and smiling. During the revival campaigns, she brought a blind friend who there met the Light of the World.

When Charles began work in a mission, he always explained, "I'll be with you until you call a national pastor." As soon as Vallecas called one, he moved to another of First Baptist Church's missions, San Blas, which met in a home.

"We love them and leave them," Indy laughed.

During the campaigns, a special folder had been distributed all over the country. The front of it pointed out that now (since Vatican Council II) Protestants and Catholics are in agreement that people should read and study the Bible.

An elderly couple happened to receive a copy of this that had first passed through several hands. After a delay of almost six months, they wrote to members of the San Blas congregation. When Charles visited them, they confided, "We feel certain that the mercy and providence of God let this little folder come to us."

Though the group in the home was small, Charles and Indy, as in whatever they undertook, were deep, steady workers with a sense of commitment. They stuck with it—not always seeing growth but knowing it would come—building relationships, building foundations.

Five years before, during another nationwide evangelistic campaign, 600 professions of faith had been recorded. Scores of those professions of faith had been made in the four missions of First Baptist Church, Madrid: San Blas, Plaza Castilla, Villaverda, and Vallecas.

In 1966, Charles agreed to be pastor of the Villaverde Mission, which was meeting in a beauty shop. Rodrigo told him, "The shop makes women beautiful on the outside during the day, and we make them beautiful on the inside at night." However, a Baptist family gave money to enable Villaverde to move into a storefront building. It was constituted as a church New Year's Day 1968, with 34 charter members.

Through the years, Charles and Joe Mefford had often worked together in stewardship revivals. Joe was a musician, but he and Charles both liked to preach. One Sunday, they had a hard time trying to decide which one would get to preach that day. Suddenly they realized that the pastor was not introducing either of them but had already begun the sermon. Neither would get to preach!

In October 1966, a group of Mississippi men at Charles's invitation led in stewardship revivals in Spain. Mostly laymen, they were led by Owen Cooper of Yazoo City. Chester L. Quarles, executive director, Mississippi Baptist Convention Board, joined the group as chaplain. Several women with them led stewardship conferences among the Spanish Baptist women. The oldest, Mrs. Ben Thompson, a former WMU president, and mother of Mrs. Owen Cooper, was 80. Walking with a cane did not deter her from being one of the more popular speakers. Hermogenes Fernandez, stewardship promoter for the Spanish Baptist Union, coordinated the men's meetings, and Indy the women's conference in Madrid, Valencia, and Barcelona.

June 5, 1967, Charles had written Hughey, "At long last we bought the property for First Baptist Church of Madrid, just to the right of the present building. After dealing with the owners for two years with very little success, today 18 people put their signatures alongside the one representing the Foreign Mission Board. To get that many people together, agreed upon a common purpose and price, was a miracle in itself."

Before Villaverde, the Whittens had helped to begin the Turo de la Peira Church as well as the Cornella Church in Barcelona. After Villaverde, they began working in another mission called Barrio del Pilar, which had started in the apartment of Antonio Alcon, a deacon in

First Baptist Church, Madrid, and a bus driver.

Alcon showed Charles his worn leather toolboxes. "In one," he said, "are tools I use to fix my bus. The other is my spiritual toolbox. In it I have tracts and New Testaments. When I see people running to the bus stop, I do not drive off and leave them like most drivers, but I wait. Usually they come up to thank me, and I tell them the reason why. And I witness to them."

A friendly man, Alcon found it easy to strike up a conversation. For instance, if a passenger boarded, shivering, he might say, "You are cold in the body. Well, you are also cold in your spirit. Take one of these tracts. It will help warm you up!" Ten years before, another bus driver named Andrew had led him to Christ. Alcon, a musician who sang in a rich baritone voice and played the *laud* (lute), said, "When I got to know Christ as my Saviour, my whole life became a song."

As Charles preached, Alcon would always be there, enthusiastic and smiling and would lay a piece of paper down in front of him. Charles would see a number, one, three, or four. "Antonio, what does this mean?" he finally asked.

"I thought you knew. I have witnessed to this number, and I have them here tonight. I hope you give them a good gospel message. I want them saved."

One Sunday while Charles was preaching at Albacete in a church which was at the moment pastorless, he had a chance to use his considerable talents as a peacemaker. Albacete, 250 kilometers south of Madrid, had one of the oldest and strongest congregations in Spain. As the Whittens arrived, they noticed a little knot of men talking, evidently in a serious frame of mind.

"What's going on?" Charles asked.

"The carpenter got a key and went in the auditorium last night and took all the backs off the pews," a deacon said. The carpenter, a member of the church, had been hired to do some work there and felt he hadn't been paid all the agreement called for. The church leaders said he had, and now they planned to call the police.

To Charles, this was a blow. He persuaded them not

to call the police until he'd had a chance to think about it. He suggested that they meet upstairs in an assembly room. This was to draw attention away from the pews without backs. While he preached, only half his mind was on his sermon. The other half was seeking a solution.

After the service he talked to each side. He said to the church leaders, "You feel the church doesn't owe this carpenter anything. But why don't you give him the benefit of the doubt and pay him this extra amount?" To the carpenter he said, "You feel they haven't paid you enough. Why don't you go an extra mile and say you will give that labor to the church?" Thus he got them together. The leaders said they were willing to pay, and the carpenter refused to accept the money. Instead, it was sent to the old folks home.

On occasions, because of his ability to be impartial, just, and compassionate, Charles was peacemaker among missionaries as well as nationals. Once at Mission Meeting, a vote went against a fellow missionary. That night Charles slept poorly as he thought and prayed. The next morning he said at the meeting, "I feel I did wrong. I cannot give my vote to such a decision." So the whole group reconsidered and a missionary remained on the field who might not otherwise have done so.

That Sunday, as the two left Albacete, someone called, "*Vaya con Dios*! May your road have no windings to tire you, no stones to trip you!"

20
Sunrise of a new day

"Whoso loves believes the impossible."—Elizabeth Barrett Browning

FIVE MEN stepped up to the door of the Zarzuela Palace: Juan Luis Rodrigo, Madrid pastor; Jose Borras, president of the Spanish Baptist Union; W. H. Jackson, Texas evangelist; Charles Whitten; and a photographer from the American Embassy.

Four entered, but the doorman reached out and stopped the fifth. "No, you are not allowed to take pictures inside the palace." It looked as if Baptists' first interview with royalty would be unphotographed.

The men expected to see Crown Prince Juan Carlos de Bourbon, designated successor to 80-year-old General Francisco Franco as head of state. But they were surprised when his wife, Princess Sofia, also came to greet them.

During the half-hour audience, the princess asked about Baptist beliefs and brought up the subject of religious freedom.

Rodrigo presented the crown prince with a copy of the Bible of the Bear, a version that had been reissued in 1971 on the 400th anniversary of its translation into Spanish. Jackson had brought Texas boots and a cowboy hat for the prince. Juan Carlos tried on the boots and they fit, but the hat was too small. He called a palace attendant to take his head measurements, so Jackson could send him another size. "Now I have hat and boots," he quipped. "I have a saddle. All I need is a horse!"

The men apologized to Princess Sofia for not bringing her a gift, since her presence had been unexpected, but she graciously thanked them for the Bible.

Saying good-bye to the future king and queen,

Charles and the others expressed disappointment that they could not have taken pictures.

"No problem," said Juan Carlos. He spoke to the doorman, who ran into the palace gardens to fetch the photographer and then watched as the royal couple posed for pictures.

Later that day, October 17, 1972, Leland Webb, then managing editor of the *Commission*, interviewed Charles and Indy in their apartment at Mateo Inurria 11.

Their guest rode up the three-person elevator to the third floor in time for *merienda* (afternoon tea). At number 3-C he saw a brass plate on the door, engraved with the Whittens' name. Light from the wide windows in the living room sent a gleam across the hardwood floor. Chairs outside on the narrow balcony looked inviting.

Since the Whittens were Southern Baptists' senior missionaries in Spain, they had been on the scene to watch the barometer shift from stormy persecution of the 1950s to this Tuesday when Baptists had been received by royalty. What factors, Webb wanted to know, had led to this change?

Charles listed several opinions. The 1953 treaty that Spain and the United States had signed to allow location of US air and navy bases in Spain had brought many Americans. The country had seen what tourism could mean to the economy. Then an improved economy had meant that more Spaniards could travel to other countries. When they did, they saw how other people lived and were no longer satisfied for Spain to be closed and isolated. Too, an improved economy had led to a rising middle class.

Another cause of change had been Vatican II. It had resulted in more interrelation between the Catholic church and evangelicals; Spanish masses instead of Latin; and the Catholic church's urging people to read the Bible. Thus, many had overcome their superstitious attitudes about evangelical churches.

A third factor was the Law of Religious Freedom, passed in 1967. On New Year's Eve, as 1967 was ushered in, Franco had broadcast a message announcing a new day of religious liberty for all the people of Spain.

"The new law was at first greatly misunderstood," Charles said, "especially the part about the churches being required to register with the government. What the churches feared about registration was that the government might control church finances and membership by putting pressure on members."

The registration question had sparked a lot of controversy. At first the Spanish Baptist Union voted to recommend that the churches not register. But at the convention in 1970 the union voted to allow churches to follow whatever course they felt led to take. The Baptist Mission had voted to register. In fact, it had become almost a necessity in order to have legal standing.

"What are some firsts Spanish Baptists have lately been able to carry out?" Webb asked.

Indy answered, "During evangelistic crusades in 1971, Baptists used radio for the first time. They used newspapers for the first time to any degree, and permission was given for open-air meetings.

"The Baptist convention in 1971 in Alcoy was held in a public place, in the best hotel," Indy continued. "Also for the first time we could fly the Christian flag alongside the Spanish flag."

Charles added, "While we do not have complete religious freedom yet, we enjoy a tolerance that enables us to do much more than we are doing."

"What is the current situation about radio?"

Indy replied, "Local Baptist radio programs are being carried in Albacete and in Alcoy, and there has been a shortwave program for a year over Trans World Radio, Monte Carlo. Joe Mefford, chairman of the committee on radio, helped to start the local programs."

After Webb had gone, Charles and Indy reviewed some of the recent changes that had taken place within their family. On May 30, 1971, Helen had been graduated from Mississippi College at the municipal auditorium in Jackson, with her mother present. On the same date, two of Indy's brothers, Bruce and H. C., had received PhD degrees in entomology from Mississippi State University.

A week later, Margaret had been graduated from Torrejon Air Base High School and now was enrolled at Mississippi College where David had gotten his degree in the spring of 1972. David was now in the Peace Corps in Jamaica. A change had come about in Indy's work schedule; she was teaching again in the seminary, this time English and a class for pastors' wives. Being adaptable and willing, and calling herself a Jill-of-all-trades, she later taught journalism, ethics, religious education, and recreation. The seminary had moved to Madrid from Barcelona in the summer of 1971.

Madrid rises from the plain suddenly like a coral reef on a wide sea bottom. On its outer edge, at Alcobendas, Baptists had bought seminary property with a picturesque view of gently sloping green hills and distant snow-dusted Guadarramas.

Because Gerald McNeely had succeeded Russell Hilliard as seminary president, the McNeelys had moved to Madrid. Once again they were the Whittens' neighbors. While new seminary buildings were under construction, classes met in Immanuel Church, and apartments were used for library, offices, and student housing. "We'll never find enough apartments!" June said. But determination shone from her blue eyes. She, Gerald, and Indy would park the car and separate to knock on doors. They dodged children playing jump rope in the courtyards to ask, "May we see the apartment for rent?" They found what they needed.

Since 70 percent of the Baptist churches were in eastern Spain, the Mission felt that seminary students in the center of the country might help to develop churches in the north and west. From the first groups of students after the move, Leopoldo Vidal was chosen to go to Burgos, 144 miles north of Madrid, on weekends to try to start a church. The seminary paid his train fare and weekend boardinghouse expenses.

Burgos, the capital of Old Castile until 1087, had been a stopping place for medieval pilgrims. El Cid, Spain's national hero, was buried in its cathedral, a wonder of Spanish Gothic art, where twin towers recalled Cologne. Burgos had no Protestant church of any kind.

Leopoldo had no funds to rent a place to hold a worship service even if anyone would rent to him. Instead, he handed out tracts and sold Bibles and Christian books and put a Bible correspondence course into the hands of as many as he could.

One April weekend two carloads of Baptist young women from First Baptist Church, Madrid, along with Charles and Indy, traveled through rain, sleet, and snow to Burgos to help Leopoldo distribute literature. They met him in front of the cathedral.

Indy took along bread, ham, cheese, and cookies enough to feed everybody. That and plenty of hot *cafe con leche* (coffee with milk) tasted good in the cold, windy city.

They visited house to house, two-by-two, giving out tracts on how to be saved, or selling books. At some apartment houses they left cards about the correspondence course in all the mailboxes. At the houses response was polite but somewhat cold. It was not hard, though, to assemble a crowd on the street. Leopoldo placed his literature suitcase on the sidewalk to divide materials among the workers. When he straightened up, children and young people stuck out their hands to receive anything he had to give.

In the boardinghouse the girls crowded into one room and talked with great emotion about how white the harvest is in Burgos.

In the fall of 1972, Spain was featured in the Foreign Mission Board's mission study series. Indy had written *Higher than Montgo* for older children, Lila Mefford's *Sylvia Goes to Spain* was previously written for younger children.

Margaret, 19, had written an article for the November *Commission,* in which she told about an August trip she and her family had made to Gijon "in the green valleys of northern Spain by the sparkling Cantabric sea." Their purpose, love in action, was to contact the great-aunt of one of Margaret's college classmates and, as the Lord led, to share Christ with her.

They inquired in a city of 100,000 about the snack-bar restaurant the great-aunt owned and were directed to a town eight miles away. As Margaret talked with the elderly woman about her relatives in the United States, tears came to the woman's eyes. "I wish I could see their faces and hug them again," she said. They left with her a New Testament which she promised to read.

"True," Margaret wrote, "missionaries do preach and teach," but their work involves "so much more." "Their main work is to gain acceptance by the people through ordinary, everyday activities."

December 20, 1972, Charles and Indy flew to Mississippi for a scheduled eight-month furlough. Charles's father had been ill. When they arrived at the missionary home of Woodland Hills Baptist Church, Jackson, they found it warm with welcome, already decorated for Christmas, tree lights burning.

21
Editor of *El Eco*

"God so loved, and we are to be channels of that love through our giving and serving."—Indy Whitten

THE WIND whistled as it hurled sheets of snow across the road. Sharp white needles broke when they struck the windshield, so that the hood of the car soon looked as white as the blurred landscape. When the three women left Wheatland on the way to Cheyenne, Wyoming, they had no idea they'd be running into a blizzard in March. Bernice Elliott of Birmingham, was driving with Pearl Steinkuehler of Wyoming beside her and Indy in back. They'd been leading conferences in Casper.

Visibility dwindled to zero, and Bernie had to stop, like all the other drivers on the road. "I'm hungry," said Indy. "I'll get some food from the trunk." But the doors had frozen shut!

"Brrr, I'm cold," chattered Bernie. Intermittently, all night, she turned the heater off and on.

In the morning the snowplow sliced into their silent white world. Rescuers said, "We can take only one at the time."

"Oh, we must all stay together," they insisted, and somehow all squeezed in. Most of the day they spent in a small hotel in Chugwater, Wyoming. Only one three-quarter-size bed stood in the room assigned them, so they took it. Though they were not small women, they slept reasonably well, taking turns as to who would sleep in the middle. They swapped stories with the other marooned travelers. Questions there arose about their religious beliefs. On furlough, Indy had spoken in 20 states, but that day gave her the most opportunities for witnessing yet.

Back home Charles had heard about the snowstorm

but didn't know how to get in touch with Indy. The two were scheduled to appear on a morning talk show, "Coffee with Judy," in Jackson, Mississippi. Margaret substituted for her mother.

On the show, Judy asked, "Margaret, do you feel you were cheated of many good things because you grew up outside the United States?"

"Oh, no!" exclaimed Margaret. "I wouldn't swap with anybody!"

En route to Madrid in the summer, they detoured by Jamaica to meet David's bride-to-be, Sharon Dennis, also in the Peace Corps. They could not stay for the August 25 wedding at Bethel Baptist Church, Kingston, but Helen would be there.

Early on an October morning in 1973, Indy climbed into a taxi at the Barcelona airport. With her she carried a small suitcase and a blue portfolio containing the copy for the December issue of *El Eco*. That was the Spanish Baptist magazine; she was its new editor.

Her editorial office was a small windowless room in the center of their apartment, meant for a live-in maid, which they no longer had. But Senor Salvado printed the magazine in Barcelona, 384 miles away. Right now she was taking the material to him.

At a corner near the Baptist Book Store, she stepped sleepily out of the taxi with her suitcase but left the blue portfolio on the floor. As the door closed and the driver pulled away from the curb, she realized she had left it. "Wait! Wait!" she called and ran down the street, but the driver never looked back. She didn't even know the number of his license plate. All day she struggled through committee meetings, her mind following her portfolio. That night at the home of Jesse and Beverly Bryan, she tried to be pleasant, but inwardly she was frantic. When she called the taxi company, they said, "If it is turned in, you can get it at our lost and found tomorrow morning."

"*If* . . ." Indy prayed, "Lord, I am convinced you gave me this job I like so much to do, and that you want me to serve you through the printed page. I put this situation into your hands. If this material is not found, you and I will just have to take it from there." It was found, and she retrieved it the next morning.

Many times during her 20 years in Spain she had thought she'd like the job, but didn't expect to have it, for she was not a native-born Spaniard, and she was not a man.

Then one night her phone rang. "Would you be editor of *El Eco*" asked Antonio Gomez, member of the Education and Publishing Board of the Spanish Baptist Union and former editor of *El Eco*.

Taking pains to act dignified, she answered, "Why yes, I'll be glad to do my best." But when the conversation ended, she threw the phone into the air and sent Bilbo Baggins, the cat, scuttling under the bed. Thus did the first non-Spaniard and the first woman become editor of *El Eco*.

Her days, already busy, grew even more so. Both she and Charles were teaching at the seminary; he was still treasurer and also pastor of Pueblo Nuevo Mission. Margaret was taking her junior year at the University of Madrid, and John, 13, was in the American School.

During her years as editor of *Nuestra Labor*, she had taught several correspondence courses for potential writers. And she had also learned that besides knowing how to write, an editor needs lots of know-how in public relations.

Potential troublemakers she handled in the spirit of Him Who said, "Love your enemy." One night a layman called her at 11:30, after his supper, and asked, "Did you know a mistake had been made in the number of magazines sent to our church? You can just cancel the whole thing."

A little gremlin of temptation told her to say, "Okay, suit yourself." Instead, she said, "I'm sure you don't really mean that. This magazine is an instrument of the Lord to inspire Christians to give the message of Christ to lost people and to promote our Baptist work in Spain. Knowing the kind of Christian person you are, I just know you will continue to support the *Eco*."

A few weeks later, she visited this man's church; he was standing in the door, selling *Ecos*.

Another time she received a letter to the editor, a bitter, undeserved attack on a leader of the Spanish Baptist Union. She declined to publish a letter that would hurt someone. Word came back, "If you don't publish this, I will resign my position in the Union."

"I'm sorry, but my reply is still the same. I cannot make it otherwise." So the man resigned.

An elderly man kept flooding *El Eco* with poetry. Though Indy published some of it, he was still not satisfied and wanted more used. He wrote her an angry letter, which she didn't answer. He sent a telegram: "Answer me something—one way or another."

Her telegram in reply: "Mr.———, you know I appreciate you."

Back came a second telegram: "Hallelujah!" In an article, she wrote, "To me, being an editor is like going fishing. I enjoy the preparation, and I feel deeply satisfied over the outcome. . . . What a reward it is to know that somebody has gone to church for the first time because of the evangelistic section in *Eco*."

After the Baptist Spanish Publishing House in El Paso published Indy's book, *Higher than Montgo*, in Spanish, censors at the customs office forbade its entering Spain. "It talks about a child becoming a Christian at the camp in Denia," they said. "All our Spanish children are already Christians." Eventually it was imported. Word spread that it had been banned. Sales zoomed.

Channels of God's love through the printed word? Yes, and through hospitality, too. The Whittens' entertainment of guests accelerated in the 1970s. Woman's Missionary Union leaders always found a warm welcome at their place. National president Marie Mathis and executive director Alma Hunt slept in the twin beds of the guest room at Mateo Inurria 11 during the 25th anniversary celebration of Spanish Baptist WMU. (Noemi Tejerina, then the national WMU president, said during the convention, "Our personal testimony is made up of all that we are and all that we do. Our smallest attitude or personal trait may make or break our testimony. We are made to be beautiful in the Lord. We are all to be missionaries.")

One sunny October day Indy drove associate executive director Bobbie Sorrill and editor Helen Allan to Toledo to see El Greco's house and other sights. On the way back, the car stopped. Two men drove them to a garage, and they returned to the car in a taxi. The car started but died again in rush-hour traffic between the Prado and the Fountain of Neptune. They pushed it up on the sidewalk, rode home in a taxi, and sent Charles back to tend to the car.

Another day Indy drove Marjean Patterson, of Mississippi WMU, to Denia. They rode past vineyards fringed with olive trees, where pruned vines looked like polka dots in the red soil, and past green wheat fields bordered with wild red poppies. Beside the road walked a shepherd leading his flock of sheep. They stopped at Cuenca, perched on a cliff. "We have no evangelical witness here," Indy said.

In a little coffee bar-restaurant, where a woman and her three children seemed to be in charge, they ordered lunch, roast lamb and a bowl of fresh fruit. It seemed to Marjean that Indy and the woman were talking a mile a minute; she strained her ears trying to understand their Spanish.

The little girl standing at the door screamed. *"Perro!"* she said. Indy jumped up to chase away the big dog that had frightened the child.

"That's something," Marjean said. "Even the dogs around here understand Spanish, and I cannot!" Turning to the mother, she asked, "May I take your little girl's picture?"

The mother spit on her finger and pushed the child's hair back from her face, straightened her collar, and stood her against the wall for posing. As she was leaving, Indy gave the woman several tracts. Later she said to Marjean, "This will be a contact. If and when we can establish a mission here, this family would remember us by the dog and the tracts and your taking her picture."

On occasion, the number in the Whittens' dinner crowd grew wildly out of control. For instance, one night in 1974, they had invited a high school friend's son and his bride to have dinner with them. The young man had finished medical school and was taking an overseas trip. Then a phone call came from a couple from Minnesota who were traveling in Spain. They had corresponded, but did not know the Whittens personally. The Whittens told them to come.

A bit later the daughter of an employee from El Paso Publishing House called to say she and her son were in town and would like to see them. So they added them to the group. The group arrived; just as they were all sitting down to eat, an Argentine woman married to a Spanish pastor came to the door. When she found out that Peggy Hart, daughter of Laura Hart Dissilkon of the El Paso Publishing House, was there, Mrs. Campederros exclaimed, "I grew up partially in the home of Peggy's grandparents, who were missionaries in Argentina!" So naturally Mrs. Campederros was invited in. They kept adding water to the soup and water to the iced tea. John later calculated that they drank 11 gallons of iced tea.

During the time that Bill Estep was on sabbatical in Spain from the faculty of Southwestern Baptist Theological Seminary, the Whittens met him when he preached at Immanuel Church, and his wife, Edna, played the organ. Indy invited them for lunch and stopped on the way home to buy fried chicken. (Often she took the easy way out and bought food already prepared, such as fresh bread from the shop beyond the flower shop next to their apartment building, or pastries from the food and beverage bar next to that. Or she ordered American pies from a place called "Helen's," which came to be known as "Indy's Bakery.")

"We've wanted to meet you a long time," Edna told the Whittens. "We prayed for you on a Wednesday night in September 1959 at First Baptist Church, Cali, Colombia, when we heard of Charles's accident. Bill was on his first sabbatical from Southwestern."

Indy gave them a copy of *We Camped at Heaven's Gate* after she wrote on the flyleaf: "Grateful for the chance to know and love you." She told Edna that she and Charles expected one day to move to another part of Spain to begin new work.

Actually, Edna and Indy had already met by phone when Edna called to ask the name of a doctor, and Indy made an appointment for her with Dr. Bill Singleton, who was a colonel in the US Air Force as well as the chief of surgery at the military base hospital.

Dr. Singleton, a lay preacher, a deacon at Immanuel Church, and a magician, sometimes traveled with Charles to speak in churches while Charles translated. He and his wife, Rosemary, and their sons Penn and Mark; along with Charles, Indy, Margaret, John, and 78 others from the air base toured Israel together. Charles wrote a commentary for the group on Scripture passages relating to places they visited. Friendship between the Singletons and Whittens was instant from the minute they met. Love kept it growing.

When the Singletons' dog, Sam, got sick, Rosemary called Indy and asked, "Would you mind going to the vet with me to translate?"

"Of course not. Come on, and we'll be ready." The Whittens had just walked into the house after being away for several days, but they didn't tell Rosemary they were tired. Indy and John jumped into the car and went to the vet.

When Bill received orders to return to the States, Indy told the Singletons, "Oh, but you can't go until you see a bullfight!" So the families got together and went to one in El Escorial.

Servant or queen, to Charles and Indy it made no difference. Their love encircled both.

One bright morning Indy hurried downstairs. If she didn't make it snappy, she'd be late for her seminary class. "*Hola!* (Hi!)" she said to the woman on her hands and knees cleaning the rug that led to the lobby door. "How's the weather?" she asked Carmen Merino, wife of the building caretaker.

"Nice and sunny."

Indy reached for the handle of the heavy door as she said, "*Adios.*"

"Wait," Carmen said hesitantly, as she pushed a strand of black hair back from her forehead and slowly got to her feet. "We have noticed how friendly you act toward us," she said. "And I've never even seen you hang out a dish towel on Sunday. You invited me to your 'mass.' I want to go next Sunday. You haven't forgotten?"

"Oh, no! I had not forgotten." She stepped into the street, her mood matching the clear, bright, sharp sunlight.

After Franco's death in 1975, Juan Carlos and Sofia were crowned king and queen. Through the queen's donation of the first million pesetas, special studies concerning the religious groups of Spain were set up with the Department of Humanities at the Autonomous University of Madrid, headed by Professor Jose de Solas. Jose Borras was invited early in 1976 to do a lecture series on Baptist beliefs. The queen herself enrolled in the studies.

When the royal couple planned to visit the US, Dr. de Solas went ahead of them to prepare for the visit. At the professor's request, the Whittens, with the help of some friends arranged for Dr. de Solas to visit a Baptist church at a home in New York. He was so impressed that when he returned, he invited the Whittens to his seminars.

That was where Indy first met the queen. At home she had practiced curtsying before the mirror. But Queen Sofia came forward and clasped both her hands and began talking to her in English, saying, "I know you are in Spain on a good mission, and I am so happy to meet you." During one class session, the queen sat in front of her and got a cough. Indy thought, "Now I'll see what queens do when they cough." She pulled out the same kind of cough drops Indy used!

Borras in his remarks emphasized that each group should have absolute freedom of worship. He said, "As a result of the seminars, we all know each other better, and so we respect and love each other more."

The king told him, "If you have any problems of religious freedom in your Baptist work do not hesitate to come to me."

This new spirit was evident too in the Madrid Roman Catholic cardinal, who had been visited by Dr. de Solas to inform him of the proposed seminars. The cardinal said, "Not only do I give you my approval, but I also give you my blessing."

To Indy, Charles said, "Only God could have made all this possible."

God Took Us to Abla

Charles, our son John, and I were traveling along the winding highway from Almeria to Granada when John began to have motion sickness. We stopped at a village and were told that the nearest pharmacy was more than five miles away.

The highway went around Abla as a bypass, and to find a pharmacy we were told to go into the central part of town. With a good bit of twisting and turning, we arrived at a quaint little plaza and had to park the car because the street became one-way. While Charles and John went to the pharmacy, I . . . walked over to where a woman was whitewashing her house. . . . I found that her name was Manuela, that she was originally from Extremadura near the Portuguese border. . . .

"And how do you feel about religion?" I asked.

"If you want me to be honest with you," she said hesitantly, "I never go to church or to confession. I haven't been since our oldest child was baptized, and he is now fifteen."

When I gave her a tract and a card offering the Correspondence Bible Course free, she suddenly lowered her voice and said, "You'd better come inside. . . . This is a . . . fanatical town, and besides, I think you have some information that I need."

So into the neat little adobe house I went. Immediately I was surrounded by Manuela's four children. . . .

When I discovered that the family had no Bible, I went back to the car to get a . . . New Testament. I looked up and read the essential verses that point out the plan of salvation. . . . When she heard Romans 3:23, . . . she said, "I never heard that before, but I know that it is true."

Before I left, Manuela served me a steaming cup of coffee and brought out some little nut cakes. She also gave me three motion-sickness tablets in case the pharmacy was closed.

Manuela soaked up the words of the Bible like dry ground drinks up the rain. She said as I left, "I knew that what you have told me had to be true. I believe with all my heart that God brought you here today."

To save my life, I couldn't think of any other way I could have gotten there!

Indy Whitten
Royal Service
October 1976

22
"Never so far from home"

"Oh, Lord, we have never asked You to give us an easy life. We do not ask for things that we ought to do for ourselves. But we do ask You to give us freedom."—Amalia Bretz

RAIN drenched Budapest the morning of Indy's arrival, but the city on the Danube was lovely even in the rain. Mrs. Gero, president of the Baptist Woman's work in Hungary, met her and delivered her—but not her luggage—to the Sport Hotel. Her suitcase had not made the transfer with her in Frankfurt.

The Executive Committee of the European Baptist Federation had invited all the editors of Baptist periodicals of Europe to meet with them September 15-21, 1976, in Budapest. Indy, in her third (and final) year as editor of *El Eco*, was representing Spanish Baptists. Some at the meeting said, "You don't look like a Spaniard, but we take your word for it!"

For six days she would room with Kerstin Ruden of Sweden, president of the European Baptist Woman's Union; Else Ohrn of Norway; and Melada Paholva of Czechoslovakia.

She hated to appear at the formal opening banquet wearing her pants suit, but she had no other clothes, not even a nightgown. But on the second night, a pastor wearing a little leather cap drove her to the airport to get her luggage. At first, he tried to talk, but his Hungarian was "Greek" to her. He began whistling a hymn tune and elbowed in her direction for her to join him in singing. Then he sang "Jesus Wants Me for a Sunbeam" in Spanish with an Argentine accent.

She exclaimed, "Argentina!"

He answered, "Argentina!" (Later, through an interpreter, she learned that a Hungarian family had lived in Argentina for a while and on their return had taught the man the song.) The pastor kept pointing up and saying something which she took to mean, "God is good!"

Eighty delegates represented the Baptist unions from 20 countries. It surprised almost everyone that Indy, a woman, should be sitting in the press section (though she met several women who were pastors). One man took her firmly by the arm, dragging her down the hall, trying to help her find her place with the women's group.

In the home of the Geros (the woman who had met her at the airport and her husband, a pastor), she ate lunch one day. Another guest, 84-year-old Amalia Bretz, had graduated from the WMU Training School in Louisville 50 years before. With tears dripping on the stiff white tablecloth, the woman told how much the love of Baptists in America had meant to her during her years there in the twenties.

Mrs. Bretz prayed in English: "Oh, Lord, we have never asked You to give us an easy life. We do not ask for things that we ought to do for ourselves. But we do ask You to give us freedom." For a long, long time, Indy thought, she would remember the faces of Hungarian Baptists she had met in Budapest.

Only the month before, during that year of America's Bicentennial celebration, she and Charles and 15-year-old John had visited Denmark and Russia. At Leningrad they had landed with anticipation but also with some anxiety. On Sunday in Leningrad they visited the Baptist church, where the crowd filled the aisles, the balcony, the back, and flowed into the street. Indy noticed that after a while the people rotated; some of those seated and some standing exchanged places with a smile and a nod. Some passed slips of paper forward with prayer requests, and the pastor raised these above his head and asked God to respond to them as He knew best.

The congregation didn't have enough Bibles and hymnbooks. Several were trying to write the Scripture passages down while they were being read. And when the choir director led "I'm Saved, Saved, Saved," Indy noticed a woman writing as fast as she could, trying to capture all the words.

The tour guide told them, "I am in the youth group of the USSR. We have no religion. I have no faith. If I want to do something of this type, I go to the tombs of our national heroes."

Indy wrote, "In philosophy and practice, I've never been so far from home. If we had not worshiped with the Baptists, we would have come away under a heavy burden of sadness and pessimism."

At Christmastime the Whittens were on furlough again, eagerly expecting their whole family, including both sets of parents, to come to celebrate the holidays with them. Helen would be there with their first grandchild, three-month-old Cristina, whom they'd never seen. Helen had married Stephen Cobb, whom she had met while teaching school in Pensacola. Their wedding had been at Poplar Flat, the church where Charles and Indy had married. Now the Cobbs were in language school in Costa Rica, preparing for missions in Honduras. Margaret would be there with her fiance, Sam Drummond. Their wedding would be at Weir two days after Christmas. Margaret had met Sam, son of a Baptist pastor, at Mississippi College while she was a Spanish instructor and he was one of her students. David and Sherry would be there from Houston, Texas, where he was studying law.

It was after 10:00 P.M., December 20, 1976, when Charles and Indy and John drove into the carport at 1625 Easy Street, Yazoo City, Mississippi. They found a Christmas tree in the living room, set up by the girls of First Baptist Church. Inside the den, one of the first things they saw was a picture gallery of the 13 couples who had previously lived at 1625. This reminded them of the beginnings of this missionary house. In 1961 Nancy Cooper had stopped to see them in Spain after a year of study in Germany and asked where they planned to live on their next furlough.

"We don't know," they said. "Housing is sometimes a problem."

"I'm going home to Yazoo City," she replied, "and see if the folks there can set up a missionary home."

And so it was that her parents, Owen and Elizabeth Cooper, initiated the purchase of the ranch-style house on Easy Street. Then First Baptist Church, Yazoo City, voted to take over the care and payments. This was one of the first missionary houses among Southern Baptists. Many think that it was the first. It was rent-free, all furnishings provided, but the missionaries paid their utility bills.

On February 28, 1977, Charles's parents celebrated their 60th wedding anniversary.

Most of the furlough was filled with speaking engagements and conferences, for they felt this an important part of their work. Yet, to renew their strength and zeal, they themselves needed the ministry of a warm and caring fellowship like they found in First Baptist Church, Yazoo City, and its pastor, James Yates. As is often the case, life on Easy Street too quickly came to an end.

23
"One step enough for me"

"The will of God comes to us as we obediently proceed one day at a time on the light we have, expecting greater light."— Albert Schweitzer

NORTHWEST Spain was like a different land from the dry plain on the other side of the Guadarramas. The train thundered along the mountain slopes, among the pine trees and the terraced vineyards and through the green valleys, past the villages of yellowish brownstone. Corn cribs on stilts supported wooden crosses, which some people said were "to bless the harvest."

In Vigo people wore wooden shoes because it rained so much. When the Whittens' train pulled into the station, the September sun was shining on the little fishing boats in the bay. Nevertheless, they could not have chosen a worse day to visit the Hales. Judith, Dennis, Kristi, and Lisa were moving.

"If you don't mind," Dennis said when he met them, "we'll go by the old place and let you take your 'last chance' bath. We don't have any hot water yet at the new Mission apartment." After the bath, Charles as treasurer officially signed for purchase of the apartment. Then the two families roasted wieners beside the Tea River, where the Hales had held summer camps for youths.

Saturday afternoon Dennis asked, "Would you help in our outdoor service?"

"I can't believe you can do that!" Indy said. "We've never spoken in a street meeting since we've been in Spain!" But Dennis parked his car at the edge of the plaza in front of the church and turned on his gift from the Baptist Student Union at Auburn University in Alabama—a loudspeaker. He began playing music while his family and Indy and Charles and John and several young people from the church handed out tracts.

After Charles spoke, he handed the microphone to Indy. As she touched the cool metal, she tingled all over as if from electrical shock. "I can't believe I'm standing here in the middle of Vigo Plaza," she thought, "telling all these people what Christ can do for them! And policemen keep walking by not even saying a word!"

Late Sunday night the Whittens' train got into Madrid. The next day Charles left by plane for Denia to sign for property for a Mission house there.

Ten years before, they had helped First Baptist, Madrid, start Villaverde Church in a beauty shop. Now Villaverde wanted to start a mission at Getafe, 12 miles south of Madrid, and asked if they would help. "Does that make us grandparents of a mission?" Charles asked.

While a storefront building was being renovated in Getafe so they could begin services in January 1978, they walked up and down the muddy streets visiting people in the neighborhood. At the ringing of one doorbell, four-feet, nine-inch-tall Manuela answered. She was hot from cooking tortillas for her invalid husband. "Come in," she said. She smiled as she wiped perspiration from her brow with a corner of her apron.

Manuela was an evangelical, the daughter and granddaughter of strong Christians leaders. Since there was no church in Getafe for her to attend, she was looking forward to the opening of the mission. "My daughter and I will take turns caring for my husband," she said, "so we can go." She had lived through days of persecution and could hardly believe religious freedom was on the way.

But Manuela died a month before her dream of a church came true. She was buried at age 75 on December 8 in a black casket, wearing a black dress and a black mantilla. The top of the casket had a large brown crucifix on a black cross. Manuela's children said, "Mother wouldn't want people to think of her Christ as dead." So, with a hammer and chisel, her sons removed the crucifix.

Charles preached the message of the Living Christ at

a service in her house and at the cemetery. Many heard the biblical plan of salvation for the first time. A neighbor told Charles, "I am going to your church when you open. Manuela and her daughter have told me of their faith."

Manuela was buried as she had asked to be, in a civil cemetery in a small fenced-off area reserved in the past for "heretics." It was such a wet day that the fire brigade had to pump water from the open grave. Then as dirt was shoveled on the casket, one daughter began to sob. Her sister said, "Don't look down! Look up! She's there with God!" And later Indy wrote, "The life she lived left a strong, beautiful, living stone to help that little mission get started."

In January, the mission opened as scheduled. Later in the year, when Charles and Indy took their guests, Earl Kelly, executive director of the Mississippi Baptist Convention Board; and his son, Bryan, 12; and daughter, Kay, 11; to Getafe, only five others showed up. But because a situation looked small or ordinary did not say to them that it was hopeless or unimportant. With patience, they kept on. As Indy said, "Never quit until the hearse comes around."

"Lead, Kindly Light!" As Charles sang his favorite hymn, his face lighted with a glow of joy. "The night is dark, and I am far from home, Lead thou me on; Keep thou my feet; I do not ask to see the distant scene; one step enough for me."

During the service, one woman asked for prayer concerning a problem she had. Then Indy told the members that Kelly's wife, Amanda, had recently died and thus he was alone now in the responsibility of caring for his children. The meeting became a memorable time of loving fellowship and sharing.

One day with the Kellys, driving across a hot, dusty plain, Charles stuck his head out the car window and brayed like a donkey. (This sometimes happened at Mission parties after the emcee entreated, "Let us bray.") The Kelly children were enthralled. In fact, the night they left, their father asked, "What did you like best about Spain? The Roman aqueduct at Segovia? The cathedral at Toledo? The windmills of La Mancha?"

"No," they replied. "When Mr. Whitten brayed like a donkey."

Hospitality was a ministry, for guests were usually infected with the Whittens' contagious love for Spain and their enthusiasm for missions in general. In Jay Massey's case, the visit had a lasting influence. His mother, Beverly, was a receptionist at the Foreign Mission Board in Richmond. At 16, Jay liked to write to missionaries, royalty, and others of note. Indy always answered; their correspondence flourished; and even before she met him, she invited him to Spain. "*Mi casa es su casa* (my house is your house)," his hosts in Madrid assured him. And he fitted in like one of the family. A few years later, in 1986, still interested in missions, he went to China to work with the Foreign Mission Board's Cooperative Services International.

One morning in Apartment 3-C the phone rang. "Would you and Charles come with us on a picnic today?" Indy recognized Esther Borras's voice. "Maybe to Case del Campo Park."

Later in the park, Esther set up a folding table and spread a cloth on it. Like most Spaniards, she made all picnics grand occasions. She placed a flower vase in the center of the table and tucked a red flower in the vase. Then she set the table with bright-colored plates, plastic glasses, and cloth napkins.

"Where is the food?" Jose asked.

"The food!" she cried. "I thought you brought the food! It was on the table by the door!"

But they all ate from the Whittens' food basket. Afterward they found a shady spot where they could sit and talk.

Jose Borras was now president of the Spanish Baptist Seminary, he and Gerald McNeely having exchanged jobs. Gerald had taken over the administrator's functions; and Borras, the president's. Both still taught in the seminary; so did Charles, Indy, and Esther. June was still librarian.

Like a jewel in its green setting, the Baptist Center building in Alcobendas was surrounded by neatly trimmed cedar hedges. The brick building included small apartments for students on the third floor. Lower floors housed seminary classrooms and offices and also offices for the Spanish Baptist Union, the Baptist Mission to Spain, and the Correspondence Bible Course.

At the picnic, they talked of many things, one of them the need for missionaries on the Canary Islands. Since the Whittens had visited the Islands twice as a family and Charles several times on treasurer's business, they had often prayed for the Islands. Long before, they had prayed for missionaries to be sent to Spain and found themselves going in answer to their own prayers. Could this be the answer again? Was God calling them to go?

On October 2, 1978, Charles wrote to J. D. Hughey:

> This is not a sudden decision. As you know, from time to time we have talked to you and expressed a desire to give up the Mission treasurer's work, which became our responsibility first in July 1953. We feel the need to give more time to promotional work, which could include more preaching, direct evangelism, and new work emphases among the churches.
>
> We have had a special interest in the Canary Islands for many years, and since no Southern Baptist missionaries are there since the summer of 1978, we feel that now is the time to make a decision. . . . We want to give up this work as of next summer's Mission Meeting.

Eternally young in spirit, they shared an adventurous heart. This decision was typical of their openness to God's leading and to new ways of serving Him. Their request was granted, effective July 1, 1979.

Through the years, Charles had had the satisfaction of channeling over $2 million into the work of Spanish Baptists for their budget, besides money for the support of missionaries of the SBC, and more or less the same amount for capital needs to acquire properties for the churches and institutions of Spanish Baptists. He had had the joy of seeing the Spanish Baptist Cooperative

Program come into being, and of watching the churches' admirable growth toward self-support and support of the Spanish Baptist Union.

At Christmas, a visit from Margaret and Sam, Southern Seminary students; and their copper-haired toddler, William, brought extra rays of sunlight. But sadness followed on the heels of joy. Indy's brother, H. C., died March 14, 1979—the little brother who cried when she went away to Colombia in 1947.

On June 23 during Mission Meeting in Denia, the missionaries gave the Whittens a farewell party at the camp where every year many children had found Christ under Charles's preaching. They had searched through their home movies and made a show of the antics of the Whittens' children. June had baked a cake and decorated it with gold-wrapped coins and the words: *Leave the moneybags here, Charles!*

Waiting in the Madrid airport to leave for the Canaries, Indy wrote a message to print in "Together," a missionary newsletter she had originated and edited: "After 32 years as a missionary—26 in Spain—I still feel like a rank beginner in the Parachute Division ready for the first jump. What will we accomplish? Absolutely nothing. Some plant; others water. But God gives the increase."

24
Sent to the Canary Islands

"It's love that takes missionary diversities and brings them into one beautiful union of caring. . . . Thank God we are different. . . . For those who are one in the bonds of His love, who would call on cornbread to be apple pie?"—Indy Whitten

ON THE morning of July 1, Charles and Indy awakened in the Hotel Las Velas on the Caravaneras Beach at Las Palmas de Gran Canaria. Though 800 miles southwest of the Iberian Peninsula and 60 miles from the coast of Africa, they had not left their adopted country, for the Canaries formed two provinces of Spain. Yet the islanders spoke and acted more like South Americans.

An important commercial link between South America and Europe, the volcanic islands with their tropical beauty and springlike climate also drew many tourists.

Flowers from every climate blossomed side by side, from the columbine to the poinsettia. Bougainvillea cascaded over walls. In well-kept parks, roses and daisies, geraniums and hibiscus, amid the green of palms and cacti, filled the air with fragrance. In contrast, rugged, rocky cliffs, and mountains reared sharply up from the sea. The islands had been named for packs of dogs that once lived there (*canaria* came from the Latin word *canis* [dog]). Canary birds, first seen there, had been named for the islands.

Each of the seven main islands (Gran Canaria, Tenerife, La Palma, Lanzarote, Fuerteventura, Gomera, and Hierro) almost seemed like a different country. For the present, the Whittens decided to live on Gran Canaria, Tafira Alta, where the Spain Baptist Mission already owned a two-story, flat-roofed, white stucco house set in a patch of greenery against the side of a hill. Dan and

Frieda White had formerly lived there, but had moved to the mainland. Charles would begin preaching as pastor of the El Fondillo Mission of First Baptist Church, Las Palmas, Gran Canaria.

On Tenerife, German was frequently spoken as well as Spanish. Men liked to play soccer on the beaches, and farmers used camels in their work. In 1960, the Whittens had visited Tenerife. Charles had preached at the Santa Cruz de Tenerife Church where Jose Beltran was pastor. One Sunday, more than 200 members had made a trip with them in buses to the foot of the 12,000-foot, snow-topped volcano, El Teide. Charles had preached there in a pine grove, and four persons had accepted Christ. Santa Cruz, a church of missionary zeal, had helped to start missions on other islands. Now, 19 years later, Santa Cruz Church was sponsoring four pastorless congregations on the island of La Palma.

On September 23, 1979, Charles (one of only three Baptist pastors on all the seven islands) preached in three of the four missions on La Palma: Llanos de Ariadne, Santa Cruz de la Palma (the island's capital), and Punta Gorda. The other, Tijarafe, had a chapel under construction.

Punta Gorda had been founded 40 years before by Senora Gonzala Martin, who had died at age 86 and left her little white house as a meeting place.

The layman, Antonio Caceres, met their plane and drove Charles and Indy to the missions. They saw how far apart they were, and realized how badly more leaders were needed on La Palma.

At Christmas they were invited to local family feasts. Nevertheless, on Christmas morning Indy still felt a pang of longing to see her mother and father, her children, and her grandchildren. Long ago, she reminded herself, she had counted the cost and set her life's priorities. For whatever she had supposedly "given up," like separations at Christmas, she felt more than compensated. That was a part of God's marvelous peace.

On Christmas Day, Benedicta Aleman, director of two private schools, made a speech at Las Palmas Baptist

Church, Gran Canaria. Destined to change many lives, it was an appeal for aid for the people of Equatorial Guinea, formerly Spanish Guinea. As she spoke of hunger and poverty she had seen there, tears streamed down her cheeks: "The people have scarcely seen bread, and many have never drunk milk."

"In my schools," she added, "we are collecting food and clothes and medicine for them. And I am urging my students to put out an extra shoe on the Day of the Kings for gifts for the children of Guinea."

The church joined with her in the drive for help. The Las Palmas pastor, Eutimio Herreros, made plans to go to Guinea to take the supplies and a box of Bibles.

Soon afterward, Charles wrote to John Mills, the Foreign Mission Board's area director for West Africa:

Has the Foreign Mission Board had any thought about the possibility of beginning work in Equatorial Guinea? . . . Another approach . . . is for Spanish Baptists to start foreign mission work there. For years, several of us have had dreams of the time when the Spanish Baptist Union would send some of their own to a foreign country to do mission work.

Two days later, Indy wrote to Sally and Woodrow Lennon in Wilmington, North Carolina, their consistent prayer partners since Indy had met Sally in 1973 during a camp in North Carolina. They had prayed for each other's families and health and missions involvements. The Lennons had visited the Whittens in Spain four times to speak and to do volunteer jobs. The Lennons were praying for more missionaries in the Canaries. Now Indy added Benedicta Aleman and Equatorial Guinea: "Benedicta goes to our church often," she wrote, "though she is not listed as a member, and it is hard to tell if she has really had a personal experience. She says she is more Baptist than Catholic."

After she had described Benedicta's dramatic appeal for Equatorial Guinea, she added, "Now the bug has bitten us! . . . Who knows? We might even end up in Equatorial Guinea. . . . Pray about this, Sally."

In March, Charles received word that his father had

died the 24th, at age 87, as the result of a car wreck in Weir and a subsequent heart attack. Charles returned home and led in the funeral service during which he played a tape of his father's testimony of faith. "Every Monday morning since I left for college, he had written me a letter," Charles told those present. "I will miss those letters and the petitions of my best prayer supporter."

The Foreign Mission Board (FMB) had begun negotiations to consider whether Spanish or Southern Baptists would establish missions work in Guinea. At the request of John Mills, Charles was to meet Mills and Bill Bullington, FMB area representative, for a survey trip to Malabo.

Charles was to take Air Afrique out of Lagos, Nigeria, on April 21 to Douala, Cameroon, but the plane was late, and he waited 9½ hours at the Lagos airport. John and Bill met him in Douala, where they got to bed at 2:45 A.M. At the Akwa Palace Hotel, John's reservations had not materialized, so the three shared one room.

Following lunch the next day in the gardens of the hotel, they lay down for a nap. Charles woke up with severe stomach cramps, the beginning of many trips to the bathroom. John gave him some pills, the same as missionary John McNair had once given him. Though Charles had already taken cholera, yellow fever, and smallpox shots, John insisted he take pills to prevent malaria. He'd spotted some suspicious mosquitoes.

On April 23 they flew in a small charter plane to Malabo, Equatorial Guinea. There they were to sleep in a Spanish ship in the harbor. In Malabo, they visited the Alcaide family, Spaniards whose children were in school in Las Palmas.

Since Senora Pilar Alcaide related well to the African people and was a good friend of the president of Equatorial Guinea, she introduced the three to some of the government officials with whom they discussed prevailing conditions.

Also she took them to a market, which had vegetables

but no meat; and to a hospital that had few medicines, little equipment, and a considerable lack of basic hygienic conditions. Recently many children had died from measles. Other frequent causes of death, they were told, were malnutrition, dysentery, and smallpox. Charles had two cameras with him; yet he could not bring himself to take pictures.

Outside later he said to Bill, "I somehow felt it would be a violation of human dignity."

"Yes, I felt the same," agreed Bill.

The next morning when they left at 5:15, it was pouring rain. Besides that, they found no food at the airport.

Bill flew on to Accra, Ghana, where he lived, and John got off the plane in Monrovia, concerned about the missionaries in Liberia because of executions there earlier in the week. Charles got into Dakar, Senegal, at 2:30 in the morning but sat in an airport chair until dawn. Then Frank and Sally Cawthon, missionaries, picked him up, fed him, drove him to bush country on a picture-taking excursion, and took him shopping. He bought Indy a "green African long dress" which he thought very pretty. That night at 9:30 he arrived in Las Palmas exhausted. The only Africa he had known previously had been Morocco. Needs of Equatorial Guinea—physical and spiritual—were so great that he had left with a heavy heart.

Shortly before this trip, on April 3, he had heard the news of the death of his good friend and fellow missionary, Tom Law, of cancer. It had been Tom who succeeded him as treasurer in Spain.

After Tom's death, the treasurer's job went to Bob Crider. Bob and his wife, Barbara, had arrived in Spain in 1970 and had, like other new missionaries, found loving care at the hands of the Whittens. In fact, Bob had first begun to think of missions work in Spain after hearing Charles speak once while he was on furlough.

Barbara took over the bookkeeping when her husband was named treasurer, and learned how by studying Charles's carefully written instructions.

The phone rang in Tafira Alta. "Charles, this is Barbara calling from Denia. I have another problem with the books." Patiently, and repeatedly, he explained to her step-by-step what she should do.

"Thanks! I don't think any of us appreciated you enough until after you left!" She meant that. He'd kept an immaculate set of books, always up-to-date. How could he have done it with eyesight so poor he could hardly see to insert a screw in a bookshelf? Especially now that she had to keep the books straight, Barbara truly admired his perfect accounting in spite of his poor vision.

In late June the Whittens flew to Denia for Mission Meeting at the Baptist camp. During the week, the pathway curving upward through trees and flowers to a hillside prayer garden was named Camino Tom Law. An artistic tile with the name was unveiled.

Saturday afternoon Karen and Reggie Quimby, new missionaries, were leaving Denia to go to their home in Jativa. "We'll drop you off in Valencia," Reggie said to Charles.

"Come go to the bathroom once more before we leave," Karen and Reggie both called to their three boys, who were across the road in front of the main building. Reggie got into the car. Karen and Indy remained standing on the steps, looking out across Denia toward the sea. Jason, seven; and Matthew, one of the four-year-old twins, crossed the road. As Michael, the other twin, approached the road, the woman who delivered bread to the dining hall came driving down the road. "Wait!" Karen called to Michael.

But Michael held his hand up toward the little car as a signal for it to stop. Then he walked out in front of it. The car knocked him down and he fell under it; the back wheel rolled over his right shoulder and his head while Indy stood watching as if in a bad dream.

"He's dead!" Karen thought. But Michael sat up screaming, blood pouring down his face. Reggie was too shaken to drive, but Charles was collected enough to put Michael into the bread woman's car, along with the Quimby family. Charles drove as fast as he dared,

181

waving a white handkerchief out the window as they went.

The national youth director for the WMU called all those still at the camp together to pray; Indy joined with them.

The doctor said the boy had no broken bones. He took a stitch or two under his eye and on his head where gravel had cut his face. As Indy wrote later in an article, "It was a miracle for Michael."

Indy continued to be an encourager to Karen through letters. "You are a good writer," she assured her. "I know you could do a good job of editing 'Together' (the newsletter Indy had started)." Karen knew she did like to write and accepted the challenge. Later Indy nominated her as secretary of the Mission.

"I can't do that," Karen said at first. But at Indy's insistence, she saw that she could.

On July 20, 1980, the Whittens moved to Pine Trails Apartments in Clinton, Mississippi, for furlough. That month Charles Bryan at the Foreign Mission Board asked J. D. Hughey to name two missionaries in his area who could serve as role models for missionaries in maintaining a simpler life-style. He chose the Whittens and Julia and Finlay Graham of Nicosia, Cyprus.

On October 24, John Mills wrote, asking, "Would you consider becoming missionaries to Equatorial Guinea?" They had only been in the Canaries a little over a year, and they would want to see more missionaries arrive there before they left.

Hence Charles answered, "We have not lost interest in Equatorial Guinea. But our answer for now is no."

That Christmas, John, a freshman at Mississippi College, spent the holidays with relatives in Weir and Louisville. Though short on cash, he bought gifts for every single family member. Later he said, "I think a person who has never spent *all he has* for those he loves is very unfortunate."

25
Exclamation point on the Atlantic

> *"As I look at the map of the island of La Palma, the very shape of the island looks like an exclamation point of urgent need."*—Indy Whitten

SUNLIGHT danced in diamonds across the blue Atlantic as the small plane from Gran Canaria circled for a landing at Santa Cruz de la Palma. Early morning of that March Sunday in 1981 promised a beautiful day. "Yes, there's Jose," said Charles. Senor Garcia was there to meet them and drive them across the mountains to Tijarafe.

Sunday School was to begin at 11:00, but the three arrived an hour early. As Indy stood in front of the new church looking down at the indigo sea beyond a banana plantation, she noticed an old woman with a cane sitting on a rock wall beside the road. Immediately she walked down the hill to greet her. The woman brushed off a place on the wall for her to sit.

"Do you sing?" Indy asked.

"No," she said, "I used to, but now my voice comes out like a crow."

"In the chapel up there on the hill, we sing, and you can if you want to come to our service."

Soon two other women joined them, the first wearing a large green straw hat, and the other a younger woman, the mother of five children. They all asked questions about the United States, and Indy told them about Mississippi and how they used to kill hogs there when she was a child.

"This is the best time we've had in years," they told her. "Nobody has time to talk anymore."

Indy got up to say good-bye, but the first two got up also and followed her to church. Inside they accepted hymnbooks, which Indy opened to the right number.

Both tried to sing, not knowing the tune. They continued to sing the stanza while the congregation sang the chorus. Indy began pointing to each line they were to sing. (That improved the sound!) The 83-year-old was exultant. She had sung again! Both said they liked the service.

At the steps, the woman in the green hat called Indy to one side. From a little cloth bag, she withdrew a brown 100-peseta bill (worth about $1.17) and handed it to her, saying, "I love you. I want to give you a gift."

In July while they took a cruise around the islands, Indy answered a couple of letters.

Dear Louise:

For four days we have been on a little cruise around the islands. John is here and is enjoying getting to see this part of Spain. He will be here until August. Right now we are on the ship.

On one of the islands (Lanzarote), we went on a camel ride up the side of the mountain. I first thought we had gotten a crippled camel but was told this was their normal way of walking. We also went to the site of the last volcano to erupt in the Canaries (in 1971). The lava ran down to the ocean and cooled and added a kilometer to the edge of the island.

Dear Sally:

Laura and Fred Dallas are to come here after they finish language study in Madrid. They are named for the island of La Palma, which has a crisis need. . . . We have decided to work on that island for a year until the Dallases are better prepared to work there. We will rent a furnished apartment, so we won't have the huge expense to ship our furniture over, and the Dallases will live in the house where we have been living in Tafira Alta.

Benedicta Aleman, the one you are praying for, offered us their old home place to fix up for camps. . . .

Our national WMU convention is to be held August 24 and 25 at Denia, and I am to speak the second day. The two main speeches are "Love God with All Your Heart" by one of my former seminary students, and my part is to be "Love Thy Neighbor as Thyself." God bless you and thank you for your prayer support.

One Sunday morning Charles and Indy invited two young men to go with them to the service at Tijarafe. The drive across the arrow-shaped island from Santa Cruz de la Palma was 51 kilometers in distance but seemed twice as far because of steep mountains and narrow, twisting roads. Reckless drivers of jeeps, sailing around the curves, added to already dangerous heights. Clouds, as Indy described them, "oozed over the mountaintops" and ran down "like frosting along the edges."

One of the young men with them was Pedro Perez, an ex-friar who had come to the church in Santa Cruz de la Palma looking for spiritual help. His experiences in several monasteries in Spain had been discouraging, and he had spent a time in Venezuela trying to recover from his dissatisfaction with the Catholic church.

The other young man, Jose Maria Ramon, who lived in Mazo near Santa Cruz de la Palma, had taken a Bible correspondence course. In his last year of high school, he needed to find purpose and direction for his life.

The Whittens wanted to be of help to the two. It would be hard to talk and drive on those roads, and so—they felt by divine inspiration—they thought of playing a tape by Jose Borras, the former priest, telling of his conversion experience, "From Monastery to Ministry." As soon as they started out, they turned on the tape.

The trip led through a tunnel and around a high mountain to another tunnel. From there the road leveled off for a little way and then began a descent into a deep volcanic crater, to the bottom, and then snaked upward out of the crater on the other side. Hardly a word was said all the way. Just as the car drove up in front of the Tijarafe Church, the tape came to an end. Both young men said simply, "Thank you for the tape."

A few days later in the Santa Cruz de la Palma Baptist Church, both made professions of faith. Pedro's family persecuted him so severely that he had to leave the island. He was baptized and married on Tenerife, then moved to Venezuela.

When Jose Maria Ramon saw what following Christ had cost Pedro, he became uneasy and stopped going to church.

During Mission Meeting near Madrid, Indy got a long-distance call at 2:30 A.M. Her father was near death. The rest of the night she prayed for a solution to her need to go to Mississippi and the need for her to be on the Canary Islands. Twelve-day evangelistic campaigns were planned, for which she was to be the chauffeur, and Charles the translator. The evangelist was to arrive in two days.

Charles bought her ticket to the States; then a call came that her father had improved. They went through the campaigns, and the day the evangelist left another phone call came. Indy flew from island to island to Madrid to New York, where she called Louisville. The relative who answered said, "Grandpa left us last night." Her parents had celebrated their 60th wedding anniversary on October 2. Indy stayed in the States 30 days after her father's death on December 12. She was glad to have the time with her mother, who showed great strength. Now her mother would be moving into a "little house" beside her brother Bruce's house.

When John drove Indy to the Jackson airport January 12, sleet was falling, and the roads were iced. Mississippi had turned into one of the coldest spots in the nation. She returned to the Canaries worn out emotionally, but she wrote to her Mission family in Spain: "Hearts that experience sorrow seem to be more capable of loving God and loving each other."

From March to July 1982, the last phase of the Five Year Mission Plan took place in La Palma. This plan had first been mapped out on January 7, 1978, by representatives of the Spanish Baptist Union meeting in Madrid, with Maximo Garcia presiding. As planned, teams of evangelists had worked in different areas of Spain several months at the time for five years strengthening existing work and beginning new churches.

The first team had begun work in the fall of 1978 in Vigo. Its members had been Joe Mefford, musician, artist, preacher, and missionary and his wife, Lila; and Fernando and Anita Vergara, Spanish Baptist pastor and wife.

Now the last team would also include Fernando Vergara, plus the Whittens, to work at Santa Cruz de la Palma; and Antonio and Deolinda Galvao, missionaries to Spain from Brazil, and Fred and Laura Dallas to work in the Tijarafe area.

As in previous campaigns, activities went on constantly inside and outside the church, publicized by loudspeaker. On March 1 all four congregations on La Palma met together in Tijarafe. A *guagua* (rented bus) transported those from Santa Cruz de la Palma. The people took their lunches and ate on a new table-tennis table.

At the beginning of the campaign there were only 20 baptized believers in all of La Palma. At Tijarafe films on the life of Christ drew large crowds. A book table on the street in Santa Cruz de la Palma attracted attention. Fernando Vergara preached on radio.

To help out in the Five Year Mission Plan, six students from Southwestern Baptist Theological Seminary spent ten weeks on La Palma.

The first Vacation Bible School the students taught was boycotted when state church leaders reacted against it. Children stood across the street from the church and said, "We want to come, but we have been told not to." The students moved the Bible school to the public park; the children went and had a great time. Later in the week they dared to come to church.

During this Bible school, a man named Antonio Vega came and asked for the "little book" spoken about on the radio programs. Students gave him a New Testament and visited his home.

They explained the plan of salvation over and over. Finally the Vegases understood. Antonio made a profession of faith and then his daughter, Maria Milagrosa, 18.

In five months, 36 made professions of faith and 9 were baptized in baptismal services. Personal contact with individuals and visits in their homes had brought the most results.

During and after the campaign, Indy continued her

ministry of love to individuals, be it giving medicine or giving advice. There was Maria Rodriguez, 60, a Christian who agonized that her husband, 4 children, and 15 grandchildren did not know the Lord. Indy prayed with her about this. And she tried to help by giving her medicine for a fungus infection on her feet. Also she invited Lydia, the youngest daughter, to a youth party at her house where she knew she would hear about the love of Christ.

And then there was Arelida of Punta Gorda, confused by Jehovah's Witnesses. She asked Indy questions about the Witnesses' beliefs. "When people say Christ is less than God, it's time to draw the line," Indy told her.

The next time Jehovah's Witnesses came, Arelida said, "You are welcome to come into my house, but I want you to leave the devil outside."

"No doubt you have been talking to your Baptist preacher!" one of them replied. And they left. On August 13, Indy wrote to Louise:

Now that the team is gone, I feel suddenly tired. But I am not sick. Just a few days of not having so much responsibility will do me good.

The sea today is so calm. The ocean looks like blue glass. I have been trying to clean the little office and throw some papers away. If you don't clean your mind out, the papers will be like Daddy used to say about the Johnson grass—it will take your place.

26
Prayer: love's magic carpet

"Through prayer you take love's magic carpet to everywhere. Through prayer you stand beside the missionaries and help them all day long."—Indy Whitten

INDY glanced at her watch. It was 2:17 A.M. She stood looking at the gigantic slab of rock that formed Montgo. Darkness blurred its outlines, but high up on a winding road, car lights and searchlights shone in eerie patterns. John was up there somewhere, lost on the mountain, maybe unconscious. She thought she heard the men calling his name on the loudspeaker.

She and Charles were at Denia for the 1982 summer Mission Meeting. John, 21, would enter Complutense University in Madrid soon for his senior year at college. The day before, around noon, he and another missionaries' kid (MK), David Simmons, had decided to climb Montgo. In late afternoon, David had returned to camp looking for John. They had become separated on the mountain when John had left his shirt at the top and gone back to get it. But no one had seen John. Darkness fell. Still no John.

Bob Crider, president of the Mission, lived at Denia and knew the mountain trails, so he left after night worship service and took a group up the mountain to begin the search.

After an hour or so they returned. Antonio Calero, Denia Baptist pastor, called the city police and the national Civil Guard. The guard arranged to meet Bob and his search party on the flanks of the mountain at the little chapel dedicated to Papa Pere, Denia's patron saint. Then at the place where the trail began, they divided into three groups, one to search the north trail, one to search the flanks, and one to go with Bob up the face of the mountain.

After the night service, Barbara Crider drove a group of missionaries to the base of the trail. They carried extra water and as many flashlights as they could find. Later she took blankets too. These didn't reach the ones on the mountaintop but helped those on the lower slopes. Missionaries' kids and volunteer workers at the camp joined the searchers.

Isam Ballenger, Foreign Mission Board director for Europe and the Middle East, was in Denia for the meeting. He and Charles drove up to the trail base about midnight. Reports kept filtering down to them as they waited there, talking and praying together. No doubt, Charles was intensely worried, but he remained calm and spoke with assurance: "The Lord will provide, whatever the outcome."

Back at camp, anxiety spread. Prayer groups formed. Indy and her Mission Meeting prayermate, Phyllis Baker, sat on two rocks and asked God to be by John's side. Her friend, Noemi Bonet, stayed nearby most of the night. Nobody slept except the youngest children.

Up on the mountain in an area of pine forest, the trail kept splitting, but Bob felt as if someone were pointing the way. It seemed clear to him which way to go. The narrow trail was treacherous even by day, with great precipices. John or anyone could have fallen.

On the jagged, hard-to-walk-on top, the five with Bob searched and called to no avail. They met the Civil Guards who had come up another trail, built a fire at the edge of the mountain, and sat around it to wait until dawn. The guard radioed down the mountain with word that search dogs from Alicante would be sent out at daylight.

At 4:00 A.M., Charles and others on the flanks went back to camp. Charles and Indy lay down to rest and try to sleep. They exchanged one phrase, "It looks bad."

Indy's thoughts turned to Jesus' words, "If you can believe, you will see the glory of God." Yet she knew God could be glorified by life or death. Suddenly the alarm clock went off. They got up, and Charles picked up the suitcase with John's clothes for the dogs to sniff.

Packing those had been the hardest part of Indy's night.

Running footsteps sounded in the hall. Dalia Gonzalez burst into the room, "Indy, they have found John! He's all right!"

"Thank God!" she said, never with more emotion.

Up on the mountain, Bob had sensed a sound, taken a light, and walked toward the sound. He saw a dark figure, standing as if dazed, and then the figure struck a match. "John, is that you?"

"I'm John," came the answer. "Who are you?"

Wearing no shirt, John was cold and hungry and thirsty. He did not remember what had happened except that he had taken a wrong trail after he left David. Perhaps he had suffered a sunstroke. He was in shock. They were glad that the lost was found; the guard radioed the message to Denia.

The rescuers had saved a little water for John but had no food. The Lord provided that. Just before sunup, two German hikers crested the mountain, their backpacks stuffed with goodies. They fed John orange juice and yogurt.

Senor Pedro Bonet, president of the Spanish Baptist Union, and Barbara Crider drove Charles and Indy up to the foot of the mountain to wait for John and his rescuers.

"Hi, Mother!" John said.

"Hi, John!" she answered. Compared with the blaze of joy in her heart, the sun rising over the Mediterranean looked to her like an anemic yellow marble.

On a cold day the following November, Indy walked up to the door of the Baptist seminary in Alcobendas on her way to see Jose and Esther Borras and ask permission to write their life story.

When they hesitated, she insisted, "All need to be mutually inspired by what God is doing around the world through His chosen instruments. It seems to me that in a special way you are chosen instruments of God. . . . Like Joseph of the Old Testament, you, Jose, lived through times of being left in the pits of discouragement, of being estranged from your family, and of suffering tremendous persecution. But God drew you out and placed you in the framework of the second half of the twentieth century to proclaim His message of salvation. . . . God can certainly use you as an object lesson of His power and grace. Would you be willing?"

"In that light, we could not refuse."

And so she began writing a book about them.

Only the month before, the Spanish Baptist Junta had sent Jorge Pastor, pastor and director of the camp at Denia, to Malabo in Equatorial Guinea to survey the situation in regard to Spanish Baptists sending a missionary there.

Though Jorge got sick and had to return to Spain shortly after Christmas, he had learned a great deal in that length of time. Charles and Indy visited him to hear his story:

I found the social conditions terrible, the poverty profound. When my plane stopped, people were running along the runway at the airport, begging for gifts. When I got off the plane, they asked, "Did you bring any food? What is in your suitcase?"

In Spain I was freezing. There at the equator I was hot! Mosquitoes covered me so thick I had to take my hand and rake them off.

I saw children carrying rats with big ears and learned their diet consists of rats and rotten fish or anything they can find. People look to see if the rats have big ears. The bigger the ears, the better they are, they say.

Jess and Peggy Thompson, Southern Baptist agricultural missionaries who had been in Equatorial Guinea for a year, met him in a Mission jeep and drove him around.

He visited in the home of a man named Gregorio, who had four wives and 17 children, all living in one small room.

"What to do with such a man when he is converted?" asked Jorge.

"Accept him. No other choice. But if a man is still single, teach him to marry only one wife," came the reply.

In Malabo, he learned the men stayed at home while the women went out into the bush to find food. "The first wife, the chief wife, sends the others out to look for food. If the man had only one wife, he would have to work himself. That would not be socially acceptable."

Gregorio asked Jorge many questions and came to hear Jorge preach at a Mission chapel. "His children sat outside to listen to the sermon," Jorge remembered, "but the wives stayed home. Gregorio came forward, knelt, and said he had accepted Jesus. He kissed my hands to show his gratitude for my coming to tell him the way."

Jorge had visited in a hospital in Malabo too. "Two hundred of 1,000 babies die in Equatorial Guinea, compared to 12 out of 1,000 in more civilized countries."

As he spoke to the Whittens, Jorge did not know they were considering going to Guinea or how much his words were influencing them.

Meanwhile, in Southern Baptists' Bold Mission Thrust, Oklahoma and Spain had become partners. In April 1983, when 203 Oklahomans traveled to 61 Baptist churches across Spain, one team arrived on Gran Canaria. Eight days later, Indy wrote to Sally and Woodrow Lennon:

We have been having the Spain/Oklahoma Partnership Evangelism Week, and we took eight team members to the airport this morning. . . .

I translated for one group, and Charles for the other. In El Fondillo we had 8 professions of faith and in Las Palmas 15.

Now the news I want to tell you is that Benedicta made a public profession of her faith. She was the last one to come last night, and how we rejoiced!

By May 1983, Joe and Chari Vasquez joined the Canaries' missionary staff. Thus, the Whittens felt more free to turn toward Africa to help Jess and Peggy Thompson start new work. Charles's May 13 letter to Mills dropped a bombshell:

We are now ready to request a transfer to go to Equatorial Guinea to do general evangelistic work, if you still need us there. . . . Really we have never been able to dismiss from our hearts and our prayers our personal involvement in the needs there. We are ready to go whenever you think best.

They had prayed for missionaries to Spain and gone themselves; they had prayed for missionaries to the Canaries and gone themselves; they had prayed for missionaries to Equatorial Guinea. Now they were going themselves. "It is dangerous to pray if you are not ready to accept the answer," Charles said.

In Georgia, Peggy Bass was praying that missionaries would be sent to Equatorial Guinea. She didn't even know the Whittens then. In North Carolina, the Lennons were praying for missionaries for Equatorial Guinea. They had no idea that God would answer by sending the Whittens. "But He knew," said Sally. "There was a need for missionaries who enjoyed starting new work. So who could do a better job than these two?"

Then during the Spanish Baptist Convention, held at Vitoria in Basque country (the first time to be held north of Madrid), August 24-26, they announced their intentions to transfer, effective January 1, 1984. Spanish Baptists presented them a plaque of appreciation for their 30 years' service.

As Pedro Bonet was leaving the presidency of the Union to become director of the Baptist Book Store in Barcelona, the Union elected Jose Borras president. Jorge Pastor gave a report of his survey of Equatorial Guinea; and Spanish Baptists, who had agreed to be partners with Southern Baptists in this venture, pledged to pray for God to call the Spanish couple who should go there.

Most of the Spain missionaries tried to talk the Whittens out of going. "At your age?" they asked, and expressed fears for their health in the tropics. They were 60 and would retire after one more term. Yet the others respected their sense of God's call and recognized their pioneer spirit and anticipation of plowing new ground.

Sometimes Indy was a little too enthusiastic, wanting to go ahead zealously, sometimes rushing ahead too soon. Yet, if she hadn't been that way, many things she did might not have been done at all. Some said both Charles and Indy were overly optimistic, that the positive approach, though good in itself, could fuzz reality if only the positive side were given and areas of potential trouble ignored.

But their co-laborers overwhelmingly agreed that they did not seek for themselves a fine house or material goods but that they loved God and they loved people far more than themselves. Their record showed that they had taken seriously, "If any among you would be great, let him be the servant of all."

IV
Africa

1984-1987

27
Sent to Equatorial Guinea

"It doesn't take a missionary long to realize that the tie with the field is not duty, but love."—Indy Whitten

THE FIRE alarm sounded. Indy and Charles on the 15th floor of the Americana Hotel woke from their siesta. "What's that?" Indy asked.

"Must be a tornado," Charles answered and switched on the television. A storm watch had been announced in Kansas City, Missouri, in early afternoon. He dialed the switchboard operator, who said, "It's a fire. Leave your room!"

Indy hobbled to the door and peeped out; smoke gushed into the room. As swiftly as she could with her right leg in an ankle cast, she grabbed her cane and broke a window. Then, holding wet towels over their faces, the two crawled along the hall.

"Where are the stairs?" they called. "Where is the exit?"

"Here. Hurry. This way." They heard voices but could see no one. Smoke boiled around them, acrid and dense. Indy inched along, dragging the cast. Finally they got to the end of the hall; the exit was at the other end! They crept back to their room and called the operator again. "Leave your room!" she repeated. They crawled in the opposite direction.

Elevators are forbidden territory during a fire, but after they finally got down one flight of stairs, firemen let them ride the rest of the way down. Indy had broken her foot while visiting Helen in Honduras.

Bartle Convention Center was only a block from the Americana, and the Southern Baptist Convention was in progress there, June 16, 1984. People who knew the Whittens gathered around them on the sidewalk. "What you won't do to get in the news!" someone said.

Since January, the Whittens had been living in the missionary house of First Baptist Church, Starkville, Mississippi. On their way there in December, they had stopped in Madrid for Charles to perform the wedding of John to Ana Mateo, a lovely dark-haired Spanish girl.

From the time they entered Spain in 1953 until the time they left in 1983, the number of Southern Baptist missionaries had increased from 2 to 44 career missionaries, 2 associate missionaries, and 7 journeymen.

In Kansas City, Indy was on program at the Southern Baptist Convention (she was heard on ACTS television across the nation) and during the WMU Annual Meeting. To the women she said, in part:

"Lord, speak through me, but first speak to me that You may be able to speak through me," my prayer has been through the years. . . .

Who can tell how God may speak through us? He can speak through an everyday life-style. It may not seem so impressive to us, but to most of the people of the world it's a powerful testimony. He can speak through a smile. He can speak through tears as we stand by the side of a person, when we may not be able to do anything but to care and to pray. He can speak through a Valentine party in the front yard of a missionary to young people who know the name of Jesus but don't know Jesus at all. He may speak in the Valley of the Shadow. He may speak in the sunshine, but He always wishes to speak.

For 37 years she and Charles on four continents had spoken for Him in an infinite variety of places and ways. Many times they felt unqualified to do certain jobs; yet because there was no one else to do them, they had tried, and the Lord had helped them. For their last term of missionary service, they were still seeing new visions, not just looking for a place "to coast out to the end." New missionaries had arrived in the Canaries, and the Whittens were moving on. In Equatorial Guinea they expected to find the rural-type situation they had first thought they might work with in Argentina. Now Charles would have more time to major in evangelism as he had always dreamed of doing.

Back in Mississippi they finished packing. Indy's book *Jose Borras: From Monastery to Ministry in Bold Commitment* had just come off the press.

From New York to Madrid took seven hours, and after seven more hours across Africa's hump, the plane set them down in Equatorial Guinea on June 30. In their map study, they had spotted two other Guineas to the north, Guinea-Bissau and Guinea. "Their" Guinea on the equator, the size of Maryland, was divided between five islands and a continental part, Rio Muni, where Bata is capital. They were headed for Malabo, capital of the main island, Bioko.

Jess and Peggy, in the country since 1981, met them in a jeep, *Mision Bautista* printed on its side. "You see the outline of land across the bay?" asked Jess. "That's the coast of Nigeria. And across there you see the Cameroons."

"It's hot all year," Peggy said, "but this rainy season is more pleasant than the dry."

"I've been hotter than this in Mississippi!" declared Charles.

On Bioko, the Thompsons had directed a campaign to vaccinate children against measles. Before their marriage, he had been a missionary in Ghana, and she in Liberia. As agricultural missionaries, they shared garden seeds and gardening and farming advice. Also they had begun two small mission points. The Whittens planned to work on beginning the church in Malabo, and the Thompsons the one in Bakake Grande, a village 21 miles away.

On their first Sunday in Malabo, the Whittens visited both preaching points. The one in Malabo was meeting in a little rented building.

Not yet fluent in Spanish, the Thompsons were slightly awed at the ease with which Charles and Indy handled the language. Surely, they thought, their superior knowledge of Spanish and Spanish ways would be an asset in obtaining various permits and in dealing with government officials as well as in getting to know the people better.

201

For centuries, until 1968, Equatorial Guinea had been Spanish Guinea. As a result, the official language was Spanish, and Spain's influence was still felt in many ways. The tribal languages, Fang, Bubi, and Combe, were also spoken. One tribe permitted plural wives, while others did not. In 1968, Equatorial Guinea had become independent from Spain, and the dictator, Francisco Macias Nguema, had ruled with an iron hand for 11 years, until 1979, when Teodore Obiang Nguema Mbasogo took the presidency and began working toward democracy. Living conditions appeared to be slightly better than they had been at the time of Macias's downfall.

On the way to Bakake Grande, the jeep pushed back the green limbs overhanging the paved but bumpy road. As they proceeded, the jungle opened before them and closed behind them. Thick along the roadsides grew coconut palms, date palms, fan palms, mango trees, banana trees, cocoa bushes, and ceiba trees. The ceiba tree centered the country's flag above the words, *Unidad, Paz, Justicia* (Unity, Peace, Justice). For the afternoon service, adults and children crowded into a home. "Hello, *Mision Bautista*," some of them called as the jeep drove up.

For the group, hymn singing was still new. One woman picked up a hymnal and said, "Oh, I want to sing ALL of these!" When the rain began, Indy thought it looked like a solid sheet of silver. And it hit the tin roof with such a noise they had to scream to be heard above it.

After the service the hostess served a snack of *name* (white yams), antelope meat in white sauce, and a French omelet in palm oil. Indy had seen people leading small antelopes, not much bigger than dogs, to market and thought they were "sweet-looking." She hadn't thought she'd like to eat one. But this was good. Both she and Charles asked for second helpings. Afterward, the people gave them a stalk of bananas, a papaya, and a white yam to take home with them.

For the next two days, Indy scratched and scratched her legs. Those little bugs, the hen-hens, had not sung or buzzed, but they bit!

In August they moved into the Thompsons' house while the Thompsons vacationed in Kenya. From the back door they could see a 10,000-foot mountain when the clouds lifted. It was like a backdrop for the house. There had been no electricity in Malabo for three months, but the Thompsons had their own generator. As usual, the Whittens took all the moves in stride—American Embassy apartment, a hotel, this house. Soon they'd move into a one-bedroom apartment on the fourth floor of the Impala Hotel to wait until their house was built next door to the Thompsons.

Their furniture arrived from the Canary Islands on August 3, a national holiday, so no one would work to unload it from the ship. The next day, Sunday, rain fell in torrents all day. Monday the two big crates were set out in the open on the dock. The Whittens arranged for a truck for Tuesday, hired a watchman, and prayed that it wouldn't rain that night.

When the truck arrived, it was too small, but port authorities loaned a big flatbed truck. By noon the crates were safe in the Thompsons' house. Suddenly Charles and Indy realized no rain had fallen for 48 hours, almost unheard of in rainy season.

Because of the food shortage at the tin-covered marketplace, they would have to fly to Douala in the Cameroons at least once a quarter to grocery shop. "That's the last one," said Charles as he stacked the sixth pasteboard box on the kitchen floor. They were back from their first grocery trip. Indy was busy pouring the water, carefully filtered, into plastic bottles. She had found a Spanish woman in Malabo who baked bread, and she planned to buy some that day. It was time, too, for their weekly dose of malaria suppressant.

One day they were sitting in the jeep in front of the post office. A lot of people, they noticed, displayed charms on their foreheads or on their babies' wrists. Superstition and animism tended to be mixed with religion here, though the Roman Catholic church was the traditional church, a legacy from Spain.

A young man left the post office carrying papers that Indy thought looked like the Bible Way Correspondence course. Since no newspapers were printed in the country, people showed great interest in anything given them to read.

When the fellow walked by, Indy said, "I believe you are taking a correspondence course."

Surprised, he said, "Yes, this is CEBICO."

"We promote the course." When he heard that, he grabbed their hands and shook them vigorously. His name, he said, was Hermenegildo. In response to their invitation: "Yes, I'll be at church Sunday!"

In her English class, Indy soon enrolled 20, aged 18 to 25, young professionals who wanted to learn English to help them get better jobs. At the end of each class, Charles would read for ten minutes in English from the *Good News Bible*. This class turned out to be one of the most satisfying things they'd ever done.

Sunday, September 2, brought more rain, and when Charles and Indy arrived for Sunday School, only Carmen Ondo was standing in the street waiting for the Malabo chapel to open. Indy started teaching just her, but then Herminia and Epifanio, two of her English students, arrived. Epifanio had asked for a Bible and was reading the book of John. At first he had wanted to learn English; now he wanted to learn more about Jesus.

That day Charles preached on the love of God. He told the story of the prodigal son and explained that God in His love always waits for the prodigal to return home. In the middle of the sermon, Carmen, mother of seven, stood and said, "I want to say here before you all that I take Jesus as my Saviour."

Then Funmi, a Nigerian Baptist whose husband was in the diplomatic service, gave her testimony. She had prayed to marry a Baptist, a real Christian man. The Lord had answered her prayers. When they were sent to Hong Kong, she was afraid to go so far from home, but her parents had said, "Don't be afraid. God will take care of you!" In Hong Kong, God had given them a wonderful Christian family in a Baptist church. When they were coming to Equatorial Guinea, she was afraid they would find no Christian church family. But here the Lord had provided this place of worship.

Funmi began to sing and clap her hands. The service did not end on time, and the Whittens did not go early to Bakake Grande as usual, but on the way home in the jeep, they remarked to each other, "The Spirit of the Lord was there!"

28
A church grows in Malabo

"Never before have we felt such a need for intercessory prayer to cut through the 'jungles' of superstition, fear, and meaningless tradition and reach the hearts of people."—Charles Whitten

We believe bold praying always precedes and empowers bold witnessing of the good news of Jesus Christ."—Indy Whitten

THE THREE sat around the Ondos' dining table—Charles, Indy, and Carmen, 38, who was to be baptized soon. Carmen's seven children stood around them; the 7-year-old girl eased closer to Indy and lovingly began stroking her arm. This answered Indy's unspoken question: "We've always worked with Latins; how will we do with Africans?"

A few days later on the morning of November 18, the Whittens in the jeep pulled up in front of the Ondo house at Ela Nguema on the edge of Malabo to pick up Carmen and her children. As they were leaving to go to the baptismal service, Carmen's husband, Cayetano, stopped them and said to the two older boys, "Get out! You must help me work here at home." The boys obeyed with sad faces.

"Won't you go with us?" Charles asked. But Cayetano refused. Later one of the boys cut across to the next street and joined another group going to see his mother baptized.

At 10:00 A.M., 21 people gathered on a beach of black sand three miles from Malabo. Jess and Peggy had brought a second jeepload. The shade of palm fronds curving over them toward the sea felt good, for dry season was beginning. The women wore cotton blouses and skirts or comfortably loose-fitting dresses. Most of the men wore short-sleeved shirts and jeans.

The two to be baptized, a young man named Jesus Mba and Carmen, had never before seen baptism by immersion. Neither had any of the other Africans. Jess explained the meaning of New Testament baptism. And then Carmen, Jesus, and Charles waded a long way into the Atlantic Ocean to deeper water, for the tide was far out. There Charles performed beautiful New Testament baptism.

Jesus had studied in the University of Madrid, and while he was there, a black friend from America had shared with him her Baptist beliefs. Back in Malabo, he saw the jeep pass one day and read the words, *Mision Bautista,* on its side. He ran after it, calling "Wait!" And then he asked the question, "Are you Baptists? I think I am a Baptist too." His wife and children watched as he was baptized.

After the service, the two jeeps transported the congregation to the church for their first observance of the Lord's Supper. Carmen and Jesus would be charter members of the church to be organized soon. They took part as Charles lifted the bread and repeated the words of Jesus. "This do in remembrance of Me."

Soon afterward, as Indy waited in front of Carmen's house, Cayetano marched up to the jeep and hissed, "I don't *ever* want to see this jeep parked here again!" Before Indy could collect her wits and answer him, he had walked away.

But Carmen's determination grew. "I can meet you a street over," she said. "I have *decided* to follow Jesus." She made this decision despite the fact that her husband drank, took drugs, and often had beaten her.

The next Sunday, Ines Buale Echek was one of four who made professions of faith. She and her husband, Salvador, had been present at the baptismal service. Ines, who worked in a bank, had enrolled in English classes and then had begun coming to church. Salvador did not want their children baptized as infants, as the state church required, so he came to church with Ines. Immediately he told Charles and Indy, "This is the message I've always wanted to hear."

Salvador lost his job and went to Madrid to take an electrical course; Charles and Indy gave him addresses of Baptist churches in Madrid. Soon they had word from him that he had been converted and was attending John and Ana's church, the congregation the Whittens had begun in Vallecas.

One morning the doorbell rang in the fourth-floor apartment. Ines, on her way to work, had brought Indy a gift of four papayas.

"I wanted to give you something," she said, "because you are always giving so much to us."

Ines sat on the plaid couch, a world map on the wall behind her, and looked at pictures of Indy's family. When she saw Margaret's little red-headed Jessie, she clapped her hands and said, "She reminds me of my Doris!"

Since French francs had replaced bipkweles in the money system, many French people had come to work in the banks. But fortunately for Ines, she had been able to keep her job as secretary to the bank director. On her salary of less than $100 a month, she was supporting her family. Since some foods were still scarce, one weekend she had paid ten times the normal price for a can of condensed milk for her baby.

Indy had been about to apologize for her small temporary apartment when she suddenly felt ridiculously rich. She wanted to snap her fingers and make her electrical appliances disappear. How could she have complained about the bitterness of antimalaria medicine when it was a luxury? Ines and her family often had malaria. What medicine Ines could get, she tried to save for her children.

To Indy, persecution, hunger, oppression, scarcity of medicine, fear of witch doctors, the lack of books to read were secondhand experiences. Always she had been surrounded with superabundance. "Why me, Lord?" she asked.

When people completed their correspondence Bible courses, the Whittens tried to get them to come to church for a diploma-awarding ceremony. When some just would not go to a Baptist church, Charles and Indy would visit them. One mother, surrounded by eight children, said she had not come because she thought she would have to pay to go in the services. They assured her, "It's free."

November 30, Indy had more news for Louise:

> We made our first trip to the continent of Equatorial Guinea this week and are thrilled with the results. We went expecting to make many contacts for the correspondence Bible course. . . . We had a wonderful contact at the little hotel where we stayed. . . . The owner, the associate, the bookkeeper, and a very trusted employee (first cousin of the owner), all were just waiting for somebody to bring them the good news. We gave Bibles to these four. . . . We are trying as hard as we can to get in enough Bibles so we won't have to distribute them on the basis of those who insist most or seem most interested. . . . With the books El Paso sent, I am going to open a reading room for those who want to read good books and magazines and even write letters or go into other rooms to talk.

Then they had definitely decided to redo the rented building where the church had been meeting, even though the owner would not sell. The front of the cream-colored stucco building already looked like a church; they would add a cross and a sign, *Iglesia Bautista*. They would enlarge the space they had by removing room partitions. The room on the side was used as a place for a reading room and social gatherings. They would repair the roof where a mango tree had fallen on it.

Their new house was under construction in a beautiful place between the Spanish Embassy and a wooded area, but delays in arrival of ships with building materials kept slowing the builders. It looked as if they would not be in it soon.

Epifanio Mohaba was baptized in April 1985, but Ines had let herself be frightened into not coming to church anymore.

Working in this isolated country was not easy. People were hesitant and suspicious about anything new in the way of religion. This move to Equatorial Guinea had been a bigger step than the Whittens had realized at the time. Yet they were happy they had taken it.

On May 26, German Nsue, 17, an orphan, would be baptized. He had first enrolled in the correspondence Bible course, then alternated between Catholic mass and Baptist services, and then had become one of the most faithful attendants at the Malabo Baptist Church. An intelligent young man, he was exceedingly shy. In a group he would not say a word. After he made a profession of faith, Charles asked him about baptism, and he replied, "I need to find an answer to that question tonight." Charles didn't want to push him so said no more to him about it.

German would come to the church and stand around as if he wanted to say something. Once he sat in the room where Charles was studying for an hour or two looking at an English book he could not read, but said not a word. Then he followed them as they walked home from church. "About the baptism," he said in a rush, "I want to be."

Though German could quickly locate Scripture passages, he had never prayed in public. Charles said to him. "Prayer is like talking to God. You don't have to use special words." In prayer meeting, he asked him, "Wouldn't you like to thank God for what He has done for you?"

Indy defined patience as "love waiting." At the moment they heard German pray, she and Charles felt their love and their waiting well rewarded.

On the same day as German's baptism, they left to go on vacation—sooner than planned. Indy had a pain which the doctor thought might be appendicitis, so they flew to Douala. It turned out to be an intestinal irritation.

For two weeks, in London, they enjoyed being cold again, sleeping under three blankets. On their 38th wedding anniversary they took a dinner cruise on the Thames River. And then in Madrid for eight days, they stayed with John and Ana and their seven-month-old Carlos, whom they had not seen before. He seemed to them most unusual and precious, for he was eager to be in contact with everybody in sight. On public buses he would pull at people's sleeves or call to them across the aisle so they would talk to him. John was teaching at the Berlitz Institute in Madrid.

From Spain they flew to the Ivory Coast and then to Togo for the annual Mission Meeting with Bill and Evelyn Bullington and with Jess and Peggy, who were ready to leave July 3 for furlough.

While on vacation, they heard that Charles's 87-year-old mother had been rushed to the hospital from Paul's house in Anniston, Alabama. She was bleeding internally and was critically ill. They talked of flying to the States, until they heard she had improved slightly.

When they got back to Malabo, the airlines which brought mail twice a week went on a strike that lasted two months. Telephone connections from Guinea to the US were almost impossible. Indy's mother, 84, had been ill with shingles. Consequently, the two of them spent a rather miserable two months anxiously wondering about their mothers. At last the strike ended and they heard that Charles's mother was so much better that she had returned to her home in Weir!

On July 16, 1985, they moved into their new house of beige-colored stucco bricks with louvered window shutters and doors of glossy hardwood; and inside, the windows with black iron grillwork. The living room floor was of tan tile. In the fence-enclosed yard they planted vegetables, flowers, and trees. Charles's bean vines grew almost as fast as those of *Jack and the Beanstalk*, and so did his turnip greens, mustard, tomatoes, and okra. Within six months, the trees were nearly as tall as the house. Coleus and elephant ears shot up like magic. They had planted a castor-bean tree but cut it down when they heard the beans were poisonous.

English classes had grown so much that Peggy had started helping to teach, but in her absence Indy was teaching alone four afternoons a week. The students sat in folding chairs at the chapel.

Their ministry in Bakake Grande had lessened in number of services; it had been a part of the Thompsons' work. Jess had started a project for bringing water down to the village from a mountain spring. This was in its final stages. (Some said why do this when the women and children could go and bring the water back on their heads.)

It wasn't easy for two to do the work of four. In August, Jerry and Jo Meeks were appointed for Equatorial Guinea, but they would study Spanish in Madrid before they went to the field.

Always when they were starting a new church, Charles preached and Indy taught the adult Sunday School class. Epifanio Mohaba, who often brought friends to church, began teaching the adult Sunday School class at Malabo. Also Jesus Mba became a fine teacher. (The Whittens were amazed at the fast growth of new Christians in Guinea, at how soon they were ready to teach and preach themselves.) So Indy then began a Sunday School class for children aged 6 to 12. The first Sunday she gave them a picture to color of a mother bird perched on the side of a nest giving a worm to her babies. The children were afraid to color, for not one of them had ever held a crayon. Indy had to show them how it was done. And then, sweat popping out on their black foreheads, they tried hard to color correctly. One little girl asked, "What color face does the mother bird have?"

This reminded Indy of the day when someone had asked her a question, "Why did God make people with different colors of faces, white and black and red?" She hadn't known exactly how to answer, but Carmen had spoken up and said, "He likes variety!"

At Christmas, Indy gave each of these children a pencil with a Bible verse on it, being careful to give each child only one.

The children left as worship service began, but in the middle of the sermon Indy saw 8-year-old Yolanda standing in the door with a pencil in her hand, holding it out to her. The child looked down at the floor and said to Indy, "I was going to take two pencils, but I know that's not right. Here, you take this one!"

"The seeds are beginning to sprout," she thought.

As in Spain, wide interests led the Whittens into many

different activities. So did they in Malabo. The American Embassy asked them to teach English to scholarship students from Guinea who would be studying in the USA to help them get some language principles and orientation on what to expect in the United States.

A Guinean friend who spoke English asked Indy to write down words from a tape of folk hymns sung by Tennessee Ernie Ford. As she listened, it was a memory experience for her. One song in particular had a special effect on her when she heard the last line of the chorus, "How long has it been since you knew that He cared for you?"

Christian workers often thought of themselves as "instruments" and felt that the Lord was only interested in them as tools to be used. Yet, Indy realized with a new forcefulness that her joy and endurance sprang from the fact that He cared for *her*. She thought, "He cares for me the same way He cares for that African child back up in the mountain with no food, no medicine, and no opportunity to hear, 'Jesus loves me, this I know, for the Bible tells me so.' "

29
A church comes to the continent

"I am to love and try to understand why people are like they are and to keep on acting among them as the love of Christ in human form. It's not an easy burden to bear, but it has great and marvelous rewards."—Indy Whitten

AS DAYS of 1985 dwindled, Charles and Indy prayed daily that there might be an opening for beginning a church on the continental part of Equatorial Guinea. They asked the Lord for one good contact there.

One afternoon they had just arrived at the church for English class when something unexpected occurred. "Good evening," a man said as he entered the church door. "My name is Crisantos. May I ask a favor?" They welcomed him and asked him to have a seat. He drew a wad of money out of his pocket and laid it on a table.

"I am a policeman," he explained, "at Mikomiseng on the continent. I plan to be married soon, and this money is my dowry for my in-laws. I drew it out of a bank here, but I'm uneasy about carrying so much around with me. Could you keep it until I can get passage to the continent?"

"I'd be glad to do you a favor," Charles answered, "but I am not a bank, and I could not be absolutely sure that nothing would happen to the money."

"Well, all right. I can understand that." So he returned the money to his pocket.

They invited him to church, and he came the next Sunday. When he visited them at their house, they gave him a Bible and literature on how to be saved and on what Baptists believe. The Thursday night before he was to return to his home in Mikomiseng, he sat in the church an hour reading his Bible before prayer meeting.

The night after his return home, he called the Whittens and said, "I feel that God sent me to Malabo, and

I'm glad He did, because I have given my heart to Jesus."

Christmas Eve 1985, Charles and Indy made morning visits to deliver Christmas greetings and Bible Way Correspondence cards. During lunch they listened to a tape of Christmas music.

In the afternoon just as their heads touched the pillow for a siesta, the doorbell rang. Since Charles was in the beginning stages of laryngitis, Indy said, "You stay in bed and save your voice for tomorrow."

The visitor turned out to be German, the timid young man who had been baptized the preceding May. "I have come to sing," he said.

"All right. We'll practice the Christmas carols we are going to sing at church tomorrow. Let's sing just the first and last verses." (Her own throat felt scratchy.) What an unusual experience! Never before had she spent Christmas Eve singing Christmas carols with an African Christian young man!

During the holidays, Cayetano got drunk and beat Carmen so cruelly she could not even get out of bed. Charles and Indy visited in their home and tried to bring words of counsel. As Charles was sitting there at the table reading Psalm 23 aloud, many women and children crowded around trying to hear. The living quarters of several families nearby opened onto a square patio.

As they were leaving, a woman came running after them to express appreciation for their coming to see about Carmen. "Wait," she said. "I want to give you a Christmas present." She laid in Indy's hand two eggs. Indy knew that Juanita only had two hens and that her family hardly ever had enough to eat. How could she eat their eggs? Yet, why should she deprive Juanita of the joy of giving?

"Thank you!" Indy said. "This is a wonderful Christmas gift. I will make a Spanish omelet. When we eat it, we will think of you."

The Sunday after Christmas a new family was present at the Malabo church (they had been praying to win whole families)—Justo, Mari Sol, and their three children. When the invitation was given, Justo made a profession of faith.

One of the couple's daughters had seizures which appeared to be epilepsy. Many who knew them said these seizures were caused by evil spirits. Charles and Indy arranged an appointment for them with a pediatrician, who told them that the child's seizures were caused by malaria, worms, and anemia. The doctor prescribed medicine which she said would clear up the illness but would take several months.

The parents bought the first medicine, but when that gave out, they returned to the native doctor. "He can cure her more quickly. He understands African diseases better," they said. The pediatrician, a Guinean woman, had studied abroad.

When Indy had started out as a missionary, she had resolved to be a burden bearer, thinking that meant lending a hand in time of great need or helping with loads too heavy for one to carry alone. But her 40 years of mission service had given her a larger capacity for bearing burdens and a greater understanding of what burdens really were. They were not isolated experiences cured when a difficulty passed.

She knew now that the worst burdens were those like this couple carried, a legacy of superstition, ignorance, fear, and poverty. The worst burden could be to exist without physical or spiritual hope.

To help clarify her thinking about burden bearing, she carefully set down some questions and answers.

How could she, only one, help bear such unrelenting burdens? She could begin by caring. That wouldn't stop anyone from dying of malaria and its complications, or of cholera, but it would be a necessary beginning. And next she could live out the "incarnation principle" among the people where God had placed her. As she had so often said, "The missionary is to be the love of Jesus in human form."

How could she keep from being overwhelmed by the enormity of the needs constantly being put before her? She could feed one or maybe even dozens. But it would be impossible to feed all the hungry, to pay medical bills for all who needed them paid, or to lend money to all those in financial trouble.

"What attitude am I to take toward people who have moral interpretations and practices far below the standards of the Commandments, not to speak of the love of God revealed in Christ?" she asked. "Polygamy; theft; violation of even the most basic of human rights; excessive fear of evil spirits."

What should she feel under these circumstances? Should she just give up and say, "These folks are hopeless and way out of my reach. I could spend 100 years here and accomplish very little."

She wrote in her notebook:

This is the point where burden bearing becomes clear. The traditions and the attitudes of the people are the burdens that the ages have pressed down on them. When I stop to realize all the advantages I have enjoyed and all the help people have given me through the years—plus all the material and spiritual blessings that have been mine, I am rather amazed that I have not done better than I have.

I am to *love* and try to understand *why* people are like they are and to keep on acting among them as the love of Christ in human form. It's not an easy burden to bear, but it has great and marvelous rewards.

Several weeks passed, and one morning Crisantos called. "Indy," Charles said when he hung up the phone, "I can't believe this! Crisantos said he has been witnessing to people in Mikomiseng, and he has 40 who are interested in the gospel and who are reading the Bible! He says they are going to build a Baptist church!" His city was 55 miles north of Bata, the capital of the continental part of the country.

A few mornings later, the doorbell rang, and Indy went to the door. "Crisantos!" she cried. There he stood, dripping wet with perspiration. He'd just gotten to Malabo and could hardly wait to see them, so he had walked as fast as he could to their house.

"My 40 friends who are reading the Bible with me took up a collection and paid my way here so I could ask you the best way to build our church," he said. "Would you lend me some paper and a ruler?"

Charles handed him what he asked for, and Crisantos drew on the paper the plan of the church they were hoping to build. "The others are out in the woods now, cutting trees for the lumber," he said.

"How in the world did you contact 40 people?" Charles asked.

"Oh, I began with 1 or 2. We would get together in the afternoons, and I would read the Bible with them. If I read just a little, they wanted to hear more. And from the 1 or 2, others began to come." And then he added rather sadly, "I liked to sing hymns when I was here, but I can't remember them. I wish we could sing in our church." So Charles taught him three hymns before he left. They practiced and practiced. (They did not have a piano at the Malabo church, but Charles led the singing without one. Sometimes they played piano tapes sent them by Grace Lovelace, a pianist in Clinton, Mississippi.)

They had prayed for "just 1 good contact" on the continent; God had given them 40.

Time passed. Again Indy stopped for Carmen. Cayetano and his brother came with her and asked if they could ride into town. Shocked, Indy said, "Of course." Carmen and Cayetano got into the front seat beside her. The rest of the jeep was filled with people.

Cayetano spoke first, "I have been awfully angry with you!"

Indy carefully dodged a hole in the street. "But I think you are not angry with me now?"

"Yes," he answered quickly. "I am!"

"But I think if I should offer you my hand in friendship that you and I could become friends."

Cayetano hesitated. Then he shifted his cigarette from his right hand to his left, and with a smile, reached across Carmen, who sat in the middle, to shake Indy's hand. Carmen was amazed.

"I want you to get me a Bible," said Cayetano. "I drive a truck for a construction company, and I want to have the Bible with me in my truck. Can you do that? Don't forget it!"

"Sure I can," she tried not to sound too eager. She thought, "Truly nothing is impossible for God."

A good surprise came in April when a Catholic friend of Indy's, a teacher in the Malabo branch of a Madrid university, called with an invitation. "I'm asking teen-aged girls over to my house on Saturday afternoons for cooking, sewing, and recreation," she said. "I think it would be a nice addition if you would come over and lead a Bible study for them every week."

Also in April the water project in Bakake Grande was finished, materials furnished by missions offerings and work done by the residents. That month, on their way to the village, the Whittens and their Malabo church companions on the trip suddenly found themselves sitting beside the road in the middle of the jungle, the jeep's gearshift jammed. On the advice of a passerby, Indy put the jeep in four-wheel traction. They chugged along the rest of the way, and later, at the same snail's pace, all the way back to Malabo. Since jeep parts were unavailable in the country, they'd have to wait for them to be shipped in. In the meantime, one of the Malabo members promised to go by bus to hold Bakake services.

For vacation in July, Charles and Indy wanted to go to Mississippi to see their mothers, children, and grandchildren. As the only missionaries on the field, they wondered how they could leave. But they worked out a plan before they left for the four strongest leaders of the congregation to take turns conducting the worship services and teaching the Sunday School classes.

When they returned, they found that attendance had not dropped. One of their Sunday School children, a little boy of 6, Jose Luis, had died suddenly, and a group from the church had gone to the home of his family (not Christians) and read from the Bible and prayed with them.

Those who taught in Sunday School had enlisted others to help also. Eduardo, 19, reported, "I taught a Sunday School class. I didn't do it so well, but I did it!"

Robbers had broken into the building and taken a couple of things. Members had discussed whether or not to call the police and decided not to, since an investigation might be damaging to the testimony of the church and to those just beginning to attend services.

At least three different tribes were represented among the members, but as Epifanio said, "We are united in our faith in Christ. We feel closer than brothers."

By early fall 1986, five missionary couples had been appointed to Equatorial Guinea. One of the couples was Larry and Lucy Driggers. Larry had been one of the Southwestern Seminary students who helped the Whittens with the last phase of the Five Year Mission Plan in the Canary Islands.

Now that more missionaries were on the way, and the Whittens had begun one church and had the nucleus of one on the continent, they were ready to make an important decision.

On September 3, Indy wrote a friend:

We had originally planned to continue here until September 20, 1987—actually some days beyond Charles's 65th birthday—and then have an eight-month furlough in the USA before our official retirement in May 1988. Now because of personal and family reasons, it seems best to leave the field around April 1, and the subsequent furlough would take us up to the retirement date in 1987.

30
"God gives the increase"

"I'd like this as my epitaph: 'Every butterfly I ever chased, I caught.'"—Indy Whitten

"MIND YOU, it hasn't all been moonlight and roses and hummingbird tongues on toast," Indy looked back at her years as a missionary. "Mixed in it all have come problems, disappointments, and failures on my part. . . . But the same Holy Spirit that communicated God's call gave me strength, understanding, and perseverance to do His work. Not mine. And I have loved it all. It has been . . . an exciting adventure of awaking to each new morning and wondering what the Lord has in mind for me that day."

This is the last are often sad words. So to the Whittens, it was a bit sad November 1, 1986, to say, "This is our last newsletter" as active missionaries of the Foreign Mission Board. Considering the needs of their mothers and several other factors, they felt they had made the right decision to leave Africa March 28, 1987, and retire soon after Charles's 65th birthday in September. The Foreign Mission Board had approved the decision.

But they had the good news to report that four couples in addition to the Thompsons would be coming to work as missionaries in Equatorial Guinea: Jerry and Jo Meeks right away, Terry and Kathy Waller, Eugene and Mary Gibbins, and Larry and Lucy Driggers after Spanish study in Costa Rica.

Both Charles and Indy had prayed for a long time for more missionaries in Equatorial Guinea. Indy's news releases and personal letters, in Spanish and English, had asked others to pray. Indy in her human interest stories, and both in many furlough addresses, had presented the needs of Equatorial Guinea. And now, in answer to prayer, four couples were on the way.

When the Guinean scholarship students left to study in the United States, the Guinean government televised the farewell and thanked Indy, Charles, and the Baptist Mission to Equatorial Guinea for the English lessons given the students.

During November Charles completed negotiations to buy land where the Malabo Baptist Church could build in a permanent location. As treasurer of the Mission (in the absence of Jess Thompson), he signed for the property.

In Friendship Spain-Equatorial Guinea, a group of children in Barcelona had asked to adopt Guinean friends. Indy had matched the pairs. In late December seven big boxes arrived with Christmas and birthday presents and a huge carton of chewable vitamins and minerals. "I'm going to drive around and deliver these today," Indy told Charles. "If I take them to Sunday School, too many children would be left out."

The Meeks family was coming to spend Christmas with them. Afterward Indy planned to fly with Jo and the boys, Justin and Jarrett, to Bata, while Charles would fly with Jerry to Douala to pick up their ranch wagon. In January 1987 Jess and Peggy returned. Two months later Charles and Indy said their farewells to the members of the Malabo Baptist Church; and to many other friends, including Pilar Alcaide, who had continued to give help in their adjustment to life in Malabo. Charles had met her on the survey trip with Mills and Bullington.

Carmen Ondo walked a long way to visit and pray with them once again and to tell them good-bye. Several times in the past when Cayetano had beaten her, they had asked, "Why don't you leave him?" She had answered, "I will stay because I love him, and I want to see him become a Christian." He had asked for a Bible, and with God anything is possible.

On March 28 they flew from Malabo to Madrid to visit with John, Ana, and Carlos. With a degree in philology in Spanish and English, John was still teaching languages and acting as translator. He also knew French and had studied German. Like others in his family, he was talented in music, especially in piano, and was putting it to good use in his church.

After only a day in Spain, they traveled to Mississippi. The next week they moved into the already furnished house of the Colonial Heights Baptist Church in Jackson, the 5lst house they had lived in since 1947. They had left their furniture in the house in Malabo for Larry and Lucy. Larry Driggers would be the next pastor of the Malabo Baptist Church, the first Baptist church ever to be organized in Equatorial Guinea.

The Foreign Mission Board's retirement dinner, during which the Whittens would be honored, was set for October 12, 1987. How fitting that it should happen to be on Columbus Day to show appreciation for two who had spent so many years in Spain! After retirement, the two planned to move to the house they owned at 108 West Lakeview, Clinton, Mississippi.

Still in good health, they didn't want simply to quit at age 65, and they had been praying that God would show them the right place to continue working as a team. An answer for 1988 came when the Foreign Mission Board invited them to be the missionaries-in-residence at the Missionary Learning Center at Rockville, Virginia.

In early summer David and his family visited them in Jackson. That meant a house full, because David and his wife, Sherry, had adopted seven children—Joel, Mary, David, Rosey, Yesenia, Viviana, and Lisa—within a three-year span. A graduate of the University of Houston Law School, David had a solo law practice in a residential neighborhood in Houston, Texas, and he and his family were active in a Baptist church there.

Following David's visit, Charles and Indy flew to Costa Rica to see Margaret and her husband, Sam Drummond. After Sam received his PhD degree in Old Testament from the Southern Baptist Theological Seminary, he and Margaret had been appointed in September 1986, by the Foreign Mission Board, SBC, as missionaries to El Salvador. They had then gone to Costa Rica to language school. Sam had been invited to teach during the fall semester at the Baptist seminary in Costa Rica.

In the summer of 1986 Margaret was assisting in the plans for the 50th anniversary celebration of the school where her parents had studied 50 years before when it was located in Medellin, Colombia. When the Whittens and Jo and Evan Holmes and their small daughter Becky had arrived in Colombia on the same plane, they had been the first Southern Baptist missionaries to enroll in that language school.

Whereas David's children all had dark hair and Helen's had light hair, Margaret and Sam's (William, Ruth, and Jessie Marie) had red hair like both their parents.

Later in the year Charles and Indy hoped to see Helen, who with her husband, Steve Cobb; and children, Cristina, Philip, Anita, and Timmy; had transferred to Quito, Ecuador, where they worked as missionaries with the Globe Missionary Society at an interdenominational Bible institute.

In his youth Charles had been a sower of seed in good Mississippi soil. Then he had become a sower of seed of the good news of Jesus Christ in the USA, and outside of it on three other continents. As he looked back across his 40 years as a missionary, he could see some of the seed producing much fruit. "Not because of me," he said. "God did it! When I left the United States in 1947, I am sure I did not know all that is involved in answering a call to serve overseas. But God had said, 'Go as my witness, and I will be with you.' I went and He has been true to His word."

In Colombia he and Indy had begun a study of Spanish, the medium through which they would communicate the gospel message; and the thread that would connect their work in South America, Europe, and Africa.

In Argentina, with the help of missionary colleagues, Argentine believers, and the prayers and money of Southern Baptists, they had spent time witnessing as pioneers at the grass-roots level. He had preached in churches and in evangelistic crusades. In seminary classrooms, both of them had trained young men and women, some of whom are Baptist leaders in Argentina today.

In Spain Charles and Indy had stood by a faithful little group of Baptists who had lost their religious freedom, loving them and encouraging them. And they had found themselves the recipients of love and encouragement generously given by the Spanish Baptists. Charles had helped to reopen the seminary in Barcelona. Both of them had taught in it, and he had directed it until another missionary could take it over. Then later, in Madrid, he had seen one of the students, an intellectual and spiritual giant, become the Spanish Baptist seminary's first Spanish director. When someone was needed to channel the funds that Southern Baptists continually sent, Charles had gladly done it for 26 years.

Planting new mission points and leading them to become churches had been Charles's favorite kind of work, and he and Indy had done that in Barcelona and Madrid and in the Canary Islands. It was always a joy to be replaced by a national worker.

To him, one of the greatest satisfactions of life had been to hear someone say, "Because of a sermon I heard you preach, I accepted Jesus as my Saviour." Of the many children who had professed their faith in Christ when he preached in camps at Denia, Marsha McNeely, one of them, was now with her husband, David Smith, as a Baptist representative in Israel. Another of those who had responded to his messages at Denia had been Sara Bonet, daughter of Pedro and Noemi Bonet. She also had entered full-time Christian service.

They had prayed for the Canary Islands, where 1,500,000 were isolated from the rest of Spain; and they had sought to call attention to the need for more missionaries there. Three other couples had been appointed.

They had urged the Foreign Mission Board to open up work in Equatorial Guinea, and had had the joy of seeing five other couples approved for service there in addition to themselves.

Wherever they had been sent, they had sought to love

first and not wait to be loved. Their lives had become lamps through which God's love could steadily shine.

One morning in Malabo, Equatorial Guinea, soon after Charles and Indy had made the decision to retire, he wrote:

Now that we go, is the work finished? No, it is only beginning.
. . .
The task really is never finished. The testimony must go forward: missionaries, nationals, humble believers all, sharing their faith with people around them.

What have we personally been able to accomplish? Perhaps not much, but the privilege was great and humbling. The privilege was to be able to plant, at times to water, the sprouting plants sowed by another; and sometimes to have the joy of harvesting the golden grain. We believers are a part of a great witnessing family that requires a great cooperation. We all work as partners, joining hands and hearts in the bold task of sharing our Lord with a lost world.

Yes, sometimes we plant; sometimes we water; and we thrill to participate in some harvesting; but we must always remember that it is God Who gives the increase (1 Cor. 3:5-9). To God be the glory.

Indy Mitchell poses for her high school graduation picture in 1939.

A happy Charles and Indy marry in June 1947.

The Whittens work in Argentina in 1948.

Charles Whitten baptizes a new Christian at Bonanova Baptist Church in Barcelona, Spain, on August 1, 1954.

Joe Mefford accompanies Charles on the accordion at Denia in 1956. Charles loves to sing.

While still prince and princess of Spain, Sofia and Juan Carlos meet with Baptists. *Pictured left to right are* Jose Borras, W. H. Jackson, Princess Sofia, Prince Juan Carlos, Juan Luis Rodrigo, and Charles Whitten.

Charles looks on as a water project is completed in Equatorial Guinea in 1986.

Charles Whitten

Indy Whitten

THE SPANISH CONNECTION (Study Section)

As the reader follows Charles and Indy Whitten from Mississippi to Colombia to Argentina to Spain to Equatorial Guinea, she will see that the connecting link between all the places they have served has been the Spanish language. The Whittens have set an example on four continents in loving, serving, giving, praying, encouraging, and witnessing.

One may study this book as an individual or with a group. Hence, the study section contains two parts. The first gives instructions, questions, and activities for study with a group. The second offers directions for individual study.

PART 1—GROUP STUDY

Before the study

1. Publicize the study. Use announcements, church bulletins, bulletin boards, invitations, and mass media to advertise the study of the Whittens. Posters could include pictures of scenes or people from the four Spanish-speaking areas where the Whittens have served: Argentina, Spain, the Canary Islands (a part of Spain), and Equatorial Guinea. Maps of the countries, plus some Spanish phrases or words, could also decorate the posters. *Enviar* means "to send." *Amor* means "love." The title of this book in Spanish is *Enviar para Amar.*

2. Collect resources needed for the study. These include:
Charles and Indy Whitten: Sent to Love (available through Baptist Book Stores)
Map of Colombia
Map of Argentina
Map of Spain's mainland
Map of the Canary Islands
Map of Equatorial Guinea
Travel posters, books, pictures, curios, and costumes from the above Spanish-speaking countries (A travel agent and/or persons who have traveled to these countries might help.)
Spanish Bibles or testaments
Hymnbooks or song sheets with "Lead, Kindly Light," Charles Whitten's favorite hymn
The Spanish version of the chorus, "I've Got Peace Like a River" (*Baptist Hymnal,* 1975 edition) and the Spanish version of the chorus of "Jesus Loves Me." Words to both are given below.

Tengo paz como un rio,	Cristo me ama
Tengo paz como un rio,	Cristo me ama
Tengo paz como un rio en me ser.	Cristo me ama
Tengo paz como un rio,	La Biblia dice asi.
Tengo paz como un rio,	
Tengo paz como un rio en me ser.	

3. At the meeting place for the study, decorate five areas to represent Colombia, Argentina, Spain, the Canary Islands, and Equatorial Guinea. Use pictures, curios, costumes, maps, books (including Spanish books and Bibles if possible). Flamenco or other Latin-type music in the background would add to the atmosphere of fiesta. Enlist tour guides—one for each display area—to help compile materials and set up her area and also to assist during the meeting. Each tour guide, if she likes, could dress in a costume representative of her area. Each guide should know some facts about her area so that as study participants arrive she can guide them in their browsing. During intermission time, the guides will continue giving verbal tours of their areas. (If five areas seems to be too many, Colombia might be omitted.)

4. Optional, but fun: At intermission time, the guides or others appointed to help them could serve Spanish snacks. If this is to be done, enlist persons to prepare and serve the snacks. The recipes for two are given below. You might think of others to add.

CHURROS (SPANISH DOUGHNUTS)

2 cups water
2 cups flour
2 tablespoons sugar
Dash of salt
1 tablespoon butter

1 egg
2 teaspoons grated lemon rind
Powdered sugar
Oil

Put the water, butter, sugar, and salt in a pan over heat. When it boils, add flour. Remove from heat and add beaten egg and lemon rind. Roll dough between your fingers to form long thin ropes. Fry in deep oil. Dust with powdered sugar. These are good served with hot cocoa.

PAPAS ARRUGADAS (WRINKLED POTATOES)

4 or 5 Irish potatoes (small to medium-size)
1 cup ice-cream salt
Water
Mexican sauce

Wash the potatoes. Do not peel them. Put the potatoes and ice-cream salt in a boiler. Cover the potatoes with cold water. Boil on medium heat 30 to 40 minutes, or until the potatoes are tender. Add more water as necessary to keep the potatoes covered. Allow to cool. Dip into Mexican sauce to eat. These are served in homes and restaurants in the Canary Islands as appetizers.

5. Read the list of activities below. Gather resources needed and make advance assignments and preparations for activities 1 and 2, to use before intermission. Choose then from the rest of the activities as many as needed to allow for a total 2½ hours of study. You will need to use at least that much time to get Church Study Course credit. Gather resources and make preparations for the other activities you have chosen.

At the study

1. Welcome and introduction: Sing Charles Whitten's favorite hymn, "Lead, Kindly Light." Lead participants in singing the choruses "I've Got Peace Like a River" and "Jesus Loves Me" in Spanish. Distribute song sheets or write the words on a chalkboard. (See list of resources above for Spanish words.)

Before the study, write the following Scripture references and verses on index cards. They are some of the verses Indy quoted in her book *We Camped at Heaven's Gate*. At the meeting, distribute the cards. After the singing of the Spanish choruses, ask those holding the cards to read them. (20 minutes)

Isa. 41:10	1 Peter 1:7	Deut. 31:6
Gal. 6:2	Isa. 48:10	Luke 22:42
Matt. 6:33	Isa. 43:21	John 5:4
Gal. 2:20	Phil. 1:12	2 Cor. 12:9

2. The book is divided geographically, according to the continents where the Whittens have lived and worked. On a world map, point out Mississippi, where they were born; Colombia, where they studied Spanish; and Argentina, Spain, the Canary Islands, and Equatorial Guinea, where they served as missionaries. Give a brief overview of happenings in these places. Divide participants into four groups. Assign each group one continent—North America, South America, Europe, Africa. Instruct each group to prepare a presentation on the Whittens' life and ministry in that area.

Each presentation will include brief information about the land and its people and their customs; facts about when the Whittens went there; how long they stayed; types of work they did there; impact of their work; unusual stories of answers to prayer and of persons they loved and helped. Groups may refer to the book and to the materials in the display areas. (The North America group could include a few furlough happenings, as well as the early years in Mississippi.) Each small group will give its presentation for the large group. (60 minutes)

3. Intermission: Tour guides will tell browsers about their areas. If Spanish snacks are to be served, now is the time. (15 minutes)

4. Before the study, write the following quotations on a poster or on a chalkboard. At the meetings read the quotations aloud and point out that they are quotes from Indy, and that all are on the theme of love. Lead in a discussion of how the Whittens applied these principles to their lives. Ask the participants to suggest ways they might apply these principles to their own lives. (10 minutes)

"We learned to love first and not wait around to see if the people were going to love us."

"In any country, the home is an effective object lesson of Christ's transforming love."

"We heard the unmistakable Voice of Love say to our troubled hearts, 'My children, lean hard. My grace is sufficient for your every need.'"

"If we could give our family anything, what would it be? (1) An understanding of the importance of love in this world."

"There is never a barrier that can continue to stand in the presence of real Christian love—whether the barrier be race, language, educational background, social position, or any other circumstance."

"God so loved, and we are to be channels of that love, through our giving and serving."

"Patience is love waiting."

"Through prayer you take love's magic carpet to everywhere."

"The missionary is to be the love of Jesus in human form."

"I am to love and try to understand why people are like they are and to keep on acting among them as the love of Christ in human form. It's not an easy burden to bear, but it has great and marvelous rewards."

5. Ask each participant to find a partner with whom to work. Instruct each pair to work together to answer the 12 questions under number 6 in Part 2—Individual Study and to answer question number 2 under Part 2—Individual Study. (20 minutes)

6. Read aloud to the group Indy's story in chapter 18, "The MKs We Left Behind." Then ask for answers to the question, What unusual problems does a missionaries' child face when he or she goes to America for college? (15 minutes)

7. When the Spanish women asked Evelyn Hughey how they could be a part of world missions, she said to them, "Be like the little duck on the boundless Atlantic Ocean. Ease yourself into world missions where it touches you." Brainstorm: Ask the participants to think of ways they can be like the little duck. Record the answers. Give time for a session of silent prayer as each participant asks the Lord to reveal to her ways that she can be a missionary, and "an arm of Christ's love" where she is. Lead in a prayer of dedication. (15 minutes)

8. Divide participants into two groups. Ask one group to look through the book, find, and list qualities that describe Indy; and the other group to find and list qualities that describe Charles. As the lists are presented to the large group, ask all to listen for ways Charles and Indy are alike and ways that they are different. Ask, Why do they make a good team? (30 minutes)

9. On his application for mission service, Charles wrote, "I want to be willing to go anywhere and to pay any price to carry out . . . Christ's will for me." Indy, in applying for foreign mission service, wrote, "I'm sure God will open up methods of serving that I never dreamed of before." Before the study, ask someone to prepare a brief report to present at the meeting, telling how these aspirations of the young Whittens worked out in their lives. (10 minutes)

10. When the Whittens were ready to leave Equatorial Guinea, to retire, many of their Christian friends from Equatorial Guinea came to their house to pray with them and for them. Some had to walk several miles. With emotion they prayed, "Lord, we thank you for sending these people to show us the way to God. And we thank you for those back in the United States who sent them." One of those who walked in order to make this visit was Carmen Ondo. Before the meeting, enlist someone to tell the story of Carmen, one of the first persons Charles baptized in Equatorial Guinea. Emphasize the Whittens' ministry of love to her and her family as they led her to the Lord.

After this story of Carmen, at the meeting, divide the participants into four groups. Assign each one a story to search for and tell from this list: a story of Charles's ministry as a peacemaker; a story of Indy's ministry as a writer; a story of the Whitten's ministry of encouragement; a story of the Whittens ministry as church planters. (45 minutes)

11. Ask each participant to find a partner with whom to work. Instruct each pair to work together to trace the theme of amazing answers to prayer throughout the book. Also ask them to look for the role that prayers of Christians in the United States played in many of these incidents in the Whittens' lives. (20 minutes)

12. Write the names of the following persons on slips of paper. At the meeting, distribute them among the participants. Ask each who received a slip of paper to identify the person whose name she received, and to tell the person's or persons' relationship or connection with Charles and Indy, and where and when. (30 minutes)

Joe Triplett	Juana Lumbreras
C. Z. Holland	Gerald and June McNeely
Louise Hill Miller	Grace Wetherell
Rosa Holquin	Rosemary Singleton
Kitty and W. Lowrey Cooper	Queen Sofia
Jose and Esther Borras	Sally Lennon
Joe and Lila Mefford	Benedicta Aleman
Roy and Joyce Wyatt	John Mills
Noemi Bonet	Crisantos
Vicenta Ramos	

13. Use item 8 under Individual Study as a closing activity.

PART 2—INDIVIDUAL STUDY

1. Read the book and the study section for group study.
2. Memorize Matthew 6:33, Charles Whitten's favorite Bible verse. How did he and Indy apply this verse to their life-style?
3. Read the quotation at the beginning of chapter 1. What phrase did Indy say best described the reason she was on the missions field? Do you think she and Charles carried out that commission? Why? Why not?
4. Make a time line of the Whittens' lives as missionaries. Include two personal events for each decade of their 40 years of service. List one world event in each of those decades.
5. List two character traits that describe Indy and two that describe Charles. Why do they make a good team? How are they different? How are they alike?
6. Write answers to the following questions:
    a) What part did a Sunday School teacher play in Indy's conversion experience? What role did Baptist Student Union play

in her call to missions? How did Charles's becoming a missionary reflect his childhood environment?
b) How did the Whittens' work in South America help prepare them for their work in Spain? List types of work both did in South America, Europe, and Africa.
c) Read the quotation at the beginning of chapter 14. What four things did the Whittens most want to teach their children? What family activities did they use to teach these?
d) What did the calendar of prayer do for Charles on his 37th birthday?
e) As legal representative for the Foreign Mission Board, SBC, in Spain, how did Charles work for the cause of religious liberty?
f) What two magazines did Indy edit?
g) Give two examples of Charles and Indy's encouragement of new missionaries.
h) What part did prayer play in the Whittens' move to Spain? to the Canary Islands? to Equatorial Guinea?
i) Retell one story of Charles's acting as peacemaker.
j) Tell the story of Indy's witnessing to a person she had just met.
k) What are some techniques Charles and Indy used in starting new missions or churches?

7. Does the title *Sent to Love* apply to you as a Christian? How can you show that you are "Christ's love in human form"?

8. Write your answers to the following:
a) Am I an encourager? How can I be?
b) Am I a peacemaker? How can I be?
c) How often do I take prayer's magic carpet to everywhere, to share my love and concern for missionaries in specific requests?
d) Have I trained my children to love first rather than waiting to be loved? What family mission action project have we engaged in? What new missions project could we plan to do as a family?
e) Do I try to be a burden bearer?
f) Am I a good steward of my possessions?
g) Am I willing to obey God? Am I willing to go any place, any time, anywhere He sends? Am I willing to do any task He sets before me?
h) How can I "be like the little duck on the boundless Atlantic"? How can I be a part of world missions where I am?

The Church Study Course
The Church Study Course is a Southern Baptist educational system consisting of more than 500 short courses for adults and youth combined with a credit and recognition system. Credit is awarded for each course completed. These credits may be applied to 1 or more of the 25 diplomas.

Complete details about the Church Study Course system, courses available, and diplomas offered may be found in a current copy of the *Church Study Course Catalog* and in the study course section of the *Church Materials Catalog*. The Church Study Course is sponsored by the Sunday School Board, Woman's Missionary Union, and the Brotherhood Commission.

Credit for the course (08130) may be obtained in two ways:(1) Read the book and participate in a 2½-hour study; (2) Read the book and follow the suggestions in "Part 2—Individual Study" in the study section.

Request credit on Form 725 "Church Study Course Enrollment/Credit Request," available from Awards Office, Sunday School Board, 127 Ninth Avenue, North, Nashville, TN 37234.

A record of your awards will be maintained by the Awards Office. Twice each year copies will be sent to churches for distribution to members.

Anne Washburn McWilliams, assistant editor of Mississippi's state Baptist paper, has been employed by the *Baptist Record* since 1953. Born in Chambers County, Alabama, she was graduated from Judson College with a major in English and a minor in Spanish. She received master's degrees from Southwestern Baptist Theological Seminary and Mississippi College, and on one sabbatical leave, studied at the University of London.

For the *Baptist Record*, she writes a column, "Faces and Places." Also she has written for many other Southern Baptist denominational publications. She is author of a Broadman Press biography of a Brazilian Baptist, *David Gomes: When Faith Triumphs*. In travels to 29 countries, she has interviewed and written articles about missionaries in 19 of them.

She and her husband, W. D. McWilliams, live in Clinton, Mississippi. They are members of the Morrison Heights Baptist Church, where she is a Girls in Action leader.